Raves for
NICOLE KNEPPER

"Nikki has a way of connecting and resonating with moms that is almost magical and pretty much guarantees a bestselling book."
—Jill Smokler, author of *Scary Mommy*

"I had this idea in my head about what mommy and daddy bloggers were all about—posts about how wonderful raising children and life with little ones were and how every day of parenting was a magical gift, like a glitter-filled fart from a baby unicorn. I wanted nothing to do with those lies. Then I found Nikki and the Moms Who Drink and Swear blog. She is honest about raising kids, being an adult child now in charge of children, and everything that comes with the parenting gig. Nikki is the parent, and writer, I want to be. Plus she smells nice. Not as nice as glittery unicorn farts, but nice."
—Chris Illuminati, author of *A**holeology: The Cheat Sheet*

"Nikki Knepper is one of a kind. She's a smart, compassionate, gritty, insightful, potty-mouthed, hilarious, fearless, silly, and generous spirit every bit deserving of the enormous online platform she's grown. I'm a proud fan of Moms Who Drink and Swear, and I can't wait to read what's next!"
—Julie Haas Brophy, author of *Sh*t My Kids Ruined:*
An A–Z Celebration of Kid-Destruction

"As a mom who despises 'mommy blogs,' discovering Nicole Knepper's writing was almost as sweet as the first time my son let me use the bathroom without him. With her biting sense of humor, Nicole has struck a chord not just with parents, but with anyone interested in answering life's biggest question, 'What the fuck?' She's all at once insightful, touching, and hilarious."
—Natalie Slater, author of *Bake and Destroy*

continued . . .

MOMS WHO DRINK AND SWEAR

TRUE TALES OF LOVING MY KIDS WHILE LOSING MY MIND

NICOLE KNEPPER

 New American Library

New American Library
Published by the Penguin Group
Penguin Group (USA) Inc., 375 Hudson Street,
New York, New York 10014, USA

USA / Canada / UK / Ireland / Australia
New Zealand / India / South Africa / China

Penguin Books Ltd., Registered Offices: 80 Strand, London WC2R 0RL, England
For more information about the Penguin Group visit penguin.com.

First published by New American Library,
a division of Penguin Group (USA) Inc.

First Printing, April 2013

 REGISTERED TRADEMARK—MARCA REGISTRADA

LIBRARY OF CONGRESS CATALOGING-IN-PUBLICATION DATA:
Knepper, Nicole.
Moms who drink and swear: true tales of loving my kids
while losing my mind/Nicole Knepper.
p. cm
ISBN 978-0-451-41814-2
1. Motherhood—Humor. 2. Parenting—Humor. I. Title.
PN6084.M6K64 2013
306.874'3'0207—dc23   2012046436

Printed in the United States of America
10 9 8 7 6 5 4 3 2 1

Set in Bembo
Designed by Spring Hoteling

PUBLISHER'S NOTE
Penguin is committed to publishing works of quality and integrity. In that spirit, we
are proud to offer this book to our readers; however the story, the experiences and the
words are the author's alone.

The publisher does not have any control over and does not assume any responsibility
for author or third-party Web sites or their content.

Mom,
your love put me at the top of the world. This book is for you.
Love, Nikki

CONTENTS

MOMS WHO
DRINK
AND SWEAR

INTRODUCTION

YOU'VE GOT MAIL AND GERMS AND A QUARTER MILLION FRIENDS ON FACEBOOK: THE STORY OF MWDAS

I resisted the computer. I saw it as the metaphorical mean girl who would mock me for my clumsy inadequacy. The bleeps and bloops and buttons intimidated me and I feared that I would be like Matthew Broderick in *War Games* and accidently almost start a nuclear war. I'm not exaggerating; I've been known to make some *big* errors when it comes to anything mechanical. But there was another reason, too. I also fought against progress because my husband wanted me to embrace it! Yes, I'm a stompy, immature, insecure, change-fearing brat with an oppositional streak. Especially when it comes to my husband, who instantly made the bloops and bleeps his BITCHES! "Come on, it's easy!" he said, to which I replied with a big "Fuck you, Math Man. Easy for you usually means mind-boggling for me!"

I had no patience for being mocked by the mean girl or micromanaged by the Math Man. I was busy trying to make sense out of all the paranormal shit on *The X-Files*, reading a book or doing the laundry. Occasionally I'd agree to attempt to form a truce with technology, but I was as impatient with the process as my husband was with me. He promised to be nice, not to mock or micromanage me, but I just had no interest in the things he thought I should be interested in online, especially playing games the way he did. Pfffth! I barely wanted to play games with him in real life (see "Fucking Family Game Night," page 272). And so I'd bitch to my friends about his whiny and demanding behavior.

I personally don't do the whole "my husband is my best friend" thing. He's my husband! In MY world, husbands are not besties—they're honeys, and that's a big diff! I consider my husband as a backup friend if I really need a plus one and my girlfriends are otherwise engaged. Don't get me wrong. I love him and like to sex up on him and spend his money and stare mindlessly at the television next to him under a blanket eating chips. But when I want to get talky and deep, I need my GIRLS!

It took him a while to think of it, but my need for girl time was how he finally coaxed me to the computer. About fifteen years ago he showed me how I could enjoy increased communication with my girlfriends via the Internet! Initially it was an uncomfortable embrace, but the lure of *free* access to my beloved friends known as the "Brat Pack" sisters encouraged me to work out the kinks. MY GIRLS! MY BFFS! Big Bossy and his ease with technology were my bridge to the Brat Pack, so I sucked it up. I figured that if I killed him in the process of trying to figure out the Internet, my friends were so loyal that they'd help me bury the body, no questions asked. So, you can see how that would motivate a technophobe to go viral. Not everybody has a friend who would hide a body for him or her, but I do. I can think of at least five off the top of my head that wouldn't think twice about it. BOOM!

So down the rabbit hole I went. As annoying as it was, that high-pitched staticky SCREEEEEEEEEEEE, clickety, pop, pop, SCREEEEEEEEEEEE, KA-Shhhhhhhhshhhh sound meant I could receive an e-mail message from one of my soul sisters, who I desperately missed since we'd all decided to conform and meet grown-up expectations like having a job and raising a family.

Change can be good, but even the good stuff can be a difficult adjustment. I wanted my friends to follow their dreams and kick some ass in their adult lives; I just didn't realize how much this dream chasing and catching would change our connection to each other. In particular, the expense of long-distance phone calls really wrecked our ability to stay in touch. As we all struggled through the early years of marriage and motherhood, we needed much more emotional support than life allowed. Time and money were tight for all of us. We didn't have hours to spend on the phone, let alone the extra cashola to cover regular three-hour cross-country marathon blabfests. The Internet was a solution to that problem. Fast, easy and CHEAP, but I'll be honest—it still scared the shit out of me. It was too much change and seemed so impersonal.

I was afraid to push any button in case I somehow managed to crash the entire computer system and then the husband would become even more bossy and annoying, trying to "help" me navigate the new and intimidating technology. Then we'd end up fighting and I'd end up feeling even more lonesome for my girlfriends. But if I wanted to cyber connect with my friends and increase the frequency (see what I did there?) of communication, I had to suck it up and embrace the computer. My increased tolerance for Eric's dictatorial interference is further evidence of how strong my need is for these women in my life. I'm talking HARD-CORE, because the hubs and I have "issues" being teacher and student.

Still, twenty or thirty years of friendship with these women made it worth sitting through his torturous technology lessons. It still stuns me that I actually survived; just as it stuns me when

I hear those numbers, twenty and thirty, roll off my tongue. Can it be that long? How can I have known and loved these ladies for that many years? When I look at our saggy boobs, age spots and laugh lines, I see that it must be true, yet when I'm with them it feels like we're still squealing teenage girls about to commence shenanigans STAT.

Our friendship started in the eighties. We had big hair and popped collars and if a guy gave one of us a mix tape, we'd spend hours on the telephone dissecting the lyrics of every single song, attaching them to special moments and using them as evidence of his undying love. Many a dude wanted to stop the world and melt with me, I'm just saying. The Brat Pack was what we called our high school powder-puff flag football team but the name stuck long after the games were over. Our lives back then certainly seemed like a combination of angsty John Hughes movies, and we had no problem comparing ourselves to the famous pack of popular young Hollywood stars. Conceited much? Damn right we were, and rightly so! We were young, beautiful and in the prime of our lives. Never again would we have such tight little asses and smooth, flawless skin. We were also incredibly close, sharing our hopes and dreams as well as our heartbreaks, teenage dramas and frustrations. In typical adolescent girl fashion, our interactions were life or death intense, freakishly histrionic, characterized by severe oversharing of personal information with alarming frequency.

Over the years, we transformed from giggly, carefree prepubescent girls into serious and focused young women, seeking education, independence and, of course, satisfying romantic relationships. College, internships, careers and marriage could separate us only physically; emotionally and spiritually, we remained as tight and dependent on each other as ever; maybe even more so. The intensity remained, but the frequency decreased. Marriage and careers had spread us out across the country and young children made our once long, uninterrupted phone conversations a rare occurrence. We had diapers to buy, butts to wipe, bills to pay, needy husbands to attend to and new friends to make.

New friends are good; each of us made some. It's just that there's something precious and unique about friendships that span decades and the kind of comfort that comes from talking to a familiar voice who knows the backstory by heart. Your shared history makes getting down to business quick, dirty and oh so easy! I had connected to other women over the years, but those relationships lacked the uninhibited freedom from judgment that I experienced with the Brat Pack.

One day, the drama queen of the group, Lisa, sent a stark-raving-mad rant that I like to call the "You've got germs" story. It was equal parts horrifying and hilarious, a truly masterful description of how, while her husband was away on business, both she and her two small children had a stomach virus causing MASSIVE amounts of diarrhea, vomit and tears to flow. She spent two days burning with a fever, trying not to shit her pants while drying tears, cleaning up leaky diapers and cradling vomiting children in her lap only to find she was too exhausted to even sleep at night but lay tossing and turning with worry over her terminally ill father five hundred miles away, her financial problems, and did I mention that she was pregnant? Oh yeah, she was also knocked up at the time. How I wish I had printed and saved that e-mail. I laughed and I cried. We all did! Lisa's rant was unique at the time. We always ranted and raved in phone conversations and in person, but to put it in print like that was a step up from our usual level of sharing and complaining. Her needs at that moment were beyond a phone call or an e-mail to just one of us. She was reaching out in a broad and bold way, to ALL of us at once.

It was glorious and it set a precedent. We all started sharing group rants as well as our usual one-to-one messages. Little did we know that there were some un-fucking-fathomable changes in store for us all. Enter marital problems, sick and dying parents, financial troubles and countless other life stressors, and eventually my grief over life's circumstances became a deep and dangerous depression. I was slogging through another graduate program without enthusiasm and missed my career as I adjusted to being a stay-at-home mom. My marriage was strained and I was becoming bitter, isolated and hopeless that I would find meaning in my future existence. I wasn't the only one struggling, but I was at an all-time low. My friends were worried. They told me so.

My friend Amy believed that Facebook would help cure what was ailing me. I was the straggler of the group—ME! Hard to believe my big mouth wasn't splatting all over a social network, but depression had sucked out my soul and shrunk my life into the four walls of my beige, aluminum-sided suburban home. I hadn't even heard of Facebook in the summer of 2008 but I soon found it gave me a way to escape the isolation I was experiencing. The status updates connected me with all my friends even faster than e-mail.

The graphic and colorful e-mails that once bounced back and forth within our group about financial stress, marital woes, hormones, postpartum depression, aging parents and our individual trips on the crazy train of parenthood were replaced by one-line status updates. It was a busy mom's dream, but as a lover of all things incoherent and rambling, I was never satisfied with the less-is-more vibe. I liked the long-winded, shambolic, stress-fueled outbursts. I had come to NEED the humor and connectedness that my brilliant friends provided. This was even more the case for me when the crazy train I was riding was derailed and I was desperately in need not just of connection but distraction. As I said, I was being destroyed by the natural disaster that seemed to be absorbing everything in my life. I was so grateful to be so regularly connected to my girlfriends. I NEEDED THEM. Was what I was going through normal? Was anyone else feeling this way, experiencing these things?

I formed a group for the Brat Pack and a few other mom pals and decided to call it "Moms Who Drink and Swear," a place where we could rant, tell stories, share ideas on everything parental and post photos of our kids. It was like a big goddamn block party/mommy and me group/PTA meeting/Bunco night all rolled into one! We laughed, confessed, chatted LIVE without having to dread the financial consequences of long-distance telephone bills, just as we had done in the old days of our Internet musings. I came back to life. As word spread, the group became a daily destination for thousands of women, seeking to share, rant or seek advice on parenting topics as well as nonparenting-related issues. At one point there were over four hundred separate discussion topics where women were actively engaged in the Moms Who Drink and Swear group. People suggested that I start a blog, so I did! Eventually readers complained that they were missing my blog posts as the group grew and the page was overrun. So, although I kept ranting, sharing and learning in the group setting, I created the "fan" page for my blog site. This allowed me to share in the group setting AND give my blog its own little showcase.

Sharing with my friends and our extended circle of moms helped me to stop feeling guilty for every last angry, bitter or negative thought or behavior toward my children. That extended circle kept extending, sort of like that commercial for shampoo from the eighties where the hot blonde's photo keeps multiplying because she's telling all her besties about shampoo: "And they told two friends, and they told two friends, and so on and so on and so on." Before long, Moms Who Drink and Swear was global. I was getting e-mail from women as far away as Australia thanking me for making them feel "normal."

So here we are now, middle-aged women flitting around a social network, knowing that needing each other and reaching out to each other will save us from ourselves (and most certainly keep us from harming our children in a moment of weakness and sheer exhaustion). We've lost parents to cancer and buried children, suffered bitter divorces, and endured numerous personal and professional traumas. What keeps us ticking is the knowledge that we are not alone. WE ARE NOT ALONE.

Today I look at myself in the mirror, not always recognizing the face staring back at me, or the body that just cannot possibly belong to the sixteen-year-old girl who lives in my mind. Being able to bridge that gap without going completely insane is possible only because of the connections I have with the other women in my life. We just *get* each other.

As the old saying goes, "Some people come into our lives and quickly go. Others lose their virginity to your brother, name his wang after a luxury hotel, and traumatize you forever by talking about how sexy he is."

Wait, that's not right. "Friends are the family we choose for ourselves," is the old saying I was thinking of.

Moms Who Drink and Swear wasn't started as something for everyone. It just WASN'T! The group was something I did on a whim while sucking down cheap white wine and stalking people from high school on Facebook. What makes MWDAS unique is that our group *still* isn't for everyone. It's just not and it never will be. We feel very comfortable telling anyone who clutches her pearls in shock, judging us for our honesty about parenthood, to feel free to SUCK IT.

Moms Who Drink and Swear is for women (and thousands of men as well) who just want to survive what is arguably the most insane, face-smacking, brain-scrambling reality that any of us could have ever imagined: we are actually somebody's parent.

PARENTHOOD. It ain't for pussies.

I have no idea who said that, but it's true. I think I saw it on a bumper sticker. And there are some serious pussies out there, afraid of the kind of raw honesty and intense emotions that are experienced when one is sharing a mostly wonderful yet often overwhelmingly chaotic and difficult life with the fruit of their loins. I was never one of those sissy types, but had I not decided to dance with the devil of technology, I might not have discovered the many "Brat Packers" beyond my crew of deep-rooted, long-standing relationships. Moms Who Drink and Swear are everywhere! I love being part of a group of like-minded parents who strive to be true to their own identities and keep growing while taking on the responsibility of trying to civilize wild beastly human cubs.

And I cannot fail to acknowledge the insane IRONY that I, the technophobic, Internet-avoiding woman who resisted the force of social media, have become a force to be reckoned with in the wide world web of cyber moms just looking to get our kids fed and watered so that we can find time to check out our friend's photos of her motherfucking kids' recent antics while slugging back an adult beverage!

I guess I should thank my husband for not only planting his fertile seed in the soil of my loins, but also for making me move my cheese by facing and conquering my fear of technology. Had

I resisted his incessant groping and bossing, I would not be sitting around in my undies every day, avoiding showers and eating Hershey bars while writing this epic known as *Moms Who Drink and Swear*. So thanks, Sugarbuns! I'm glad I didn't dump you in college for that nerdy Jesus freak who didn't appreciate my naked waterslide antics. I heart you and will be forever grateful to you, but remember this: I've now got half a million bitches who not only got my back, but also know where to bury a body if you get out of line. BOOM!

BATHROOM WARS PART I

ZACH   What are you doing, Mom?

ME   (On the toilet) WHAT DOES IT LOOK LIKE I AM DOING?

ZACH   You don't have to yell about it.

ME   I am not feeling well and I need some privacy. Please leave now.

ZACH   I was just wondering where you were. I was worried.

ME   Awww, that would be sweet if you didn't pick the lock and barge in on me after I told you I was in here and feeling sick to my stomach. NOW GET OUT!

ZACH   What's in that box?

ME   Tampons. GET OUT OF HERE NOW!

ZACH   Oh! That explains why you are yelling. You are going through puberty. Again.

ME   OH MY GOD! GET OUT OF HERE RIGHT NOW!

SISTERHOOD OF
THE STATUS UPDATES:
Girlfriends, Genitals and Growing Up

"Whether you are throwing up or
breaking up, you want your girlfriends
right there. I don't trust women who
don't go to their girlfriends."

—Drew Barrymore

KITTY'S GOT PMS

I have no idea how I've managed almost two decades of marriage without killing my husband or at least "accidentally" hurting him when I'm suffering from PMS. My tender humanity leaves me and I become an angry feline, hijacked by my hormones. I've tried to warn him, to explain that even though I like him well enough, at times like these I may have violent fantasies of slicing his throat when he breathes too loudly around me. Yet he continues to risk his life, sitting on my lap and farting on me during this dangerous and unpredictable time. Nothing I say sticks in his man brain, and he ends up reacting to my PMS-fueled behavior like a scared puppy who's been clawed by the momma house kitty, cowering in the corner, confused.

Why is it that his testosterone-filled melon cannot absorb even the most basic and surprisingly simple truth about women: that I BLEED FROM MY LADY PARTS EVERY MONTH FOR ANYWHERE FROM THREE TO SEVEN DAYS and he needs to accept it and take safety precautions? When the pretty kitty gets sick, she *will* bare her claws and lash out in pain!

He's not alone. Men just don't like to think about their women having tomato pants, let alone talk about it. There should be a class or a support group for them, but unfortunately there isn't, so I've prepared the following trifecta: the hat trick, the veritable HOLY TRINITY of free information and support for men when their woman is off riding the cotton pony. Here we go, guys, GIDDYUP!

The first simple truth:

If chocolate doesn't take the edge off when a woman is raging with PMS, you need to get her MORE chocolate, and probably some ice cream. These are her "medicines" and she needs them to get well. Don't get too close to her or ask her what's wrong. Don't make eye contact. This can be taken as a sign of aggression by an angry feline. Just give her the medicine and back away.

Slowly.

Don't eat ANY of the medicine in the house unless you have determined that she has enough to treat her symptoms. Not . . . one . . . bite. She needs all of it.

You can eat the nonmedicinal foods; however, if you choose cereal and use the last of the milk, you must get more milk (as in YESTERDAY, especially if you don't have a kid or two to take the blame for the empty milk carton). It's bad enough to be inconsiderate when your woman isn't a hot mess of hormonal madness, but it's just suicide to engage in such risky behavior when she is.

The second simple truth:

During this time, a woman will spew venomous, short-tempered insults in your direction just because you are breathing. This is because she often finds herself feeling ravenously hungry after eating a quart of ice cream and an entire package of Oreos. Accompanying this insatiable hunger is a dull, thumping lower-back pain interspersed with stabbing pains in her junk and a throbbing headache. Some days she is experiencing an overall feeling that her skeletal system could burst out of her skin any moment AND her breasts are sore in the way your nuts are after being kicked.

What would *your* mood be like after two or three nights of restless, unsatisfying sleep while experiencing all of the above physical symptoms? You need to understand that she is at Defcon 1, the highest state of readiness to defend herself, a cocked pistol! So, if a kitty hisses at you, do NOT keep trying to pet the kitty—unless you want to get your fingers ripped off by her claws. **Leave Kitty alone.**

The third simple truth:

Take care of the things that need to be taken care of. ALL OF THE THINGS. Don't ask what they are—KNOW that you need to do something. ANYTHING. Look around. You cannot claim ignorance or stupidity after one or two menstrual cycles. Your lady will just see you as a lazy, lying moron instead of the powerful and virile man that you'd like her to see once she returns to good health. Remember that during ovulation, kitty will purr. She can't help it, and she will be clearheaded enough to remember and recognize your actions, making you an attractive potential father of her kittens. You will be invited to pet her, stroke her and refer to her using terms of endearment such as "my sweet pussycat." So, clean something, launder something, and pick up after yourself and your kitten children, if you already have them. (Oh, and for the love of the gods, do NOT leave an empty roll where the toilet paper should be. People have been killed for less serious offenses and PMS has been used successfully as a defense in a court of law.) Everybody knows that Kitty hates a dirty litter box. You are the metaphorical corner she will piss in if her box isn't in order. Remember you are dealing with an injured animal.

If this all seems too complicated for you, then maybe you

aren't ready for a kitty of your own. You should stick to looking at kitties on the Internet until you can memorize, internalize and implement these three simple things.

1) Get her "medicine" and don't touch it.

2) Accept and understand her condition. You'd have more luck trying to reason with an angry toddler or argue with a sloppy drunk than thinking you can understand how she is feeling. Just shut your mouth!

3) Help out. Put on your thinking cap and move. Your. ASS.

Fellas, your kitty's got a crime scene in her pants every month. Deal with it. Consider this not only a warning by a kitty who has been there, but a public service from an expert in the field of kitty mood management.

THE VAGINA DIALOGUES

"Your baby daddy makes good fajitas," I told Dagmar while stuffing my face with leftovers. I was starving. She nodded, her mouth full as well, and started pouring us some of those nasty ready-mixed mojitos into tiny juice glasses. We were sitting outside on her deck, enjoying the last bit of light on a warm summer night. "Shit, I forgot ice for the drinks," she sighed. She started to get up to fetch some when I told her, "Sit your skinny ass down and relax. I'll get it." She had spent the day inside with her three sick kids, breaking up fights and cleaning up puke. My pal was too pooped to party, so girl's night out had turned into girl's night in. Leftovers and drinks on her deck!

I hopped up quickly, planning to go inside and grab not only some ice cubes but also some larger glasses, because what the hell was she thinking with those itty-bitty things anyway? I was planning to get my mojito buzz ON and I needed a big, frosty mug! When I returned with the supplies, she was talking on her cell phone. "Is it your baby daddy?" I whispered, giggling. She started laughing and rolled her eyes.

I rolled mine as well. "He wants to know if we're talking about our vaginas," she told me. "What else would we be talking about?" I replied, leaning over and talking loudly into the receiver. "And after we get all shit-faced here on the deck, we're going up to your bedroom to have a pillow fight wearing only our panties."

Just a half hour earlier, I had checked in by text with Eric. "Hey, Sugarbuns. Remember, I'm at Dag's. Going to talk girly and drown my sorrow in mojitos."

"Say hi to her for me. I assume the two of you will spend the bulk of your evening drinking and talking about penises."

"Seriously," I said to Dagmar after she hung up, "do they really think we sit around talking about vaginas and penises? I can't imagine calling you up to talk about all things genitalia. Ring Ring—'Hey, girlfriend, I hate getting your voice mail when I have a penis emergency. Hurry and call me back as soon as you get this message.' Or, knock knock, 'Surprise!' There I am at your front door. 'I brought over some wine and snacks and thought we could just sit around comparing vaginas.'"

Do all men really think this way? Do they really think we gals get together and spend our precious, kid-free time talking about our sex organs?

It seems like every time I am out with one of my girlfriends and we take the time to check in with our husbands, they mention a minimum of two (but usually all) of the following: their penis, whether or not we miss their penis, what they would like us to do with their penis, our vaginas, how much they miss our vaginas, what they would like to do with our vaginas, boobs, what they want to do with our boobs, what they would like us to do with our boobs and whether or not we are talking about, looking at or doing anything to each other's boobs and if so, can we PLEASE get it on film (okay, fine, that's just my husband)?

Oh, and no matter what time we check in, they want to know what time we will be home. If we are walking out the door and telling them that we will be home after the kids are asleep, they will call or text us about ten seconds after we drive away to ask what time the kids actually go to sleep and how long after they are asleep will we be home so that we can sex each other up. It's predictable, irritating and also confusing. Why are men always so damn focused on all things vag and peen? WHY?

And why do I continue to spend any time at all trying to figure it out? That and why men can't understand how completely unattractive it is when they take every opportunity to work sex organ chatter into every damn conversation. Do I think that understanding how men think will change it, or make it easier to help them understand why it's so fucking annoying?

I refuse to believe men can't help themselves! They're not Neanderthals anymore. Men have walked on the moon, for fuck sake! They no longer have to fight for territory, food or mates. With eHarmony and one hundred types of cereal to choose from at the grocery store, the biological urge to feed and breed just can't be used as an excuse for any man to perpetually posture and pimp his penis, but they do. They must *choose* to think this way. There's just no other explanation.

It's so frustrating. The minds of men are obvious and mysterious at the same time. That is why we need our girlfriends so much. We understand each other and if we get in an argument or have a misunderstanding, we know how to approach any problem and solve it without genital involvement.

Dagmar and I are sure that our husbands' preoccupation with their penises and the things their penises preoccupy them with prevent them from taking proper care of themselves. That self-neglect, along with the reality that men statistically do not live as long as women, means that they will most likely die before we do. Once they are both six feet under, we are moving in together. We are getting at least sixteen cats, merging our wardrobes and bank accounts and wearing themed outfits for every holiday of the year with our mom jeans and Crocs. And without constant reminders from men to think about our vaginas, we will probably forget we even have them.

> God grant me the serenity to accept the things I cannot change, a sledgehammer to smash the motherfucking shit out of the toys that are loud, broken, obnoxious and constantly being fought over, and the wisdom NOT to smash said toys because it would scare my children and it would really just be easier to uncork the wine and drink the entire bottle. Amen.

MOMMY'S DRINKING PROBLEM

I have a drinking problem.

The problem is, I waste wine.

Don't try to make me feel better by saying I drink cheap, shitty wine so it's not a big deal. There are wineless mothers in China who would give their left eyeball for the cheap wine I so carelessly waste. Sometimes the guilt overwhelms me and I feel ashamed, but I do have an explanation for my seemingly irresponsible and inconsiderate behavior.

I never, EVER intend to waste the magical elixir that makes my mind hum with happiness, but as they say, the road to hell is paved with good intentions. It starts with me innocently pouring a glass of wine when I'm done with Mom/hausfrau duties for the day. I've worked hard and kept my shit together so I feel quite justified in sucking down a glass of tangy goodness. I feel immediately happy as the first sip trickles down my throat while I'm reading, watching TV or writing. All set? YOU BET! Let the Me time begin!

Before the liquid hits my belly, I hear the back doorbells ringing, which means that one of the dogs has to go out. Some people think it's so cool that we have our dogs bell trained. It's not cool. It's fucking annoying. Especially since one of them is senile, and the other one just has a screw loose, so they play the in and out game repeatedly even when they don't have to make. I get up and let one or both of them out to make yuck, wait for them to finish making yuck, and then give them a doggie treat for making said yuck in the backyard instead of under the piano bench. If one dog is out and the other dog is curled up somewhere else sleeping, it's inevitable that once I re-snuggle up I hear the RING-RING-RING of the other dog, who needs to make yuck. I always think I should just take my glass of wine with me, but inevitably I forget and miss out on the sippy goodness. SIGH.

When the dogs have finished their business, and realize that ringing the goddamn bell and going out a few more times is *not* going to result in additional treats, they settle down for a snooze. Knowing they are content, I'll get all snuggled up for the second time and just as I greet my sweet drink with a little slurp, I hear the buzzer of the dryer go off—BUUUUUUUUUZZZZZ! I know that if I don't get up, I'm going to end up having to re-wash the whole damn load or iron some crap that is too wrinkled even for me to wear. Hey, I have *some* standards! And since neither of my kids understands the idea of coordinating tops and bottoms, at least their color-blind, freak-show clothes combos are clean. Again, I think I should take the glass with me but I'm easily distracted and end up forgetting. SIGH.

After I fluff and fold, I run the piles upstairs and inevitably one of the kids (who I've tucked in sixteen times at this point) wants another snuggle or a drink or to be retucked in. I think to myself, Self, you should run downstairs and get your wine because you could sip and snuggle, but no sooner do I have the thought than it vanishes. My kids are SO cute and warm and deliciously sweet at night when they are tired, snuggling them gives me a natural buzz. Also, if I did bring the wine upstairs,

Murphy's Law of wine drinking around children states that no matter where you put your wine, they will manage to spill it, so between rule-following and forgetting, the wine just sits all lonely waiting for me. Right, another SIGH.

At this point, anywhere from five to thirty minutes after getting sucked into the kid vortex, I make my way downstairs (assuming I don't fall asleep in one of the beds with my kids post-snuggle, thereby wasting the entire glass of wine), and I take a sip of my beloved white wine treat, only to find that the chill is gone. I buy cheap wine, and trust me when I tell you that warm, cheap white wine is like flat, stale Froot Loop-flavored beer, and it coats your tongue with a furrylike film that makes morning mouth seem tasty in comparison. So, I have to get up, again, but of course this time I remember to bring the wine.

I transfer my piss-warm wine into another glass with ice, 'cause I lack any semblance of class when it comes to wine drinking, and wait for the chill to come back. Of course it's watered down and not as buzzy good now. (Insert frown face.)

Now, when I'm throwing all caution to the wind, I dump the warm stuff down the sink and pour a fresh glass! This happens only if we have a surplus of cash for the month or I have found a ten-dollar bill that day while walking down the street. Neither of these things has actually happened over the last ten years, but I like to pretend that they do sometimes and then I get CRAZY CARELESS WITH THE WINE. Look at me; I have a money tree in the backyard! I feel rebellious, wasteful and oh so naughty! This is usually when I've actually thrown back a glass *before* getting all distracted so I have a teeny buzzy wuzzy and I'm all cavalier with the vino and subject to bad judgment. Basically I act like a Kardashian (not the one who made the pee pee sex video, the tall, smart-ass one. I think I'd actually enjoy warm wine if I were drinking it with her).

At this point, the dogs are aroused by my movement and either they start in with the bell-ringing shit or one of the kids inevitably decides to put on a dramatic performance in order to get me upstairs AGAIN or I have to pee within two minutes of sitting down and snugglefying myself. As usual, I forget to bring my wine when tending to the dogs or kids and seriously, who brings their drink into the bathroom unless they are at a party and trying to avoid getting roofied?

Many times when I'm in the bathroom I notice that either A) there is no toilet paper on the roll or B) there is a roll of toilet paper, but it's almost empty and there are no spare rolls in the bathroom or C) there is something disgusting that needs my immediate attention because it's a bodily fluid thing and I just HAVE to clean it.

Once I've tied up the loose ends with regard to the shitter and shitter supplies, I head back to snuggleville and I rejoice in the fact that my wineglass is still FULL; but seeing how it's leaky with condensation I need to suck that drink down STAT before it cools down completely. This makes me grin and forget my woes. Chugging wine? Sounds like a great time! I take one sip and another and then a gulp or two once I've got the groove. I feel warm and cozy. I sink farther into whatever place I'm chill-axing until I realize that I'm too horizontal to drink without spilling so I have to get vertical again to enjoy my beverage. How annoying! But I'll just have to get up again if I spill it all over the sofa and I've already been up and down a dozen times, so I just stop my bellyaching and sit the fuck up. I shouldn't bitch when there are wineless women in China who would love to drink my glass of cheap vino.

I have about two of those horizontal-to-vertical adjustments in me before I'm snoring like a rhino with a head cold, unless of course a dog needs to go out, a kid needs a hit of momma, my weak bladder doesn't betray me or the dryer doesn't taunt me.

See what I mean? I have a major drinking problem! The first step is admitting it and I'm doing that right now. Hello, my name is Nikki and I have a problem wasting wine, forgetting wine and being too distracted to drink my wine. I need fucking help.

Live-in help.

MAKING NEW McFRIENDS

One Sunday, not so long ago, I was cranky for no particular reason. I was also as close to brain-dead as you can be without actually being brain-dead. My daughter and her friend were as close to bouncing off the walls as kids can be without actually bouncing off the walls. I thought about taking them to the town pool but it didn't seem particularly safe, given how zoned out and aggravated I was. So, I settled on the next best thing: McDonald's. I figured that having my kid and her buddy swim around in E. coli and grease was probably a much safer Sunday afternoon activity than drowning or being kidnapped.

Judge me. Tell me about my other options. List them. Thank you, I never considered any of those things. You have changed my life forever, possibly saved a life. Moving on.

After Cate and her buddy shoveled their Happy Meals in their faces at six hundred miles per hour, they put on their socks and took off running towards the monstrosity of plastic tubes and slides that was jam-packed with screaming crotchfruit. I think it's ridonkulous that the people in McCharge at the McPlayplace require kids to wear socks, on the basis that covered feet decrease the chance that kids will catch a fungus or whatnot. Who are they fucking kidding? The kiddos are pressing their lips to the plastic windows, making their cheeks puff out, and wiping their greasy, grimy fingers on every inch of the gigantic germ house. I have personally watched my daughter give a tongue bath to the side of the curly slide at the McPlay area. Socks? Please.

Anyhow . . . I whipped out my notebook to make a grocery list. I considered starting a blog post, but I figured I was more likely to successfully shit out a baby rhino than to think creatively while the loudspeaker played "Quack Quack" by the Wiggles on full blast. I know my limits. Now, I have seen the Wiggles live—three times—and I love the memories I have of watching my kids dance and sing to those entertaining Australians, but that particular song was one of my least favorite. Wishing I had brought my earbuds, I started looking around for napkins to shove in my ears. The lady at the table next to me was sitting alone. I smiled at her and she smiled back. I was going to initiate a conversation, but she beat me to it.

"I was sitting here wondering if this is hell. Are we in hell? Maybe this IS hell and I just don't know it and everyone else does," she said, giggling.

"Well, if you're thinking that way, I'd say you're either experiencing an intense existential enlightenment, or the high level of stress induced by sensory overload is signaling an impending heart attack," I answered, giggling back.

We were cracking up when the theme from *Dora the Explorer* started blasting.

"Kill me," she deadpanned.

"No, you kill me!" I responded.

More cracking up. I noticed we were both wearing pajama pants. I was falling in love with her. Not in the sexual, "I want to jump her mom bones" way, but in the "OH MY GOD I LOVE THE WAY THIS BITCH THINKS" way. Know what I mean?

"Okay, same time; we kill each other at the same time," she suggested.

"Do you have any nightlock?" I asked.

"Oh my GOD—*Hunger Games* reference?" she half yelled at me. "I can't kill you because I love you."

"And I you," I responded.

Now we were choking with laughter.

The theme song from *Little Einsteins* started blaring.

"Before we started talking, I was lamenting the fact that I didn't bring my earbuds to drown out the music, and by lamenting, I mean considering poking out my eardrums with a fork," I said, sighing.

"I was thinking I should have brought a flask."

"Will you marry me?"

Yeah, we were BFFs by this point, and the witty banter and giggles just kept coming. It made me so happy. My brain was sparking, turning on again! That's when my daughter strolled up to the table to report a "very dangerous situation."

"Right, dangerous, tell me what's up, sister."

"There is a total DOUCHE BAG up there in the tunnels who keeps pushing me, hard, down the slide before I'm ready, and saying inappropriate things! I'm going to kick him in the nuts if he doesn't stop bothering us," she whined loudly while dramatically flinging herself in my lap.

I wasn't exactly embarrassed—remember, my new BFF sitting right next to me had the mouth of a truck driver—but it occurred to me that she might not like hearing my eight-year-old threaten to assault another child while calling said child a douche bag. Just because she was shooting the shit with me, dropping profanity liberally, that didn't necessarily mean she would find the humor in a kid using such language.

And honestly, I really don't approve of kids casually swearing, and my daughter rarely repeats any of my potty-mouthed ranting. But douche bag is one of my favorite words. On the plus side, I'm sure she has no idea what it means. My kids think it's a term of endearment when I tell them they are dumb asses. It's also not uncommon for her to hear me threatening to kick my son and husband in the nuts when they leave their man crap everywhere on a daily basis.

Judge. Comment and make suggestions as to how I could clean up my mouth (swear jar, counseling) and educate me about the potential harm I am causing to my children. Your suggestions and advice could be just what I need to change. I know that my father's gratuitous use of profanity traumatized me so much that I'm on disability and in twice-daily therapy in order to deal with it.

Not.

Anyway. I knew better than to act all shocked and tell her not to use such language or threaten another child; it would just backfire and she'd say "But, Mom, *you* say it." So, I simply told her to ignore the boy, that it would be wrong to hurt him, and that I realized that she wasn't really going to kick him in the nuts, but since he didn't know that, she ought not to say it. I also asked her not to call names, using the "two wrongs don't make a right" analogy. I told her to apologize to the kid and try to avoid him for the duration of our visit.

She had stopped listening to me before I finished speaking. Frankly, I was surprised she even came down to report this incident in the first place. Of course before going back to play, she grabbed two fistfuls of fries, shoved them in her mouth, and then tried to wash them down with ten huge, noisy gulps of her Hi-C. OH—that's why she came down. The "dangerous situation" was just a dramatic extra. My daughter is the moth drawn to the flame of French fries. She walked away still chewing.

"Wait," said my new BFF. "Is the boy wearing an orange shirt?" Cate turned around and nodded in the affirmative. "Did he tell you that you smell like dog shit?"

"Yep!" Cate kept nodding.

"Goddammit," BFF chuckled, "he's been saying that a lot. His older sister says it to him, and she's not just saying it to be cruel. He really does tend to have that dog shit scent. Not that he doesn't have the opportunity to choose from a litany of four-letter words that roll out of my mouth regularly."

"Well, I wish I could blame Cate's older brother for the douche bag comment and the nut-kicking threat, but those are all me." I grinned. I couldn't help it. It was all so funny.

"Listen up, honey," she said to Cate, "tell him that if he keeps acting like a thug, he will not only be cleaning up our dog's shit, but I'll let the neighbors know he is available for free dog shit pickup in their yards all week. Okay? Now go on, tell that little douche bag what his momma said."

Cate looked at me for confirmation. I shrugged and tilted my head in the direction of my new BFF and said, "You heard her. Go!" And off she went. The two of us started laughing again, just as the theme song for *The Wonder Pets* came on.

"I hate that duck," my BFF said, referring to a character from the cartoon theme song that was playing. "She's bossy and never fucking learns her lesson, right? But she's not as bad as Ruby the bunny. I used to have to leave the room when this show was on. I just couldn't TAKE it."

"Girl, I feel you, but I can't help feeling sorry for Ruby, you know? Her parents are nowhere to be found, her brother is a mute with oppositional defiant disorder and developmental delays, and I'm pretty sure Grandma Bunny is too high to give a shit. Oh, and that turtle, Tuck? He whines more than Caillou, and all that bald little bastard ever does is whine. His mom just sits there with her thumb up her ass, not doing a thing about it. I think it's irresponsible of PBS to run that kind of dysfunctional shit."

"Oh, don't get me started on Caillou," she said, looking up at the Playplace. She was getting started on Caillou, I could tell, and I couldn't wait to hear her take on it, but instead she burst into laughter and pointed up at the yellow tunnel with the triangle-shaped windows. "Oh yeah, look at that! LOOK! Look up!"

So I looked up, and saw both of our kids' faces in the windows. Cate's forehead and shit-eating grin were plastered against the filthy plastic window, and she was waving at me with one hand while pointing to the kid next to her with the other. BFF's kid was not smiling or waving. He looked like he was staring at a bloody crime scene: frozen stiff, mouth hanging open, with both his hands pressed up against the glass. I said, "I think you scared him. He looks like he shit his pants."

"God, I hope not," she laughed. "I want to hang out with you and talk about that little fucker Calliou."

Twenty hundred is not a real number, but for a few seconds I believed it could be and that maybe third grade math really was too difficult for me. I'm that tired.

THE BACKUP PLAN

"Oh my god! Your pussy is pulsating!" was probably a completely inappropriate thing to bark out as I was holding up my best friend's puffy, limp leg and staring at her exploding lady parts, but in my defense, her pussy WAS pulsating and I'm not known for having much of a verbal filter. My best friend, Dagmar, knew there would be some colorful language and chaotic ridiculousness when she asked me to be in the delivery room. As a matter of fact, I'm sure she was counting on it as a welcome distraction from labor. As mouthy and misplaced as my observations about her vagina might have been, at the time I was watching it explode, vibrate and leak with life, I finally understood what a gift I had been given.

When she had asked if I would be willing to be her second string labor coach, I didn't hesitate. "Of course I'll be your backup plan!" I squealed like a twelve-year-old girl at a Justin Bieber concert. "I am so honored that you asked me." Her husband, John, was constantly out of town on business and she knew there was only a fifty/fifty chance that he would be around when the baby decided to come. This was her first pregnancy and she needed an experienced mom-sidekick. I was excited and made no secret that I hoped that her husband *would* be out of town. I WANTED to be there. Hell, I had already been thinking about asking her if I could be there. I imagined an estrogen fest, the ultimate girl's night out!

On the flip side, it would also be the first time I would ever witness childbirth, and that's some serious shit. I'd be up close and personal, watching a three-dimensional, live-action birth complete with skin ripping, fluids leaking and potential poops popping out with pushes. This wasn't going to be like the movie *Beaches* where the Bette Midler character gets all dramatic and flirty with the doctor and then passes out. I would need to be the heroic wind beneath her wings. Wind beneath her wings? FUCK YEAH, I could do that. Like I said, this was some severe responsibility and I was **all** in. I'll be honest here; it made me squeamy to think about having that vag view, but what the hell? I wouldn't have to worry about it for another eight months.

As I said, I was all IN and totally committed. I felt flattered and so grateful to be trusted with sharing such a sacred and important life event with Dagmar, even if I had to see her vagina turn inside out.

Sure, I had two of my own crotchfruit, but I didn't have a front row seat to their exit from my lady parts. When they were born, there was no time for anyone to grab a mirror so that I could watch either of them slithering out—not that I WANTED one! And of course I banned video cameras during the birthing process, because that's truly just not something I figured anyone, including myself, would be interested in watching. EVER. The therapist in me imagined a twisted family tradition: the annual birth video viewing party! I estimated that the cost of future therapy brought on by the trauma would never be worth the hilariousness of even one viewing of the blessed event. Still I giggled at the thought of me rounding them up each year on their birthday and saying:

"Hey, guys! It's time to celebrate your birthday by watching hemorrhoids pop out of Mom's ass like Jiffy Pop! Oooohhh, look at how BIG Mommy's vagina gets! Can you believe it? Of course it's not that big anymore, but WOW, isn't that something? Do you guys think this popcorn has enough butter? Can you pause the video so that I can microwave more butter? It's hard to really enjoy a show without popcorn, which I don't know WHY reminds me of hemorrhoids! Damn, you kids ruined my loins! Oh, just joking. I love you even if you completely destroyed my body and my mind, which reminds me that I forgot to take my pills today. Could one of you pour me a glass of wine while I'm melting the butter and taking my meds?"

Good solid entertainment guaranteed to traumatize the *entire* family and maybe the friends attending a party after a nice game of pin the tail on the donkey. My husband, a full-fledged grown-up, admits that he's still not quite over the experience of witnessing his children swim out of my vag. Please understand that I don't judge others who like seeing it all up close and reliving the shredding of twat year after year, but for me, the use of mirrors and filming the live-action purging of a baby person is a very personal choice that I chose not to make.

Hells N.O.P.E. Even with my commitment to avoiding the messy aftermath during my own birthing experiences, I got a peek at some of the gore, thanks to the doctor who was hell-bent on showing me the placentas—HORK! But that was the worst of it, placenta in a pan. The births of my kids were events I merely witnessed through a slow-motion, narcotic haze that made me understand my beloved Elvis Presley's addiction to the downers SOOOOO much better.

But this time, the choices were not mine to make. It was Dagmar's birth plan, Dagmar's baby, and there was a good possibility that I was going to witness some serious bloodshed. God, I might even be asked to hold the camera! This time around it wouldn't be me all whacked out on Stadol, blowing kisses to nurses and flirting with the hot British anesthesiologist with the sexy accent. Yeah, I worried a bit. But since having kids myself, I had learned how to shed my worries quickly and consistently, like a snake molting out of her skin. Nothing, I mean nothing smacks a person into the acceptance of powerlessness like having kids. Each time a delusion of control is shattered by a screaming toddler or an exploding diaper, it becomes less possible to harbor further delusions of control, and more possible to embrace semi-controlled chaos. So, I ordered myself to let it go, to molt and shrug off thoughts of seeing my girl's girl parts expand to ten times their normal size and to stop worrying about whether or not her entire butthole was going to turn inside out right before my eyes. I was sure Dagmar was worrying enough for the both of us, anyway. Today, as the mother of three, she is no longer a complete control freak, but at the time the girl was truly a woman worrier extraordinaire.

Yep, Dagmar worries. She's also a meticulous organizer and a planner. She worries about everything including the organizing and planning she's doing in order to decrease her worries about what she is worrying about. She is the Germanic stereotype through and through: disciplined, organized and efficient. Sometimes I think she is also psychic, because I get a thank-you note for a gift five minutes after arriving home from giving her said gift. But with all her planning, she didn't anticipate getting knocked up practically the first time she and her hubs knocked boots with the intent of starting a family. Or to be due to give birth just as he would be attending THE most important trade show and conference of the year. She immediately started worrying and planning, firmly insisting that I be her backup birth companion. At the stage of pregnancy when most people don't even know they have a bun in the oven, she had her birth plan complete and practically notarized. I promised I would be there! Notarize THAT, bitch!

Given John's job, Frau Dagmar knew full well that there was a very good chance that her enthusiastic, hyper-verbal, disorganized and often late girlfriend, ME, would be the one with her during labor and delivery. I'm sure she even calculated the odds that I would be late due to A) my cheapness resulting in an empty tank of gas, B) my frequent efforts to drive as far as possible on fumes just to break my previous record of miles driven on empty or C) getting lost driving to a place that I had likely driven past no less than fifty times; yet she stood her ground month after month. I was to be there, no matter what! And I would be. Even though I thought she could have made a more responsible choice, I wasn't going to tell her that. I wanted to be there like I wanted to breathe. All I had to do was strategically find a way to avoid viewing the vag without being obvious or shirking my responsibilities as the birth buddy.

I felt like each of my pregnancies lasted two years, but Dagmar's sure went by quick; at least it seemed to. I suppose that's because I wasn't starving all the time from growing a person in my body or feeling all barfy, fat and zitty with sore tits and grape-sized veins playing peekaboo out of my asshole. As Baby Girl's due date approached, each ring of the phone made my heart thump with excitement. Was it D-day? Would I make it to the hospital on time? Would Dagmar and the baby be okay? Would I be able to avoid the yucky vag view? Would I even be there? Maybe John would be in town and I would be uninvited. I was alternately excited and disgusted. What the HELL was wrong with me?

I have a vagina and I like it well enough. So, why was I so worried about seeing someone else's, especially someone so important in my life? Women had been doing this birthing biznazz together for thousands of years, standing on rocks in the middle of fields, shoving their hands inside one another to turn a breech baby around and helping each other as only another woman truly can! And I had given birth twice for fuck sake and nobody puked or passed out during my deliveries.

Of course, I was lucky enough not to push poop. You know what I mean by that, right? Everyone knows someone who did, and everyone who did will tell you that they were horrified despite the normalcy and frequency of the phenomenon. I had certainly heard a few stories that had me concerned.

My favorite was the one about how my friend Chris puked and passed out when his wife went into labor and then she pooped while she was on all fours trying to grunt out their firstborn. (In his defense, he had just had a huge Mexican fiesta complete with a pitcher of margaritas.) They laugh about it, but it's a nervous laugh and the smell of fear permeates the room each time I hear that story. Nasty!

And then my friend Lisa told me the grossest push poop story I ever didn't want to hear. She actually got to see herself crap in the reflection of a mirror, so . . . never mind. You can see why I was concerned. There was much to consider in terms of how I could be a responsible friend and NOT screw up the moment by taking precautions not to put myself in a position (literally and figuratively) where I was at risk for such inappropriate and irresponsible behavior as hurling or wilting like a sissy.

Aarrgghh, why *did* she choose me? And please GOD just let her have an easy, turd-free delivery.

When the phone rang and Dagmar's mother, Margaret, told me that they were pretty sure she was in labor and on their way to the hospital, I started leaping around like a lunatic. "YES! YES! YES!" I exclaimed as my family sat at the dinner table watching my uncoordinated happy dance complete with half-assed attempts at old cheerleading jumps! I kept punching the air and frolicking around until I realized that I had almost forgotten why I wasn't eating dinner with the rest of my family. Oh yeah, oh yeah, oh yeah, yeah, yeah! I was really IN! John was gone and I was to be the labor coach! BOOM! BOOM! A few more sky punches and then I had to focus. A BABY WAS ON THE WAY!

As jazzed and spazzed up as I was after hanging up the phone, I knew that I was going to the show, so the leaping and squealing had to stop. I needed to move horizontally, not vertically, and get my buns to the hospital—STAT. Or did I? I would wait for the call. It could be a false alarm. Still I was excited and prepared to leave immediately once it was confirmed that she was officially in labor. Having done the baby birthing a couple of times my own self, I figured I had plenty of time to gas up the minivan and make it to the hospital. But even knowing this, I rushed around acting all slapstick and clumsy like a maniac first-time father on a silly sitcom. Stupid, I know, but when you love someone and their dream is coming true, it's hard not to feel it too.

And I love my friend so much. She had made my life better, loved me in my most unlovable moments for over twenty-five years. I was not going to disappoint her! HELL TO THE NO, I WAS NOT! I'd be German for a day, leaving my Irish at home with my lephrechaun-ish dance moves. I *was* the wind on my way to be beneath her wings. I'd hold her hand, wipe her sweaty brow and make sure her needs for order and efficiency were met. IT WAS FINALLY HAPPENING! My mind flashed back to the day she told me about her pregnancy and I found myself spacing out, incredulous that it was finally GO TIME!

Another phone call snapped me out of the trance—it really

was go time. Dagmar's mom said they had checked into the hospital and her water had broken. There was no time to reminisce or fuck around acting all dreamy and heroic. I hadn't even made it out of the house. FOCUS!

Quickly my mind snapped back into the present. THE NOW! It was happening. It was really happening, and after a few more air punches and jump spins, I froze again. Out of nowhere my mind flashed forward and was invaded by creepy and disturbing thoughts about my best friend's VAGINA! How distracting and buzz killing. I shook it off and flew out the door, intent on formulating my vag-avoiding plan during the drive to the hospital.

Breathe, I told myself as I ripped down the Stevenson Expressway toward the city. I'd seen her naked plenty of times; what was all this vag-phobia about? And then it hit me! I KNEW! I remembered the mortified look on my husband's face when I was pushing my firstborn out of my own baby maker. His already large and expressive eyes expanding into cartoonlike saucers, the expression on his face morphing slowly from surprised to afraid to confused to incredulous, and then the sucking in of his breath and clenching of his teeth as the doctor said, "The head is out, Nikki!" When I looked at Eric, the poor lamb was white as rice, hands on either side of his head with his mouth hanging wide open. What must he be thinking? Seeing? Better him than me, I recalled thinking, glad I had turned down the mirror. I'm lucky I was up at the top.

Of course!

I needed to be near the top during the birth of Dagmar's baby! The shoulders!

I was a genius.

My husband was at the bottom when my kids were born, holding my leg and looking into the eye of the beast! For months after the birth of my son, I asked him for details, but he said he just couldn't discuss it, that he was still recovering from the trauma and trying to get back to seeing my lady parts as his personal playground. A guy friend of mine said that it's sort of like watching a train wreck or a car accident. You want to look away because of the carnage, yet you keep looking at the wreckage for signs of life, hoping for the best. Now, *that* I understood, because I made the mistake of taking a look down there a few days after my son was born.

I would plant myself firmly at Dagmar's shoulders, the brow-wiping, forehead-kissing, and cheerleader position. Nobody could stop me. It was suddenly so simple, and I felt incredible relief. I had a tank full of gas, I had printed out a map so that I would *not* get lost, and I was going to be on time for the big show.

Piece of cake, I thought, relaxing. Now I could be all over this birth coaching business, doing what I do best. Dagmar had chosen me because I've always been the one who could turn tears into laughter, solve problems and make the impossible possible. Who said I had to hold a leg? I would maneuver my way into the position most comfy for me, which would provide a view similar to the one I had during the births of my own babies, only this time I would be the one doing the shushing, stroking and snuggling, not the one shooting a slimy blob of baby out of my junk.

My plan meant that I would be free to really enjoy what was sure to be one of the most important days of my life. My best friend, my beautiful and loyal friend, was about to give birth to her first child. I would be there to witness her miraculous transformation into a mother. And fortunately, her mother would also be there with us. THIS I considered a serious bonus in terms of my positioning. I figured that she would totally want the front row seat to the birth of her first grandbaby. I also knew that mother and daughter would be too nervous and distracted to argue with me. "Hey, Margaret, take a leg!" I would say. "I'm up here shushing and sweat mopping!" It was too perfect. I would look without really seeing. Take a leg, Margaret, I chuckled to myself, my confidence now soaring along with my excitement.

I made it to the city in record time without getting lost. I was focused and ready for action. I ran into the birthing room and threw a few air punches and hugs around: I was just so excited! One look at Dagmar's face underlined the reason she had wanted me there! She was laboring comfortably, albeit VERY anxiously, watching her mother pace around the room. Nerves were aplenty for a few reasons. Dagmar had never given birth before, obviously, but neither had her mother; Dagmar was adopted, and an only child, so neither of them had any idea what to expect. On top of which these are two of the most orderly, controlled, neat, efficient and disciplined broads on the planet. (They're so similar I find it impossible to believe they aren't related by blood!) So, these gals needed a big ol' dose of Nikki: an experienced birth mother with some flexibility and facetiousness. I answered a few questions and mocked a few medical professionals and we all relaxed!

Our friend Amy showed up soon after and it was truly all I had dreamed. An epic estrogen fest with tears, bonding and conversation that would make the manliest man lactate within minutes. Motherhood magic: we were making it happen. My uterus throbbed with joy. Dagmar relaxed and decided to try for a bit of a nap, so Amy and I waited for the big event by wandering around the hospital, reminiscing about our own experiences, so excited for our friend.

Now I can't prove this, but I believe that the estrogen fest magic and Dagmar's single-minded focus moved her labor along at an alarmingly quick pace (along with an effective epidural and some Pitocin). A mere three hours passed, and very suddenly it was time to take our places! But I looked up and the shoulders were *taken*. Where was my shoulder where I'd commence my job of shushing and soothing while looking without really seeing? FUCKITY SHIT—THIS WAS NOT THE PLAN. It's what happens when a vag-phobic bitch gets a little too big for her britches and her friend is giving birth at a teaching hospital where the room is full of spectators, one of whom was obviously assigned to shushing.

Dagmar's mother had snagged the other shoulder and the coveted position of brow wiper, hair stroker and co-shusher, which was not only the role I wanted but also the one I truly believed best suited me. When the blue-haired hippie obstetrician with a nose ring handed me a leg, I was in shock. "Take a leg," she said. HEY, that's MY line, I thought to myself, but I took the leg. And just like that, I was looking at what I didn't really want to see. I wanted to ask for help, to pull a switcheroo, but I am nothing if not obedient and very good with direction. I was told to hold the leg so there I was, holding the leg, and watching something try to bust its way through my bestie's labia. My knees buckled a bit when I laid eyes on the oozing, bleeding, gushing and pulsating-like-something-from-a-horror-movie, not-so-private parts of my friend. I froze.

At least my body froze; my mouth kept moving. Thankfully I didn't say her "cunt" was pulsating because even with all the between-the-legs action, I got a dirty look from one of the junior docs I had previously mocked—which I thought was sort of rude, considering she had bogarted my shoulder-position shushing role, so I gave her the stink eye and smirked. Wasn't she supposed to be helping out *down here*? I was just the wise-cracking sidekick!

This reminded me that a sidekick is a very important role that I needed to take seriously. I had been trusted by the super-hero whose leg I was holding as she struggled to give birth to her daughter, and WOW was she doing superhero stuff! She was doing the most incredibly cool and fascinating and powerful thing I had ever seen her do. I found that even with my peepers completely focused on her lady parts, I wasn't grossed out at all. As a matter of fact, I was totally in awe of her amazing expanding vagina!

And there I was, looking *and* seeing! The first push revealed a tiny glimpse of the baby's head before it quickly vanished again. There was hair! I couldn't tell what color but I shrieked, "She has so much hair!" My heart was beating so hard, I SWORE it was a fist trying to explode out of my rib cage and punch me out of the severe state of shock I was in. My entire body tingled and a flood of some sort of good-feely chemicals began to bathe my brain in a river of ecstasy. I had never seen anything like it. A baby was being born right before my eyes. I was actually seeing it happen.

Another push and another and the matted blond hair of my mighty and brave friend's daughter refused to go back into the darkness. She was a blondie like her momma! Another big push and her head was out, followed by all kinds of gunkish stuff that was blocking my view of her beauty.

GET OUT OF THE WAY, GUNK, I thought to myself. I NEED TO SEE HER FACE!

And then I saw it. Even covered with blood and baby goop, I saw her tiny, perfect face. I saw her father in that face almost immediately, even amidst the pink, squished up-ness of her cheeks and her tightly closed eyes. My friend John was now a father! Another push and her flawless, healthy body swam out of Dagmar into the arms of the doctor, the sound of her quivering baby cries filling the air. I had never seen anything so absolutely gloriously miraculously beautiful in my entire life. I was fearless, overwhelmed, aching with complete love and admiration for my friends and grateful beyond words for the opportunity to witness such a magnificent event. I wanted to clap my hands and give a standing ovation for the best show I had ever seen in my life, but I couldn't. I was holding Dagmar's leg and looking at the incredulous expression on her face as the doctor placed her daughter, Zoey, in her arms.

I've told Dagmar in detail about what I saw when I was trying not to look and ended up looking. I mean REALLY looking. (My meticulous friend is a stickler for detail and not easily grossed out.) I've told her everything at least ten times over. There is nothing in the world like seeing what the human body can do. My favorite parts of the story that I tell and retell are about seeing Zoey's face for the first time and the speed at which she slid out of her momma. Just like that, a person was there, and I know that I could see it a thousand times over and still be as awestruck as I was the first time. And although her daddy was absent for her birth, his presence in her face made it seem as though the goo was invisible. There was only Zoey, the daughter of John and Dagmar. Through the blood and nasty placenta goo and tears, I saw both of them in the face of their daughter! If I had been a shoulder hugger and shusher, I would have missed that magic. To this day, I play it back in my mind at random moments when I see my friend and her daughter together.

She hasn't mentioned it, so I'm pretty sure Dagmar never realized the extent of my anxiety over having a front row seat to her junk. She was too busy trusting me and needing me and believing in me and giving birth to a human to notice that anything extra weird might be going on with me. I think I proved that when the going gets weird, the weird turn pro, so even though I briefly dissociated into a superhero sidekick (sans tights) who delivers shitty one-liners, in Dagmar's mind and memory I was merely her mouthy friend—who she invited back into the delivery room for baby number two.

CONVERSATIONS with CROTCHFRUIT

BATHROOM WARS PART II

ZACH   What are you doing, Mom?

ME   WHAT DOES IT LOOK LIKE I AM DOING?

ZACH   Why are you yelling at me?

ME   BECAUSE I'M FRUSTRATED THAT YOU WON'T GIVE ME ANY PRIVACY!

ZACH   I was just wondering where you were. I was worried.

ME   Awww, that would be sweet if I hadn't told you a hundred times to give me privacy in the bathroom! GET OUT! I'm trying to get dressed.

ZACH   Can I ask you something?

ME   No.

ZACH   Just one thing?

ME   Fine, one thing and then you GET OUT!

ZACH   Why do you wear underwear that goes straight up your butt?

ME   Thongs? I wear these so underpants lines don't show through my pants, okay?

ZACH   And it probably doesn't get stuck in all those dents all over your butt either. I get it.

ME   OH MY GOD! GET OUT!

FUCK YOU, DINNER, MAKE YOURSELF:
Domestic Frustrations and Failures

"My theory . . . is, that if the item
doesn't multiply, smell, catch fire, or
block the refrigerator door, let it be.
No one else cares. Why should you?"

—Erma Bombeck

DINNER IS LIKE HERPES

Dinner is the herpes of the mom world.

You may be wondering why I am comparing an innocent meal like dinner to a blistery, stubborn virus like herpes. Well, I believe the two are strikingly analogous: they both are repugnantly pesky pains in the ass.

You can go all day and try not to think about making dinner, but it's still there, lingering, lurking and mocking you. You can't always see it, but it's a permanent condition, a symptom of the virus known as "children," who need to be fed as long as they are alive. Because yes, what you've heard is all too true: many of them never leave, even when they are old enough to get the hell out of your house!

These days, kids—and when I say kids I mean all loin-fruit between eighteen and one hundred who can no longer claim that you are legally responsible for taking care of them, but can guilt you into doing it anyway—are all too prone to either never moving out of your house or needing to move back into your house because of some catastrophe. Of course, that might not happen to you. I mean, hopefully they will get the hell out and grow the fuck up and you just have to feed them on holidays and sporadic weekends and this will actually be a pleasure if you like to cook. But sorry to tell you, it could go down either way. For those of you who have a "plan" for your retirement and life as empty nesters and might not have allowed yourself to consider this at all: I swear I'm not trying to scare you as much as I'm trying to mock you for planning. Man plans, God laughs. Somebody cool said that.

But back to the herp and dinner comparison! That's right. Just like herpes, the dinner blister just never goes away, waiting to flare up and irritate the living shit out of you. No matter how stress free the rest of your day has been, thoughts of preparing the evening meal keep popping up like an oozing, festering sore you can't ignore. Dinner, children and the herp—these things are forever.

One of the reasons that dinner annoys ME as much as a disgusting, festering sore in my nether regions (not that I have experienced this kind of genital issue, but I had pregnancy hemorrhoids the size of a toddler's fist, so I know whereof I speak when it comes to sore private parts, okay?) is that it coincides with the time of day when everyone around my house, including me, is losing their minds. When it's dinnertime, it seems like everything and everyone is getting ready to break out into a breakdown. The kids are tattling on and clobbering each other while fighting over who is breathing too loud.

"Can you tell her to shut up? Can you tell him to stop touching me? MOM—she's hogging the computer! When is DAD coming home? I'm bored. My homework is too hard. Help me. He farted on me. She's in my room. Do you want to see my Christmas list full of expensive toys that you can't afford and just thinking about them will stress you out?" Of course by third grade, my oldest kid surpassed me in smartness, so I can't even help him, and that's just another painful blister that belongs in another story.

(That last part about Christmas toys? My kids would never

say that thing about how we can't afford them. They truly think money grows on trees or they wouldn't constantly ask for stuff that makes me feel like I'm going to stroke out, because I cannot help wanting to make Christmas awesome and get them cool stuff at least once a year.)

Some people call the onset of evening "the witching hour." This makes sense. It's like some supernatural force is meddling and corrupting every creature under my roof, including the ones that go "woof." Oh yeah, the fur babies are losing it too. Maybe losing it is the wrong expression to describe the animal behavior. It's more like they are choosing it, as in choosing to be awake and on high alert after snoring, shedding and drooling on the furniture all day. Like clockwork, both of my dogs seem to have an "on" switch that gets flipped just as my dimmer switch has been activated by sheer exhaustion. Without fail, they are barking at *nothing*, wanting to be let in and out (and in and out and out and in and in and . . .) and sniffing around hoping scraps fall while I try to prepare the damn food that will eventually become the dinner everyone will complain about. I'm tripping over them and the kids, who are either underfoot or wrapped around one of my limbs, asking when dinner will be ready.

At this point, I'm usually feeling my blood pressure rise; like each kid and dog has shrunk to microscopic size and they are playing a game of tag or hide-and-seek inside my arteries. I imagine that I can actually feel their little feet kicking me and pointy claws scratching me and the only relief from this feeling of being physically possessed would be to bleed them out . . . which reminds me to be more careful with the knife I'm probably using to chop up some shit because if I did end up accidently cutting one of them ('cause sometimes they literally stick their fingers next to whatever I'm chopping and I do NOT know why) I'd never hear the end of it and neither would their therapists.

Or what if I accidentally cut myself; then who the fuck would cook dinner?

Truly sometimes I am just overwhelmed by how much I'm needed, how much they all get under my skin. I yearn for relief, both the human and liquid variety, and just as I start to wonder when I'll have a little of both, I get a phone call.

Yep, my human relief (or so he likes to call himself), the husband, likes to call right around dinnertime and ask what I'm doing and what I'm wearing and try to get me into some dirty phone talk. This is not what I call relief. Relief is when he walks in the door, and the kids are so sick of me that they maul him like in that scene from *The Lion King* when Simba pounces on Mufasa. It's adorable and always manages to suck out my crankiness. But the phone calls? Those I consider harassment. "Baby, what 'cha doin'?" he asks.

Is he kidding? WHAT DOES HE THINK I'M DOING?

Oh, hi, honey, I was just thinking of you. Daydreaming really, you know, just sitting around hoping you'd call me for some phone sex because I have NOTHING going on.

Nothing but waiting desperately for you to get here already, so that I can have a few minutes of peace and quiet while the proof of our eternal love uses YOU as a human jungle gym for a bit.

And of course making his and everybody else's dinner, that's what I'm fucking doing! So that when he walks in the house starving after a long day at work, he's not eating Hot Pockets and mandarin oranges from a can with his evening cocktail in the leather recliner that has the shape of his ass permanently outlined on the seat while the kids climb on his head.

"What are you wearing?" he asks.

And really, WHAT DOES HE THINK I'M WEARING?

Does he think I'm strutting around here in front of the kids (and frequently a handful of their friends as well) in my dominatrix pleather (not that I actually have any) or a sexy nightgown (I don't have one of these either) and kitten heels (for fuck sake, do women with small children really own shoes like this?), counting the minutes until we can have wild, acrobatic sex?

Of course the poor guy's just trying to get a little phone sex, but sex reminds me too much of herpes—which I'm glad I don't have, but continues to be the only metaphor that is tenaciously agitating enough to remind me of how the phone is a symptom of the dinner virus. FUCK!

And it's not just my husband calling. The constantly ringing phone is TRULY as gnawingly annoying as dinner and herpes, because solicitors love to call around dinnertime. "Hello, is this Mrs. Kepenenereifkrk?" (Nobody gets it right. Nobody.) They put on their best sexy-smooth voice. "And how are we this evening?"

We?

Who are these WE that you are asking about?

Do you have a mouse in your pocket, sir? Or are you asking about the collective WE that are going bloody bonkers from overstimulation and the day's exhaustion? I need some clarification, Mr. Smooth-Talker, because if you really want to know how I am, this is the time of day I could really use someone to LISTEN!

But no, he just wants to know if I want to be one of the one hundred lucky women who will be given a key, one of which might just open the door to a custom-built home. Ooooh—yes please! Well, it's my lucky day then, Mr. Smooth informs me.

To become one of those one hundred lucky ladies, I only have to subscribe to *Forty and Fashionable Weekly*, because everyone knows that forty is the new twenty.

Everyone except me, obviously, because although I could say, "Yes, plllllleeeease, I was just thinking about how I wanted to subscribe to some fashion magazine full of clothes I'm too poor to afford and too fat to wear," instead I just hang up on the bastard, hoping he spreads the word throughout the telemarketing community that Mrs. Knenepsnenrsrs (or however the fuck they pronounce it wherever they are calling from) is the angriest bitch on the list. (But not before asking him for his phone number so that I can call him back to ask him how he's doing when he is at home with his screaming kids.) I truly am an angry bitch at that time of day. Angry as in "If you call during the dinner hour ever again, I'll find you and CUT you" angry. I sound terrible, I know. But it's just me acting outrageous. I wouldn't actually cut anyone and not just because I don't want to end up in jail, but IF I was in jail, who would make dinner?

But I digress—AGAIN!

I mean obviously most women want very much to make huge financial decisions about real estate like buying a time-share in Bora Bora over the phone, and OF COURSE I have time to take a ten-minute survey about my preferences in lawn care services (no hidden sales involved—WE PROMISE). Most of all, I really want to talk to some smarmy politician about the upcoming election. But I'm going to have to get back to you pesky jerks right after I finish up with this guy on the other line who wants me to answer a few questions about the quality of my water, because a mere five minutes of my time will get me a coupon for a free gallon of ice cream from Oberweis. Although to be honest, I do usually take the coupons because these come

in handy when I'm bribing my kids to eat the foods they constantly complain about at dinner. Also we are big dessert people
around here. BIG-TIME!

I must confess that there are times when I just throw Lucky
Charms in a bowl and consider the variety of artificial colors a
good substitute for having all the food groups represented.
When I do, it feels like I've been given a dose of medicine to
relieve the pain associated with my symptoms, or that my disease is in remission. And desperate times call for ordering a
pizza, which makes me everybody's hero and then instead of
slugs I get hugs, and I LOVE HUGS, especially when I am not
holding raw meat or knives or trying to time the pasta so that
it's not a congealed mass of slop before the chicken breasts are
off-white enough to safely eat. And WHY does everybody
ignore me when I'm in perfect hug position, but paw at me relentlessly when I'm otherwise engaged?

But I digress again, sorry! I think I have a digression disorder. Does that even exist?

I enjoy blowing off the overwhelming responsibility of dinner for a night (or two or three) and pretending that the pesti-
lence hasn't invaded my body and soul, but in the back of my
mind I know it's temporary. For while both dinner and herpes
have periods when they are dormant, they are ever present.
They both make you feel tingly (and not in the good way, from
what I've heard) when you realize they are about to make an
appearance and ooze all over any peaceful or successful feelings
that you might have experienced pre–witching hour. So, I must
accept that I suffer from the disease of dinner. This affliction is
and will always be in my blood, and as much as I scream "FUCK
YOU, DINNER, MAKE YOURSELF," it never fucking does.

Thus I stand by my disgusting analogy between herpes and

dinner. They are both forever because as everyone knows, there is no cure for dinner, or herpes. And because this story solves none of your current dinner problems, I recommend you answer at least one of the calls about a time-share and buy that shit if you can, so that you have somewhere to go when your retirement/empty nest plan becomes the joke not even your teenage grandkids (who either never left your home or are moving back in with their parents, who have quite possibly also either never left your home or are moving back in) think is funny. Not in the least.

And I hope you don't think I'm also comparing having kids to having herpes the way I'm comparing having to constantly make dinner to having herpes, because who the hell would do a disgusting thing like that? I mean, I wouldn't buy a book written by a heartless bitch of an ungrateful psycho like that, even if I was the heartless bitch who wrote it.

We prayed for, planned and wanted both of our kids. They weren't unwanted viruses caught by unprotected, high-risk sexual activity. I wanted the virus of motherhood, much like I want a full-time chef named Sven, who can also answer the phone and pick out *something* at Kohl's for me to wear that doesn't make my ass look like all I do is eat everybody's leftover dinner after I snarf up my own. I just didn't stop to think that these constantly hungry little people we created would require SO MUCH FEEDING AND WATERING! It's endless!

So if you lend this book to your friends, could you help a bitch out and make sure they understand this? Because I'm pretty stressed out from worrying about dinner and I don't want anyone calling to tell me how horrible I am while I'm trying to cook, okay? I might not have stress-induced herp breakouts, but too much anxiety gives me hives and then I would have to take

Benadryl, which would put me straight to sleep, and then who would make dinner?

Thanks.

> The girl can film and edit a stop-motion Littlest Pet Shop video on her iPad, but she can't pour herself a glass of orange juice because it's too hard? ARE YOU FUCKING KIDDING ME?

NO SHIT, SHERLOCK

Call me crazy, but I like my toilet to be puke-ready at all times. Puke-ready means it won't make me have to puke more than I'm already puking because it's a filthy, poop-stained pool of horror. And since I'm being honest, even though I don't give a shit what people think of how I look or dress, I occasionally worry that if we get murdered and my bathrooms are dirty, the detectives will see it and if they're married and their wives say, "How was your day?" they might say, "Aside from that horrifying quadruple homicide at the Knepper house, where it looked like Poo-casso painted all the toilets, it was great. I mean really, no wonder some psychopath took them out. Filthy bastards had shit stains in every single toilet! I had to hold in my piss all day and that's why my eyes are yellow!" And the wife would understand because she probably likes her toilets poop streak–free. Most people do.

The rest of the house can be in disarray and I barely notice the chaos, but for some reason I simply cannot tolerate a nasty commode. And this is a huge problem since I just happen to live with sloppy, sneaky poopers who aren't concerned about the puke-worthiness of toilets or the distress it causes me when they don't clean up their crapola. Like, how about when they don't flush a load, leaving me a rotten pile of "surprise" when I open the bathroom door and it smells like something died in the bathroom, except there is no dead body, but I WISH there was, because it would be nobody's fault that an animal crawled up the pipes through our potty and died in the bathroom? It IS somebody's fault when there is shit in the shitter and I realize that they are just not bothering with the one teeny-tiny thing that's really quite easy to do—FLUSH THE FUCKING TOILET!

Around here, everybody leaves the occasional dump or at least regularly leaves poop skids in the toilet, but nobody will fess up to being the lazy flusher or the poop skidder. I have been investigating this case for a number of years and I'm telling you, the trail goes cold quick.

The evidence poses a real problem for me. Short of conducting a crime scene investigation involving some sort of poop DNA comparison or twenty-four-hour bathroom video surveillance, what can I really do? I file these mostly cold cases under the letter "A" for ASSHOLES (because I think I'm funny like that) but this doesn't mean that I've given up on the investigating. That's just what doo-doo delinquents want, but god help the poop-ertrator I bust fleeing the scene of the grime! See what I did there? I made a funny. But that doesn't mean I'm not mad.

I do that when I'm upset. I make a joke, but even more so when I'm talking about poop because poop is almost always funny. Except when it's dried up and all nasty looking in my toilets, even if I do not have to puke, guests aren't expected, or the police aren't here because we are all alive. But in all seriousness, I'm one hundred and twenty-seven percent committed to keeping toilets clean by getting my family on board with my weird issue. Seriously, how fucking hard is it to A) FLUSH down the dung OR B) Whip out the toilet brush that happens to be two inches from the turd-let and just give the shit streak a quick swipe away?

I refuse to believe that any member of my family is less capable than I when it comes to this task and it upsets me to acknowledge how little it bothers them to walk away from such nastiness. It is a small thing to ask, right? It's so basic and uncomplicated, but after 659 reminders (give or take a few) and toilet-cleaning demos, I've been successful only approximately zero out of 10,499 times in getting them to clean up their own shit streaks.

It would seem that the bathroom would be the easiest room to patrol, because the person goes in alone and comes out alone, unable to blame someone else or make a clean getaway. But around here we don't frequently announce our visits to the bathroom. So, my family gets their sneak on much easier than if they were in the common areas of the house. My success rate in busting them for slobbery is much higher in the bedrooms, kitchen and family room, because in those rooms, the evidence usually betrays the perpetrator.

Take the family room, which looks a lot like the hidden pictures section of *Highlights* magazine.

What doesn't belong here? Oh yeah, that power screwdriver on top of the television, the lone, naked Monster High doll sticking out from under the sofa and the broken squirt gun leaking water on the expensive-as-fuck wooden end tables. Like I don't know whose Littlest Pet Shop underpants are under the piano bench. BUSTED! Pay the fine.

But in the bathroom, UNSUBS (unknown subjects in investigator lingo for those of you who don't live and breathe crime shows) leave evidence that I am unable to substantiate for obvious reasons. You might think that size matters and might lead me to a suspect, but I've never found that to be the case because even my little ones poop as much as a baby elephant (I've seen both a baby elephant and my daughter poop and I can say that each one shocked me with its hugeness). Unless I catch them in the act, the crapper remains clandestine.

Suspect #1 is the girl. Sure she's tiny and adorable, but she can outshit a grown man (and a baby elephant). She is still a bit wary of the flushing part of the potty process, so she conveniently forgets that part unless I catch her in the act (which is usually because she needs help wiping). She's a big fan of cheese and she never hydrates properly, so I can never really rule her out as a suspect. Dairy + dry bowels = Silly Putty poop. But she's not the only one around here that can tell a bold-faced lie or merely just deny all responsibility when confronted with the evidence after she visits the loo. "That was there when I came in, I swear!" And I can't prove her claims of innocence are untrue, even though she's quite often full of shit, literally and figuratively.

Suspect #2 is, of course, the husband. He's the king of the fake tummy ache. This man-child is a former momma's boy who never had to lift a finger around the house growing up. He is still in training. The bathroom is his hideout. We haven't even cleared the plates after a meal before he makes his claim to the throne. He hides in the can, reading or playing Sudoku until the cleanup noises from the kitchen stop. Because I'm busy shuffling around, trying to make sure the dogs don't gag on chicken bones, I really don't even notice he's gone until I'm three-quarters done with cleanup. I'm certain that the King has never considered the purpose of a toilet brush other than to have to pick it up after he knocks it over with whatever magazine he tosses on the floor after a leisurely "avoid the cleanup" dump. At least he closes the door. I don't care how many years we've been married: I just don't want to see him on the throne. Seeing a person poop is the best way to suck even a strong sex drive out of most people. Moving on.

Suspect #3—The boy, who is NOT allowed to screw around on his Nintendo, iPod or any other electronic device before school, will use the shitter to hide his addiction to technology. "I'm pooping in here," he'll holler, followed by a loud grunt to increase the likelihood that I'll buy into his fib, yet I can hear the annoying beeping noises and his whispered exclamations of "YES" when he levels up. Of course he attempts to drown out the noise with the bathroom fan, which only makes it so that he has to turn the volume up on whatever device he is sneaking and I bust his two-faced tush. The problem here is that although I can take the technology away as a consequence for using it when he's not supposed to, the truth is that most of the time, he truly IS pooping. And like his father before him, this kid is surely destined to have a future filled with visits to the proctologist, due to the hemorrhoids that are an inevitable result of using the toilet as a reading recliner/video game chair. And the kid is like clockwork, too. A more regular pooper I have never known. I think it's because, unlike his little sister, he hydrates and avoids cheese. But regular doesn't mean that he's quick, so I don't sit there waiting for him to finish so that I can see if he's left anything. I have two other bathrooms that I'm probably cleaning while he's taking a forty-three-hour dump.

And we have three bathrooms, so what if one of them is in each bathroom? I can't very well be standing outside all three doors at once. I have so many other things to clean! CLEAN ALL THE THINGS isn't just a cartoon in a great blog—it's my life!

And the poop isn't the only bathroom-related mystery.

Another mystery is who is responsible for using the last of the toilet paper (two-ply if I did the grocery shopping because the one-ply cheap stuff just does NOT feel right or do the job, amiright?) and either

A) Doesn't bother to replace the empty roll with a full one OR,

B) Gets out a new roll, but doesn't put it on the dispenser and instead leaves it on the floor for the dog to find and shred into ten thousand pieces.

It's almost comical. I say almost, because I'm the one who ends up cleaning up the trail of sopping-wet tissue the dog has created and I'm usually too pissed off to laugh about it. I'm like the cop who shows up at the crime scene after the perps are long gone, and ends up doing hours of paperwork after interviewing the eighty-nine-year-old blind-in-one-eye victim who speaks only Portuguese and can't provide any reliable details aside from making his hand look like a gun and yelling, "Bang bang." It's tough on the ego to fail so often, but each successful bust encourages me to carry on.

For example, I'm a whiz at deducing who did what to the bathroom sink, but that's much less of a challenge. Christ on a cracker, have they no shame at all? I never have to wonder if they have brushed their teeth because the evidence is everyfuckingwhere! A pea-sized amount of toothpaste around here is more like a plum, and most of this expensive, freaky-flavored glittery goop ends up stuck to the sink in dried-up globs of pink and blue plaster. Ratted out by color, the culprits can be forced to pay for their crime with blood, sweat, tears and some soft soap. (My husband has his own sink. I don't touch that shit with a two-inch sponge unless we are having overnight guests who might use our bathroom.)

But back to the toilet.

Of course they all consider me as suspect #4, which is about as ridiculous as accusing a kitten of clubbing a baby harp seal. I'm an efficient pooper and toothbrusher and I rarely spend more than the minimum amount of time it takes to blow-dry my hair into the "homeless and mentally ill" style I rock on the daily. I don't linger. I don't putter. I don't hide. The bathroom is truly the only room in the house I can walk into and actually remember why the hell I'm there!

When I walk into any room, I have a purpose, but the bathroom is small enough that even MY overwhelming ADHD doesn't cause me to lose focus and forget that purpose. In other parts of the house, distractions really fuck with my flow. Example: Let's say I'm washing dishes and happen to notice a pile of laundry on the kitchen table. I struggle to resist the urge to make a quick run upstairs to put it on my bed, just to get it out of my sight. This decision is pretty much guaranteed to result in me completely forgetting to return to the dishes, because I happen to notice another mess or dirt pile that I can't ignore, because as I said before, I CLEAN ALL THE THINGS! Because of this problem, the ability to complete a task in the bathroom makes me feel a kind of joy that is disproportionate to the actual event. I even clean the bath/shower combo, during my shower, WHILE I'm letting conditioner work its magic in my hair. This is one of those rare times when my extreme distractibility works in my favor. I also shower in the kids' bathroom once a week so that I can do the same thing there. The bath and shower are really the only things in the bathroom that don't piss me off, because there're no turds or toothpaste globs in there. This clever multitasking makes me feel like a winner, even if it's only temporary because as soon as I step OUT of the shower, there's a chance I'll be staring down a scummy sink or toilet. I take the victories where I can.

Now even though I am the quickest groomer/pooper in the family, I'm the one who spends the most time in the bathroom. Why? Because apparently I am the only one who notices the dried shit, snot, toothpaste, pubic hair, dog hair, shredded toilet paper and soaking-wet towels and washrags slopped from floor to ceiling. Or am I? Is it possible that the 659 reminders (give or take a few) are not so much being forgotten but ignored? Maybe a clean bathroom doesn't really matter to these derelict dumpers in my family! So, why do I bother? I told you why! Remember the murder and the not wanting to puke more than I have to if I'm sick? And what if I win the Publishers ~~Cleaning~~ Clearing House sweepstakes and they surprise me and someone from the camera crew has to use the bathroom and sees the poop skids? I have to maintain some sense of dignity!

Speaking of dignity, you might think my obsession undignified. I CARE NOT! Any sane person would just toss these skid marks of crime into the cold case files and accept the reality that sometimes SHIT HAPPENS and you just have to accept it, right? Luckily I don't have to concern myself with that because it's well established that I'm not a sane person. If my abnormal fixation with having a pristine potty could be construed as something that also requires further investigation, then so be it. In the meantime, this mental momma isn't giving up until the poop-ertrators are caught in the act, crime show style—and I've watched enough of them to know that the villain often gets caught with their pants down.

FOCUS GIRL

Today I am focused. My superhero name today will be Focus Girl. I shall stay on task and be the mom I've always not been, that I rarely am, but that I want to be, because I have a list and I am f.o.c.u.s.e.d.

First on the list is laundry. I so totally and completely got this. This day is my BITCH! I shall take the laundry and hypnotize it with my super focus. Ima get shit DONE! Maybe my superhero name should be Focus Mom, instead of Focus Girl? I'm really no longer a girl. Focus Woman would be fine, but since my goal is having focus on my mom duties today, I think Focus Mom is good. I wonder if wearing a cape would increase this focus and make me feel very superheroey-ish. Sort of like a reminder in case I lose the list.

Why am I in the garage? Is this even on my list?

Zach: Can I go to Chuck's house?

Me: Yes.

Zach: Will you please drive me?

Me: YES.

Zach: When?

Me: YES.

Zach: MOM! ARE YOU EVEN LISTENING?

Me: No, I don't have any cash, sweetheart.

Zach: What?

Me: Mmmm, yes?

Zach: Forget it, I'll skateboard over.

Me: Skateboard where? Where are you going? Why do you need money?

Zach: MOM!!! Can you please listen?

Me: Yes, I promise. I was just focused on the laundry.

Zach: Then why are you in the garage?

Me: I think I was looking for a cape.

Zach: Seriously, can I go to Chuck's? Will you please drive me? And NO, I don't need money.

Me: You don't have to be a rude little dude about it. Let me go upstairs and get my keys.

I'm overwhelmed the lion's share of the time. I just love using that phrase, lion's share. But I don't even know what it means. I have a book on all those fun phrases. I should look it up. SHIT! Not now, woman! There's no time to read about lions, although I do know that lions are powerful and beautiful and that the female lions do all the hunting while the cubs play and the males sleep all day. I can't imagine the focus it takes to hunt in the wild. I wonder if it takes as long to kill dinner as it does to make dinner, and if the lioness ladies bitch about it like

I do. "I'm so fucking sick of killing shit for you lazy asses who lick your balls and sleep all damn day!" That makes me giggle, because I'm so hilarious, but now I'm not focused. I need to focus.

I roar a little and laugh again. It would be hilarious if I were wearing a cape and roaring. ENOUGH! I am no longer laughing. I am focusing. I am Focus Mom AND I need to get back to the list. And the boy needs a ride. I'll drive him to Chuck's, and then I can start working on the list. Shit, he needs money too. I should put that on the list and bring the list with me and we can get cash on the way to Chuck's house. I'm organized and focused.

ROOOOOOOOOOOAAAAAAAAARRRRR-RRRRR!

My inner dialogue becomes a mantra: get the keys; get money (why does he even need money? I need to ask him), keys, money, money, keys, drive the boy, get the keys, and drive the boy. Roar and giggle. My keys are upstairs in my bedroom. I need to go upstairs. I'm standing in the middle of my bedroom upstairs. Why am I even in the room? Am I in here because I need to be, or because someone needed something? I am an expert finder.

But aren't all moms expert finders? My girlfriends and I think it's because we actually take the time to look or because we do the lion's share of the straightening and cleaning, which reminds me that I need to call my friend Cathy. I'm going to put that on the list. And I need to put "look for book of funny sayings about lions" on the list. But seriously, I'm the only one who can find ANYFUCKINGTHING around here. So, what am I looking for again? Am I in the room looking for said lost/misplaced something for someone else or was it my idea? If I had my list I'd know.

OMG I have a bunch of new things to put on my list. I hope I remember! I should have a little list carrier so that I can keep the list with me at all times. I could write a list on my cape if I was wearing one. Pffth, I'd never find a cape in this discombobulated disarray. I practically had to use a shovel to clear a path to my bedroom, which I notice is a real mess! GAH!

Fucking FUCK! What a mess. I'm totally adding this room to my list. I WISH I WERE WEARING A CAPE WITH A LIST WRITTEN ALL OVER IT! I'd roar all over the house! I throw my head back and roar, and when I'm looking up I see the ceiling fan. The ceiling fan is GOD-awful disgusting. At night, when I'm in bed, I'm always too tired to get up and clean it. I should have a list next to my bed. I'm putting that on my list. Put list next to bed for when I remember important things at bedtime. I'll just clean it now real quick, and then I won't have to add it to my list. I am so focused. What next? My list is downstairs. I don't know why I was upstairs anyway. I probably came up here to get another load of laundry.

LAUNDRY! Husband person really needs his pants today. Gawd, nobody is going to have clean clothes if I don't get focused right fucking NOW! I'd better bring another load downstairs, but first I should get whatever I came upstairs for because I am focused. KEYS! Yesh! I turn around to get the KEYS and ARE YOU KIDDING ME—How many glasses are upstairs? I'll bring them downstairs because I can't very well bring them down with the laundry that I'll be bringing down after I find my keys and drive Zach to Chuck's. Even with a cape I couldn't. I'll just put these glasses in the dishwasher right quick!

Cate: Can I watch TV?

Me: Yes.

Cate: Can you please make me some cheese and crackers?

Me: YES.

Hell, I'm already in the kitchen. I start making cheese and crackers.

My husband does the loud walk through the kitchen, stomping and mumbling something about his pants. He REALLY needs those pants today. I hear the "bazrrrrrrrrr" of the dryer going off, and since I've washed the same damn load of laundry no less than four times because I've let it sit in the washer too long and don't want to do that again I zoom to the laundry room. Not only am I focused, but also I am fast. I'd be faster with a cape. I should just get the cape before I continue completing the tasks on my list so I don't keep forgetting about it and wishing I had my list with me. Find a cape. I start to quickly fold the stuff in the dryer with the intent of switching the wet, clean stuff over, PRONTO, because the man needs his pants. I'm totally focused. This list is helping, but I need to add some shit to it as soon as I'm done folding. Another mantra. Add shit to cape list . . . add shit to cape list . . . add shit to cape list . . . add—

Cate: MOM, can I have some cheese and crackers? I'm so HUNGRY!

Me: Yeah, baby, sorry, sorry, sorry.

I leave the laundry room to finish making cheese and crackers. My sweet hungry girl! Awwwww, she is so adorable. Filling her belly trumps anything on the stupid-ass list!

Zach: Are you still driving me to Chuck's?

Me: Oh, sorry. Yes. Yep. Gimme just a sec. . . .

Me: WHY ARE YOU WATCHING TV? I TOLD YOU THAT YOU COULDN'T WATCH TV UNTIL YOUR ROOM WAS CLEAN.

Cate: I asked you and you said YES!

Eric: You did say that. You did. I mean, I'm just saying that I heard you say YES so . . .

Holy hell, I'm sweating like a whore in church and I'm about to roar for real. I have to walk away. I need a quiet minute to think and get focused. I walk to my happy room, with the piano and my favorite pictures and—DOG CRAP UNDER THE PIANO BENCH! Since it is already dried up, I'll just put that on my list. I need to stay focused. But it's funny that I was talking about adding shit to my list and now I literally have to add "clean up dog shit" to my list.

Hilarious! I am adding SHIT to my list, which makes me feel all better and this refocuses me. I should go to the kitchen and get my list before I forget and transfer the stuff to a cape, which I will wear all day as I am getting shit done and staying focused. I should find a cape before I do anything else!

OH MY GOD I KNOW WHERE I CAN FIND A CAPE! I run to the basement and dig through the dress-up clothes. YES!! Red and shiny and just the thing I need to keep my sense of humor along with my focus. Today I am totally the mom I've always wanted to be. I am so focused. I need to add the dog shit to the list. Speaking of shit, OH FUCKITY SHIT . . . the laundry!

I run through the kitchen towards the laundry room, and my family is waiting, all three of them: Snack-less, Ride-less and Pants-less. They are standing there just staring at me, shaking their heads. If they have shit lists, I'm sure my name is at the tippy top right now.

> **Me:** WHAT? No, seriously, you guys, if you need something, you should put it on my list.

If my kid responds to one more question with the text acronym, IDK, I'm going to ROTFL-MAO as I take away his fucking phone for a week and give him the 411 about appropriate responses. He won't LOL about it, but he'll understand that I'm a BAMF capable of FUBAR-ing his YOLO.

MEATLOAF MAYHEM, OR WHY I LEARNED TO FUCKING COOK

As a teenager, I found myself wondering what all the fuss was about when it came to feminism. Women could vote and work and had the same freedoms as men, I thought; what more do these feminists want? I always believed the sky was the limit for me. I could be whatever I wanted to be and do whatever I wanted to do. I had big plans! I didn't spend time dreaming about my future husband, imagining my wedding day or naming my future children. I was planning to become a neurosurgeon after my career as an Olympic gymnast was over, stuff I found way more interesting than a boring life as a wife and mother. Up until my junior year in college, I still hadn't given much thought to where marriage and motherhood would fit into my life. Then I met Eric.

Marriage? Yes. Career? Moving ahead as planned. Motherhood? We'd have to see about that.

I had never lived with a man before and I was only twenty-four years old, which today seems to me to be about a minute removed from teething. But I figured it would all work out. Eric knew I did not plan to be a housewife, content to cook, clean and breed. My career would be my first priority. I figured we'd have a modern marriage, equally sharing the household responsibilities. I sure as shit wasn't about to do all the cleaning and cooking! I had watched my mom role model the *Good Housekeeping* standard of never bitching about cooking or cleaning. I respected her choices, but I did NOT embrace the 1950s housewife mentality as she had. I would not be greeting my husband at the door with a smile and a cocktail, catering to his every whim. Fuck that. I had more of the "go-braless, pro-choice, storm the Capitol and protest shit" attitude. I wanted and expected equality.

So when I ended up cleaning up Eric's crap every damn day and being the only one to run the vacuum or clean the bathroom, I was disappointed in both of us. Almost instantly my modern marriage fantasies were fading away.

Eric often worked evening hours, and I couldn't cook for shit, so I ate a lot of dry cereal, drive-through and takeout for dinner. Our apartment was always a mess; Eric never lifted a finger to clean or tidy up, so why should I? But as time passed, I couldn't stand to live in squalor, so I started to clean every day and make simple meals for us, like pasta with sauce from a jar or scrambled eggs.

At first I felt as if I was being disloyal to the feminist movement by taking up traditional housewifery without putting up a fight or demanding equality, but I was just so sick of living in a filthy mess and hungry for home-cooked meals. (Basically, I missed my mommy. I hadn't realized just how hard her job really was.) But I did it reluctantly, still believing that a real feminist didn't do the domestic thing. It was only from sheer desperation for food that didn't come in a sack that I decided to up my cooking game.

After all, didn't feminism mean I could have it all! Marriage and a career! Surely I'd be able to bring home the bacon to my tidy house and fry it up in a pan with ease.

Because of this and numerous other domestic failures, I made some carefully considered observations that, although totally subjective, I believe everyone should agree with. These experiences and observations led to the opinion that every fucking one no matter who they are needs to be able to cook. NOT microwave, but cook up a decent meal that won't give the people eating it food poisoning or butt-fire diarrhea. Cooking is the toughest of the tough domestic duties. Single or married, if you are going to live on your own, cooking is a must-learn skill.

My failures taught me that embracing and excelling in the traditional female role of a housewife isn't for the weak, ignorant or anti-feminist type of woman. Learning how to be an awesome cook is not any easier than learning how to become a good attorney, nurse or teacher. It takes practice, hard work and dedication. A feminist doesn't judge or belittle other women for their choices, thinking themselves superior to women in traditional roles. A feminist seeks to make sure that women in all walks of life are empowered, respected and celebrated in the same manner as men. It's just that simple. I learned this the hard way. That's why I've learned to cook and I can cook a bunch of kick-ass meals. I think everyone needs to learn to fucking cook and cook well.

Why learn to cook well? I'm sure you have also observed the simple biological fact that humans need to eat and aside from people who are truly too mentally or physically ill to enjoy it, eating is also FUN AS HELL. What is not fun as hell, at least for me, is cooking. I do it because I have to, or else I won't get to do the fun-as-hell part, which is the eating! I also have people depending on me to feed them nutritious meals so they don't become malnourished or dead, but even before I had baby birds constantly needing to be fed and watered, I needed to be nourished myself. We all do. I couldn't take much more reheated pizza. I was hungry for a home-cooked meal! I would have to learn to fucking cook. There was no mom around to do the cooking and Eric wasn't doing it either. If I wanted to eat good food, I would have to fucking make it myself.

I would learn to fucking cook and I was going to start with a home-cooked MEATLOAF! Why meatloaf? Because it's chock-full of MEAT—which is my favorite ever food. Meat is fun to eat (and THAT is fun to say, isn't it? Say It!). What kind of meat do I like best? I LOVE any and all meat: fresh meat, potted meat, canned meat and lunch meat. You get what I'm saying here, right? I'm trying to express how very much I love meaty meat. Plus I had observed my mom making my favorite meaty meatloaf a hundred times when I was growing up and she made it look fun AND easy so I figured it would be fun and easy for me too. Having meatloaf would be like having a little bit of mom around. I missed her and goddammit I was starving!

Looking back, I feel sorry for my naïve newlywed self. I was as excited and hopeful as Charlie Bucket, chasing around an impossible dream of a golden ticket, the odds stacked against me. I wanted the unattainable: to be a great cook immediately, to make something out of nothing with very few resources to draw on! I dreamed about cooking up some stick-to-the-ribs kind of grub for my large and always hungry new husband and myself.

To fully appreciate the magnitude of the task I was about to attempt, you have to imagine a spoiled, immature princess of a woman-child surrounded by pristine, top-of-the-line appliances still in their original boxes. The kitchen was like a foreign country to me, but I was keen to take the road less traveled. Calphalon, KitchenAid, Oneida. You name it, we had it. We had a big wedding with generous gift givers, setting me up for housekeeping success. If only I could figure out what the hell to do with all of it!

Sadly, this was also before the Internet was in every household. My version of Google at the time was my parents! I had always gone directly to them when I had a problem or a question and they did not disappoint. EVER. No matter how many times a day my innocent ignorance necessitated their assistance, I could count on them to be the 411 and 911, 24/7. They may no longer be cooking my meals for me, but they sure could help me learn to do it for myself.

But seriously, I smugly chuckled to myself, how hard could it be to make a meatloaf? I didn't need them! I'd observed what I imagined was my mom's joy and ease in doing it many times over. Granted, I hadn't observed the details very carefully, but I was feeling fabulously confident. I have always been an excellent direction follower and had a basic idea of what I needed to do. I was all over this meatloaf making! I was going to learn to fucking cook!

After rummaging through boxes of wedding gifts I found a baking pan just right for the loaf of perfection I was hoping to create! Thus far *Joy of Cooking* had served solely as a holder for take-out menus, but now I would follow the directions to the letter like a good listening grown-up!

Drunk with the power of innocence, I cracked the spine on *Joy of Cooking*. "Meatloaf; about, p. 431."

About Meatloaf. Blah, blah, ★&$^★%@# . . . what the WHAT? What language was this nonsense?

And what's this "About meatloaf" bullshit? NO, not *about* meatloaf; MEATLOAF! I wanted step-by-step, "do it this way and don't deviate from it" directions about how to make a marvelous loaf of meat. But there were two different recipes listed and both of those tricky bastards contained ingredients, words and concepts that may as well have been written in hieroglyphs: baste at intervals, invert the mold, mounding, folding and creating an attractive service.

WHAT. THE. HELL? There was no way I was going to be able to do this without either a translator or parental assistance.

FUCK YOU, *Joy of Cooking.* I tossed it aside, and channeled my inner Veruca Salt while I dialed up my parents. My father answered the phone. He knew how to cook, although he didn't do it often. I pleaded for help.

"Daaaaaad, I need to cook a meatloaf and the stupid cook-booooook doesn't say how to dooooooo it," I whined in my best helpless daughter voice. "I NEED you to help me." (And I also want an Oompa Loompa with that golden ticket.) "Can you come here?" (I want an Oompa Loompa NOW!)

"Just follow the recipe," he answered matter-of-factly and not at all sympathetic and daddylike. I was pretty sure he was watching television so I needed to up my game in order to get him focused on ME, ME, ME! I was so hungry. I wanted meatloaf and I wanted it NOW!

"But, DAAAAAAAAAAAAAAAAAD, I don't have any of these exotic ingredients in the apartment. I mean what the fuck is vegetable stock or onion juice? How do I invert a mold and what's a mold? And there are two recipes, so how do I know which one to choose and . . ." I just kept yapping and complaining, totally convinced that he would not only explain the concept of mixing lightly, but also zip right on over and help me. The meatloaf I knew and loved was made of meat, not all the other mystery ingredients. How could anything be this complicated and why didn't I hear him say, "I'll be right there"? I was sure we must have gotten disconnected until I heard his laugh.

"Stop laughing," I demanded.

He laughed a little more and then was silent. Was he ignoring me? I turned up the volume and added a little drama.

"DAD, THIS IS SERIOUS," I yelled into the receiver.

"Mmm-hmm," was his reply.

I looked at the clock and figured he must be sitting in his recliner drinking bourbon and watching *Coach* or some other shitty sitcom in reruns, because that's what he did after work: he vegged out in front of the boob tube while my mom made dinner. I prodded Veruca Nikki to work a bit harder in order to get my metaphorical Oompa Loompa engaged. The man was ignoring me! Then instead of offering up any specific tips or advice he told me to read the directions more carefully, which I fucking WAS trying to do, but I needed him to *decipher* the directions for me. HE needed to listen more carefully, but I knew that while the television was on, bombs could be going off all around him and he wouldn't notice. I demanded to talk to my mother since my father was being an inconsiderate dick. THIS is why I feared domestication. There was no equality in my parents' relationship. As usual, he was drinking and chilling and my mom was cooking. I wouldn't tolerate that kind of behavior from Eric. Yeah, I was making a meatloaf, but it was more for me than it was for him.

"I WANT MOM!" I barked.

"Jesus, Judy," I heard him call out to my mother, not even trying to hide the fact that he was cracking up, "pick up the phone. Nikki wants to talk about making an exotic meatloaf so pick up please." Um, NO, I didn't want to *talk* about meatloaf. I wanted to *make* a meatloaf, and I needed to know why the hell my one and only cookbook, America's bestselling cookbook for that matter, touted for years as the best reference for new cooks so that learning to cook could be joyful, was written in gibber-ish. I was feeling hostile enough to strangle a puppy. The damn thing was like a book of World War II secret recipes in fucking spy code! The JOY of cooking, my ASS!

And then I heard my mom burst out laughing in the back-ground. Hell to the NO she didn't! Not her too!

"FINE—DON'T HELP ME!" I yelled and I hung up the phone.

I wasn't going to tolerate mockery from either of my par-ents; I was a grown-up and deserved more respect than that. I talked myself down, telling my mad mind that I really shouldn't need their help anyway, right? If I wanted to be treated like a grown-up, I'd have to act like one. And that's when it came to me, the dumbest, most egomaniacal fantasy I had ever enter-tained in my twenty-four years of life: I would make a hybrid-specialty meatloaf, combining the stuff I understood from the two recipes in my book of Joy, because FUCK YOU, mockers, I am a college graduate. I am a wife who cooks dinner because I want to, not because I have to, though I did hope that when big guy got a taste my cooking, he was going to do more than *kiss* the cook. My food art was going to make him want to plant a million man seeds in me to make a million babies, IF I were to decide that I wanted to have babies at all. God, where the fuck did that thought come from? I was getting carried away. I'd have to be careful about that stuff in the future if I was to get my equality. This domesticity was sneaky indeed!

So I got to work on my masterpiece. I shall call it "Miracle loaf," I chuckled to myself, because realistically I knew that if I were to pull this off, it would indeed be miraculous. I plowed ahead, mixing the meat, catsup, salt, pepper, and onion and crushed-up saltine crackers with some butter and parsley. That would do it. My loaf had no need for herbs and spices I'd never even heard of, no onion juice, lemon juice or bread crumbs. Well, I had a vague suspicion that it did need bread crumbs, but since I didn't have a car in which to go buy the bread crumbs (or an Oompa Loompa to run out and fetch me some), I figured that a crumbled handful of saltines would do the trick. I just had to estimate. I mean did Julia Child and her hoity-toity French chef friends who used sixty thousand herbs and spices write these recipes? Whatever happened to good old American meatloaf made with MEAT?

I popped the mound of meat into the oven at 350 degrees, feeling quite satisfied and darn proud of my "can-do" attitude. In a mere forty-five minutes, I was going to change my husband's LIFE! And this was only the beginning. There was no end to the marvelous and magical delights I was going to churn out in the future. Like Wonka himself, I would confound them all with MY secret recipes for delicious food creations!

But forty-five minutes later, I was dumbfounded. The Miracle loaf was just as moist and gooey as when I had put it in the oven. I poked at the wet, pink blob of raw meat, wondering if I should suck it up and call my dad again. I was running out of time and the stuffing was starting to shrivel up in the saucepan on the stove top.

WHAT WAS WRONG WITH MY MEATLOAF?

Maybe it just needed to cook a bit longer? After all, I had used my own special recipe so of course I should have also modified the cooking time! Silly me, how could I have not thought of this? THAT WAS IT! It had to be. And I adjusted the temperature as well, cranking it up a bit and praying for a miracle.

Please, please, please cook, you meaty meat miracle! PLEASE!

I set the timer for fifteen more minutes, but even after turning up the temperature and giving it extra time, the thing was still a gelatinous blob. After fifteen minutes I set it for fifteen more. More blob.

WHY WASN'T IT GETTING FIRM AND CRUSTY-LIKE?

I didn't know what to do and the book of Joy wasn't going to be of any help. If ever I needed an Oompa Loompa it was that day. I could send him to Boston Market to pick me up some ready-made meatloaf! I considered calling my parents and the thought of that was unbearable. My dad was probably STILL sitting in his recliner watching television, and based on my previous tantrum, I was pretty sure he would either not answer the phone in order to make me suffer OR he would answer and make me suck it up and apologize for acting like a spoiled toddler. NO. I WOULDN'T CALL! More prayers and problem solving were needed. Okay, Miracle loaf, now would be a good time to miracle-ize!

Maybe if I turned up the oven to 450? Maybe our oven was broken? I hadn't used it yet so THAT could be the problem. Eric was due home any minute. The blob of soggy dead cow was just sitting in my oven, refusing to be cooked and mocking me. I felt like my heart was going to burst into flames and explode out of my chest at any moment, the humiliation so overwhelming that it became physically painful.

Looking at that sticky, raw hunk of meat, all I could think was that I was not a good wife, or a joyful cook. It was hurting my face to hold back the tears because I didn't want my husband to walk in and see me crying. I wanted so badly to be amazing, to be everything, to do it myself and I had failed miserably. Was I ever NOT going to be the helpless child who needed to rely on others to make a simple meal? Goddammit, why hadn't I learned to fucking cook?

I needed to pull myself together and somehow try to avert a full-on dinner disaster, but the sadness overcame me and the tears began to flow. I was sobbing the total ugly cry and I felt so embarrassed. My stomach was grumbling louder than my sobs and twisting in pain from hunger. Not only was I a failure, I was a starving failure, and that only increased the power of my meltdown over this uncooked mess of a meatloaf.

Sometime during my pity party, Eric had entered the kitchen and was looking at the hunk of raw meat sitting on top of the stove. "I don't know what I did wrong," I managed to choke out from the corner of the kitchen where I was grieving over my lost dream of being a superwife whipping up gloriously magnificent meals that melted in your mouth. I could bring home the bacon, but I was a failure at frying it up in a pan. FUCK! I felt as if I deserved this sadness as punishment for looking down on women like my mom who eschewed a career for full-time family life. Karma's a bitch.

"Shit," I cried, "I'm sorry." And I cried some more because seriously, a TEAM of Oompa Loompas couldn't have saved my meatloaf that day. I felt small and insignificant, Veruca turned Charlie Bucket. I wanted to be joyful but at this point I would have settled for being a halfway-decent cook. It was the first time I had tried to do the housewife thing and I had failed. FAILED! That's when my husband put some of the joy back into me.

He scooped me up off the floor and said, "Let's have a quickie and go out for beers and a bucket of mussels. I'm starving!" And so we did both of these things. And he not only thanked me for the sex and for trying to cook a meal, but also agreed with my opinion that something had to be done about my parents' rude behavior and my father's television addiction. After all, he was watching reruns of *M*A*S*H* a week earlier when I called him up to come fix the flat tire on my car and he told me to call a tow truck. A TOW TRUCK? You'd think under the influence of the sensitive Alan Alda he would have come running with a tire jack and a smile, but nope. The man had a problem.

In time I realized that the meatloaf debacle was a stroke of luck, a shove towards independence and maturity that I sorely needed. My parents let me go it alone, knowing I needed to grow the fuck up. I began to appreciate my mother so much more and eventually did read up about feminism. I had it all wrong. I could enjoy being a wife and all that came with it, even if that did include the unequal division of domestic duties.

Not everybody has a grown-up husband who gets turned on by tears and is satisfied eating shellfish that wallow in their own piss. Most men prefer a meal that isn't basted in tears and E. coli as well, even if they won't admit it to your face. Eric continued to have a great sense of humor in the years to come as I fucked up many a meal beyond all recognition. We ate at a lot of restaurants in the early years. He cooked more and cleaned more too. It wasn't perfect equality, but that's only because it's impossible to have that in any relationship and I needed a lot of practice if I was going to learn to fucking cook well.

I went into marriage and motherhood thinking I'd be so much better at them than I am, that it would come as easy to me as everything else in my life had up to that point. At the time of the meatloaf debacle, my lack of knowledge and skill in the kitchen was a considerable blow to my self-confidence, but I kept at it, and now I make a mean motherfucking turkey meatloaf with pepper jack cheese that would knock your socks off!

But thinking back to that day still stings my ego. It hurt. It was VERY embarrassing. The meatloaf mayhem incident, as I call it today, was the beginning of the end of me demanding the metaphorical Oompa Loompas from my parents, and the beginning of me solving my own problems and figuring out how to get golden tickets on my own—like a big girl. Of course I still fail miserably at times, but I use the Internet as an Oompa Loompa of sorts when I'm in a pickle. I log on to Domino's Pizza, order online and save my family from starvation in thirty minutes or less (or it's free). My children know that even after all these years, when Mom cooks, there is still a chance there will be a dinner disaster and they will end up being rescued from whatever mess I made by a hot, delicious cheese pizza, which they most likely begged for before I fucked up the meal I had planned.

I am going to teach both of my kids what feminism actually means! I will make sure they understand that being married will not provide either of them a guarantee of support, understanding or equality. But more importantly, they will not be allowed to leave this house until they learn to fucking cook.

They *need* to know that although fast food, processed food and candy are always consistently satisfying and mood improving good (and reaching for this crap when you are exhausted or on the run is part of modern life for many busy people), they will eventually tire of it and be grateful they can cook. I think the road to independence often starts with being able to provide one's self with a meal that rivals a delicious beef and sausage combo with cheese fries from Portillo's. Eventually these novelty foods not only lose their luster, leaving you with a perpetual grease-induced hangover, but also cause you to need pants a size bigger. These are just a few more reasons that everyone needs to learn to fucking cook. They will learn. Everyone should learn to cook. Every fucking one.

You will thank you, your partner will thank you, and even though your kids say that they would like to eat junky food or candy for every meal, the truth is that they would eventually hate it, and think you suck, and wonder why the hell you didn't just figure out how to cook a few things really well. The point being that learning how to cook should be as optional as breathing. I don't care who you are. Learn to fucking cook. I did it and you can too.

KEEP CALM AND MOM ON

"Ouch! That hurts!" Zach whined, sitting on the floor between my legs as I combed tangles out of his mop of shoulder-length hair.

Normally I didn't get this involved with his do, even if it looked like a haystack atop his head, but it was school picture day. I rarely fork out the big bucks for the poor-quality school photos. In my experience it doesn't matter how nice they look when they leave the house; by the time they actually get their pictures taken they look like filthy hobos. But since the grandmas had been nagging me for current pictures, I coughed up the cash. Going to a professional photographer wasn't worth the copayments for the numerous therapy sessions I would inevitably need in order to recover from the trauma of fighting to clean, dress and transport them to the picture place and then getting them to behave. Just brushing their hair was torture.

"What are you squirting on me? It smells like sadness," he complained, coughing for maximum effect.

"What the *hell* does sadness smell like?" I replied, still yanking knots out of his hair. The detangler was watermelon scented. What was sad about the smell of watermelons? I started laughing. How does he come up with this stuff? Zach wasn't amused.

"I told you what sadness smells like—this detangler! It doesn't smell like watermelons! It smells like shit!" he howled back at me.

"Cussing like a tough guy *and* whining wike a wittle baby about having your hair brushed?" I mocked him. "Hilarious!" He started wiggling away so I used my legs to drag him back toward me, locking them around his waist. He tried again to escape.

"Let me GO! Why are you laughing? What's so funny?" He squirmed and turned his head around to glare at me. His angry little face made me laugh even harder.

"You! That's what's funny," I chuckled. "I've never heard anyone say something smelled like sadness before. Sorry I'm spraying you with sadness, but you better act happy when they take your picture at school because if you screw up your school pictures, I'll be sad. You don't want that. Haven't you heard? If Momma ain't happy, ain't nobody happy. Sit still and let me finish!"

Never missing an opportunity to irritate her brother, Cate chimed in. "Yeah, Zach, sit still and stop swearing!"

"Shut up!" he barked. He always took the bait, as she knew he would.

"No, YOU shut up!" she snorted.

"Both of you shut up!" I said, still snickering, but on alert for potential trouble. Things got ugly fast between these two.

"He started it." As usual, Cate insisted on having the last word.

That set him off! "Mom, I didn't. . . . You heard her. . . . SHE STARTED IT!" He thrashed a bit, trying to get away from me and go after his sister. I squeezed my legs around his waist again. She sat on the bottom stair with a shit-eating grin plastered on her face, quite pleased with herself for provoking her brother while I continued brushing out his mane.

"Yeah, well, you're next!" he hissed.

Her smile vanished instantly and she sprinted up the stairs. Having her hair brushed often sent my darling daughter into full-blown tantrums, second only to brushing her teeth. You'd think they'd give each other a little support, considering their mutual hatred of all things grooming, but fighting had become as natural to them as breathing. Jerks, I thought. I was proud of myself for not saying it out loud. I'd been working hard at keeping my mouth in check, decreasing the amount of smart remarks and ill-tempered outbursts in response to their crappy behavior.

I finished spewing sadness on my son and released him. "Cate," I called out, "get down here and get your hair brushed—now!"

"I DON'T WANT TO! I DON'T WANT YOU TO BRUSH MY HAIR!"

I desperately wanted to yell back at her, "I don't care what you want. Get your ass down here or I'll beat it," but since I was on a verbal-control roll, I just mumbled it under my breath.

"You aren't funny, you know," Zach said and stomped away still with that sour look on his face. It was hopeless. I couldn't resist the urge to instigate.

My kids were used to my swearing and sarcasm, but if I had managed to tick off Zach, who almost always responded well to silliness, there was no telling what ferocious reaction it would get from Cate, who still hadn't yet grasped the concept of sarcasm.

"YOU are the one who doesn't know. I am actually hilarious!" I hooted. So much for verbal control. I hollered again for

Cate, who was nowhere in sight. Who was I kidding? She would not come willingly. I chased her down, trapped her between my legs and started in on the second rat's nest of the morning. With the first stroke of the brush, she erupted.

"OH MY GOD WHY ARE YOU TRYING TO KILL ME? YOU ARE KILLING ME! LET ME GO! STOP KILLING ME. . . ." She went on and on with the accusations and started flailing and clawing at my hand with her tiny fists of fury. God, she was strong! Suddenly her elbow delivered a forceful blow to my left boob. My tender, swollen, premenstrual left tit. Now Momma wasn't happy. Soon nobody else would be either. I wiggled away from Cate, scrambled up off the floor and exploded!

"Why does it have to be this way every fucking day? If either of you have one more fit over your hair, I swear to GOD I'm going to shave you bald!"

I threw the brush across the room and stormed upstairs. I had to get away from them. It was bad enough I had lost my temper; I didn't want to keep shooting my mouth off, saying things I didn't mean and making empty threats. *Obviously* they would have more fits, many more in fact, and I wasn't *really* going to shave their heads. That was just plain stupid talk.

I knew better than to toss out consequences for which I had no plans to follow through. I wondered what was wrong with me. Just a few weeks earlier I'd had an even more massive meltdown.

It was a blistering hot August day, and I had been breaking up fights, making meals and snacks and cleaning up messes all day long. August is audit time for Eric at work; he leaves before the kids are up in the morning and comes home long after they are tucked in at night. By the end of the month, I'm a frazzled mess, desperately in need of a break. On day number twenty-five of parenting solo, I was ripe for a raging rant.

The kids were killing time playing in the backyard before dinner, and I was counting the minutes until I could put them to bed. It was the only thing keeping me even partially sane that night. Well, that and the light at the end of the tunnel—school would be starting in a few weeks. I sat on a lawn chair, drinking a glass of wine, watching them play. Cate was scaling the wall on the oversized play set and hurtling herself down the slide over and over and over. *Apparently*, she wanted me to watch.

"Mom, watch me! Are you watching? Do you see me? Watch this! Hey, are you looking? I thought you said you were watching! Did you see what I did that time? Now watch how I do it this time. Watch me, Mom! Moooom, watch THIS!"

She asked me to watch her do the same fucking thing over and over.

"Are you still watching? Watch meeeeeeeeeeeeeeeeeeeeee!" she'd squeal as she flew down the slide.

Oh my god, shut up! I thought to myself. I heard you the first zillion times. I'm watching! It was impossible *not* to watch her. I felt a twinge of guilt for my ugly thoughts, but the glass of wine I was drinking was hard at work, washing that nonsense away. At least I didn't say "shut up" out loud.

Zach was monkeying around on the trapeze on the other side of the play set. "MOM, DID YOU SEE WHAT I JUST DID?" he hollered. I did not. I was watching Cate. I hopped up from my chair and walked towards the swing set so I could see what he wanted me to see. Hooray! Now I have both of them wanting me to watch them do the same trick over and over.

"On my way, pal, I'm coming around to see you." I made my way around the monster play set that took up half of my backyard. Cate had made it to the top of the climbing wall and noticed that I was not watching her. Ah yes, let the jealous bullshit begin!

"MOM! YOU LIED! You said you were watching ME!" she wailed, throwing herself down on the platform for dramatic effect.

Now, remember, I was overheated, tired and hungry. I went off.

"I have been doing nothing but watch you for the entire summer! I've watched you walk, run, skip, hop, swim, jump into the pool, jump rope, color, paint, dance, sleep, read, eat, poop and breathe! All I *do* is watch you, Cate! I have been watching your every move for the past twenty minutes and the one time I pay attention to your brother, you lose your mind? I CANNOT WATCH YOU EVERY SECOND OF EVERY DAY AND IF THAT MAKES ME A LIAR, SO BE IT!"

I spun on my heel and was on my way inside when I heard Zach say, "Yeah, Cate! You suck!"

"No, you suck! MOM, ZACH JUST TOLD ME I SUCK!"

Now they were *fighting*? Hell to the no *fucking* way! I turned around and ripped off a raging rant.

"YOU BOTH SUCK! I AM SICK TO DEATH OF BOTH OF YOU! I AM GOING INSIDE AND YOU NEED TO LEAVE . . . ME . . . ALONE!"

Oh, yes, I did. I told my kids they sucked. Two surprised little faces stared at me silently for a few seconds. I felt terrible and was about to apologize, but then they both resumed their climbing, sliding and flipping. "Hey, Zach, watch this!" Cate called out to him as she slid.

"Awesome! Watch this!" he yelled as he flipped himself upside down. They both started giggling. "Mom, did you see that?"

What? How could they be so unfazed by my hateful rant?

And how did they always manage to go from enemies to BFFs in the blink of an eye? I couldn't help but stare back at them in silence for a few minutes before going into the house to check on dinner. Like nothing happened, they talked and giggled through dinner, dessert and bedtime routines, oblivious to my internal struggle. I was so disgusted with myself for telling them they sucked. They were just kids doing what kids do, not trying to be sucky. I was the one who sucked! BIG-TIME. I had to make it right, even if it did seem like my tirade hadn't had any effect on them whatsoever.

At tuck-in time, I invited both of them into my bedroom, making an extra effort to cuddle up and smother them with love. I had them pick out some books and we snuggled up to read together. Once they were all calmed down and sleepy, I apologized for my harsh words. Summer was ending and it would be nice if *some* of their memories of it didn't include me yelling, swearing, losing my temper or nitpicking at them about stuff like chewing with their mouths open or chasing the dogs around trying to milk them.

"You know I don't think you suck, right? I'm crazy about you guys. I think you guys are the most unique, funny, clever, kind, nonsucky kids I know and I love you more than anything in the world. I've been a big, fat grouch lately. Please forgive me for losing my temper and saying mean things." Phew. I said it. I was making it right.

"You *are* a little fat and grouchy," Cate agreed.

"She's not fat. Mom, you aren't fat. But you are grouchy." A very nice effort from Zach.

"But she is mean," said Cate.

"No, she's not," said Zach.

"Yeah, she is. She's the meanest." Cate got up and threw her arms around my neck. "Just kidding!" she squealed.

I felt a little better. They didn't suck and I only sucked a little.

"But you *are* a fun ender," said Cate. "You always end the fun, but you can't help it because you are the mom."

Both kids started giggling and hopping around on the bed, shoving each other and flopping around pretending to be boneless. Wow, now that hurt. Moms are "fun enders?" And now instead of settling down, they were revved up. It was long past their bedtime, but telling them to sit down and shut up would just confirm my role as a mean, fun-ending mom. I decided to tolerate the chaos until they chilled out by choice, which was thankfully pretty quick since they were exhausted. I apologized one more time to Zach as I tucked him into bed.

"Oh, it's okay. But I think you should do something about your anger problem."

My anger problem?

Did he just say I should do something about my anger problem?

SHIT! Really? Just like that, I went back to believing I sucked.

"I'll look into that, pal," I said and then kissed him on the head. "And thanks for being so understanding about today."

"Oh, no problem," he replied as he shimmied down under his covers.

I went downstairs to get some thinking food. After hogging down two bowls of ice cream, wallowing in sucky parent guilt, I had an epiphany! If I really had an anger problem, I would have gotten angry when he accused me of having an anger problem. I would have gone off right then and there! Pfffth! What anger problem?

Yeah, I had done wrong that day, but I'd be damned if I was going to let a couple of grade school kids cause me to question my sanity when I was just doing what all moms have to do. If trying to civilize them makes me a meanie, so be it. I just needed to hang in there for a few more weeks until school started. Just keep calm and be mom, I told myself. Hey, that would be my new mantra—Keep calm and be mom.

Which brings me back around to the school picture day incident. It was like déjà vu. I was all "keeping calm and being mom" until I wasn't, and suddenly I was in a self-imposed time-out and riddled with guilt. I flung myself backwards on the bed. Every single day I said something I didn't want to say . . . but you know what? Nobody's perfect and who the hell wouldn't react to the kind of bullshit I had dealt with all morning from my kids? If anyone sucked that morning, it was those knuckle-heads!

That's when I heard the yelling. I guess they had decided to continue inciting each other and arguing the entire time I was upstairs. Yep, I sighed, those two sucked. Keep calm and be mom, I told myself as I hustled downstairs. They were on the floor, yelling, pounding on each other and pulling each other's hair.

Really? The hair?

"*What* is going on?" I asked, trying to separate them. This was the second round of shit fits I'd had to deal with that morning and my boob was still super sore. If anyone had a good reason to be angry, it was me, but I had pulled myself together! I couldn't understand a word of their blather and honestly, I didn't care who said or did what. Under different circumstances I would have let the argument play out naturally, but it was picture day and they had *messed up their hair*!

"Both of you, knock it off right now!" I raised my voice, but I wasn't yelling. I call it my firm but friendly voice. Keep calm and be mom.

Zach and Cate both spoke at once.

"You don't have to talk so mean!" she snipped, crossing her arms in front of her chest defensively.

"Why are you yelling at us again?" Zach accused me with a furrowed brow.

The plan was still in place. I needed to keep calm and be mom, but first I had to get their attention.

"I'm not yelling. THIS IS YELLING!" I screamed as loud as I could. They both flinched and stopped talking. Good, I'd scared the shit out of them.

"It's my turn to talk and you need to listen very carefully because I am only going to say this one time. If you choose not to listen and cooperate, know that you will lose all television, computer and friend privileges for a week. Is that understood?"

Calm Mom was not yelling. Both kids nodded their heads slowly in the affirmative. Calm Mom carried on.

"Very good. Now, *if* I were a mean person neither of you would have a fraction of the nice toys or warm clothes you have. *If* I were a mean person, I would call you terrible names, hit you or refuse to feed you when I was mad at you instead of putting myself in a time-out so that I could regroup and care for you safely. *If* I were a mean person, I would break or throw out your toys when you leave them everyfuckingwhere instead of asking you ten times to clean them up. *If* I were a mean person, I would use a hairbrush to beat you until you were bruised and bloody, instead of trying not to hurt you when I brush your hair, because I know you have sensitive heads. Mean moms don't want to look at their kids. I want pictures because I love you so much that I want to be able to see your faces any time of the day or night."

I was so calm I considered checking my pulse.

"I am sorry if I scared you when I lost my temper this morning and threw the brush. I was frustrated by all the hairbrushing drama, and when Cate accidentally elbowed me in the boob, it hurt. It hurt a real lot, so I had to get away from the both of you so that I didn't say or do anything meaner than I already had. Now get up, go get your shoes and backpacks and come back to me. I am going to run a brush through your hair again quickly because you mussed each other up while trying to kill each other, and I don't want to hear a peep out of either of you while I'm doing it. You remember the consequences if you don't cooperate?"

Slow nodding. Now we were all calm. I turned around and walked toward the kitchen. I needed to get their lunches made. Cate started giggling. I heard her whisper.

"Mean."

"Anger problem," Zach added, trying not to crack up.

I was laughing too, but I let those sucky little bastards have their moment. Keep calm and be mom, I told myself. Mom the fuck on.

Me:	Why do you put your clothes on backwards every day?
Cate:	Why do you care? Am I breaking the law?
Me:	Carry on then.

TOO POOPED TO GIVE A SHIT

I don't trust people who dislike kids. Because what the fuck? They were kids once and someone liked them despite their kid-ness. It's unnatural to think that babies and children are not cute. Human beings are programmed to dig the faces of little ones—that's just a fact. I cannot fathom what it's like to be able to resist smiling at a precious little baby. I think that shit's just cold. I don't trust people who don't like dogs either. The only dog-hating people who I don't want to pinch are the ones who got attacked by a crazy one and had half their face torn off, but let's face it, that's rare. Kid and dog haters are often heartless bastards; however, I completely understand why people *choose* not to have kids or dogs, even if they do like them. Both these beasts trash your life and personal possessions on such an epic level, the only reason they survive at all is because of their ador-ableness. At least that's the case in my home. I confess that I used to have some pretty significant anxiety about keeping things not only neat and tidy, but also clean. Notice I said *used* to. That was before I had my first four-legged fleabag. Having an epileptic mutt that puked everyfuckingwhere, chewed up my shoes and left clumps of hair on every single piece of furniture in my house began the process of desensitizing me to disgustingness. Now that I have two dogs and two kids, the only neat and tidy anything that can be found in my house is my days of the week pill organizer, because fuckin' A, if I'm going to survive this phase of my life, it's going to take more than adorable faces to get me through.

For years I wasn't sure if I'd *overcome* the anxiety that plagued me all my life or I was just overmedicated. My cozy fabulous sectional sofa is extra soft due to the fine layer of dog hair that covers the fabric and if I'm feeling particularly hungry and lazy, there's a good chance I can find a cracker or something to snack on if I reach between the snot-smeared cushions. A few years ago I spotted a pile of dried-up dog poop under the piano bench when we were on our way out the door. The old perfectionist me would have cleaned it up and sanitized that shit PRONTO. The new, realistic me shrugged, laughed and said, "Meh, that thing is bone dry. I'll take care of it when we get home." And when we got home, I was tired so I just went straight up to bed. I didn't lose one wink of sleep over it, either. And the grosser version of me was happier than the anxious perfectionist. There are those who think this confession pathetic. I don't blame you.

But since becoming a mother, I no longer feel guilty or gross when I fall asleep with dishes in the sink, clothes in the washer AND dryer, toys in my bed, clothes on the floor, and unbrushed teeth. I'm not fucking superwoman. I do what I can, but when I hit my wall, I am done. DONE! If I'm unloading the dishwasher and a wave of fatigue hits me, I'll stop what I'm doing and trudge up to bed. The dishes aren't going anywhere. This bitch needs her sleep.

I am either hauling ass or comatose; with me, there's no in between.

I sleep soundly even when the hooligan neighbor kids set off M80s, making the dogs bark and sending the kids running to our room in the middle of the night to pile on top of me in bed. I'm clueless until the dog licks my face to wake me the next day, and even then, sometimes I'm sleepwalking. I'm often so exhausted that a few minutes of "resting my eyes" while listening to one of my children reading at night results in me waking up next to them at three a.m., drooling on their pillow and bogarting their favorite stuffed animal. I forgive myself for not supervising my kid's nighttime reading, and sign the slip that says they read for twenty minutes, even if I snored through fifteen of them. I accept occasionally having to kick clothes and toys out of my way to get to my own bed at night, because being all things to all people is *tiring*. I just cannot do it all.

In other words, I've accepted the reality that having a neat and clean house is next to impossible while having kids and pets, and I've stopped trying to keep things picked up unless it's a holiday or company we have to impress is coming. My mantra is, "This ain't Pottery Barn—people live here." This prevents me from getting all worked up on the days when I feel like the walls are closing in on me because there is just too much trash and muck everywhere. There is no OFF button to stop the flow of stuff that comes along with living a life.

My acceptance of living with mess does have a *few* limits. There is stuff that is just too fucking disgusting and unsanitary. Bodily fluids—puke, urine, poop, gooey boogers and drool with food chunks in it—are hard limits. I must clean all varieties of person juice as soon as I come across it. But dog shit sometimes gets ignored, as long as it's not runny or fresh. I know it's awful and I SHOULD BE ASHAMED. But I'm not.

Why not? you ask. Well, it was a small thing, really, that made me stop giving a shit about dog shit. One morning, in the wee hours of zero dark thirty o'clock, I felt something scratchy against my foot. I figured it was the dog's nails or one of the bones she is always burying under the covers. Maybe a toy or a book that one of the kids left in my room? Was I even awake or was I dreaming? I was stuck somewhere between sleep stages when the itch became too much to ignore. I knew that if I didn't pop open my peepers, check it out and do something about the scratchy thing, I'd be ruined for the day, too tired to function. So I did. I squinted enough to see where my cell phone was. I grabbed it and activated the flashlight application, lifted up the covers and there it was: an itty, bitty dried-up puppy turd.

IN MY BED!

God help me, I couldn't believe it either, but I have cleaned up enough of these dried-up nuggets of nasty that I knew what I was looking at. And if it was unthinkable that I was snuggled up with one for most of the night (hell, maybe even a few nights), it was even more unthinkable that I could possibly muster up the energy to get up and change the linens. AAAAAARRRRRGGGGGGGGHH! I WAS SO STINKIN' TIRED!

I started the sleepy self-talk, trying to deny reality. Maybe it wasn't a turd, after all. Maybe it was a broken crayon. Beef jerky. A Tootsie Roll. A stick.

DAMMIT. There was no denying it. It was poo. POO! But it was all dry and so little! I could just go back to sleep, clean it up in the morning. OH HOLY FUCKBALLS! What was I doing? What was I telling myself? Had I sunk this low? Had I lost every shred of dignity?

Sure the turd was bone dry and an inch long at best, but still—it was POOP! A person with any standards at all, even a psychotic refrigerator box–dwelling hobo sauced up on hooch, would change the sheets, right? But I was merely an exhausted parent, tasked with the care and keeping of adults, children and four-legged souls who need me to be ON and alert to their needs, night and day. I needed to get back to dreaming about getting a full-body massage from a naked and very enthusiastic Ryan Reynolds.

So I did what any drained and mentally depleted mother would do. Rather than strip the bed, I chose sleep. I chose the option that would make me a happy, kind and well-rested mother the next day as opposed to an irritable, short-tempered and useless bitch. I wrapped the petite poop up in a few tissues, put it in the trash and went back to sleep!

What did you think I was going to say? That I just left it there? That I kicked it on the floor? I do have *some* standards. And although I wouldn't swear on my father's grave to this, I *think* I changed the sheets the next day. At least that's what I tell myself. I just can't remember if I remembered, so I tell myself that I did. That's how I am able to sleep at night now.

I'm not embarrassed that I had learned to pick and choose my housekeeping battles and prioritize having quality time with my kids over a spic-and-span house, but it is curious how I could have sunk so low that I would actually contemplate sharing my bed with shit flakes. What did this behavior communicate to my children? What kind of example does it set?

Here's my justification: I have to sleep. I need to sleep. I refuse to forgo sleep unless somebody I love is bleeding, puking or dying. If the house isn't burning to the ground and nobody has a fever or needs snuggling to chase away a bad dream, then nobody better fucking wake me up when I'm trying to get my sleep on. If I don't get a minimum of six hours of uninterrupted sleep, I teeter on the edge of sanity. If I don't sleep for more than a few nights in a row, I lose my grasp of reality. I cannot effectively take care of my own needs, let alone take responsibility for children, when I'm hallucinating from exhaustion. Lunatics make shitty parents no matter how much they love their kids. I love my family. I would rather stab myself in the armpit with one of those little things that you poke into the end of an ear of corn than hurt them with my bitter words or make them witness a monumental meltdown that requires a call to 911. And so if my desperate need for z's means that once in a while I end up having a slumber party with a turd, well, fuck it.

I know others will judge me for my disgusting dealings with dog poo and you know what? I JUST DON'T GIVE A SHIT!

DELUSIONS OF READINESS:
A FOLIE À DEUX

Some people think that you can be "ready" to be parents. What makes a person ready?

Is it having enough money? I know folks who are loaded, and quite frankly they are some of the shittiest parents I know. I base this statement on the behavior of their kids, and their admission that they mistakenly thought they could just buy what they needed for the care and keeping of their crotchfruit.

Another sign of readiness? Relying on your instincts, as in, "It just feels like the right time!" You know what? Sometimes I feel like I have to fart and end up shitting my pants. Feelings are not facts.

Some argue that being educated and well traveled has them feeling ready to devote all the time and money they previously spent on selfish pursuits, such as cavorting around naked and drinking until they pass out, to a kid. Wrong again. There is never enough naked cavorting time. EVER.

Some people think kids are just a natural progression of marriage. Um . . . no. There are people who have no urge to breed, or can't breed because their sperms have forked heads or their ovaries are defective or their uterus is deemed a "hostile environment." Some folks get married for green cards and conjugal visits. To say breeding is the natural progression of marriage is nonsense.

For some couples, having kids serves the purpose of silencing the strangers, friends and parents who will not fucking stop asking when they will start a family. And of course for some, procreation is merely an attempt to fill a void or to correct the perceived failures of their own lives by doing the parent thing right, which is epic horseshit and quite possibly the worst reason to breed. Those boneheads need to get therapy, not pregnant.

In case you think I'm a judgmental asshole, I will admit that there was a time when I thought there was a "right time." I suffered the same delusion of grandeur that all parents have prior to starting a family: the dumb-ass belief that you can actually be prepared, that you will not just do it right, but you will do it better than anyone else. Every parent has been there. We somehow entertained a jacked-up happily-ever-after idea that after we have done X, or Y has happened, we are *ready*. Unfortunately you won't know until after you've done the deed and merged your seed that none of these ideas make a bit of sense. Because, mi compadres, walking the floors at three a.m. with an infant screaming in pain from an ear infection or driving to the emergency room, one hand on the steering wheel, the other applying direct pressure on your teenager's blood-gushing head wound, are not things one can prepare for. Makes you wonder how the hell you even imagined you could possibly have been prepared. What were you thinking? I feel that way. *All the time.* I mean WHAT was I thinking before having kids when I thought I knew what I was thinking?

As the old saying goes, hindsight is twenty/twenty. I certainly know now that there is NO WAY to know if you are ready to be a parent even if you think you are ready to be a parent, and I'm going to tell you exactly how I fucking know this.

What I thought was my supporting evidence for readiness was actually a complete delusion. Fact: there is nothing that proves anyone's readiness to be a parent. Ever. This is the end of my rant, but the beginning of my cautionary tale.

When I got married, kids were merely a maybe in my future. I didn't think I had a fraction of the knowledge and skill required to be a parent, let alone a *good* parent. I was too selfish, too flaky and irresponsible. Through college and the early years of my marriage, I continued caring only for myself. My husband did his own laundry, and the majority of the cooking (because we would have starved to death waiting for me to learn). Years passed. We grew together and then we grew apart. It seemed we struggled more than we snuggled, so unlike some idiots who think having a kid will help bring them together, we did what any *smart* couple would do—we decided to get a pet.

I grew up around animals, but I didn't have much responsibility for them. Don't get me wrong. I begrudgingly picked up dog crap from the yard, filled up water and food dishes and walked each of our dogs, but only because I was told to, and I bitched about it like a typical kid. I loved our pets, but my mom did the majority of the caregiving. Eric was the same way, but because he's really allergic to cats and mildly allergic to dogs, house pets weren't as much a part of his life as they were in mine. He grew up in one of those nerdy allergy-kid families where even a small, hypoallergenic dog was the source of bucket loads of snot. He had one dog. No cats. He hates cats.

But despite our lack of experience as committed animal caregivers, we felt we could work together to take care of a pet. We discussed it at length, and I decided that a cat would be the perfect pet for people like us who work a lot and have busy lives. Cats are low maintenance, don't need to be let outside to do their business multiple times a day, and when they aren't purring on your lap or making all sorts of racket about being fed, they mostly just lie sleeping in a sunbeam. MEOW! Eric was allergic to cats, and did I mention he hates them? Yet he convinced me that if he took allergy medicine and got shots, he'd be fine. Not only could he live with a cat, but also he wouldn't put it in the microwave no matter how pissed off he was at me, or how much he hated the thing. He knew how much I loved cats and wanted me to be happy. We'd soon be three: kitty, him and me! So, one crisp fall Sunday, we were off to the animal shelter!

Technically the cat would be "ours," but really the kitty would be mine and I didn't want to wait. I wanted to get a kitty immediately. Eric insisted he wanted to be part of the kitty-choosing process, but I wasn't buying his fake, "Oh honey, I just want to spend the day with you and share the experience" act. The man had been on me like white on rice ever since I went out one afternoon to look at cars and ended up buying one without him. I suppose I couldn't blame him for wanting to supervise me. If I was merely looking at cars and brought one home, imagine the damage an animal lover like me could do in a shelter. Instead of drinking beers in his standard horizontal Sunday football pose, he would have to accompany me to make sure I didn't get carried away and become a cat hoarder. Fine, I'd let him tag along, but I wasn't planning on taking his opinion into consideration. His hatred for cats was already well documented, so be it a tabby or a calico, he would always have to fight the urge to pop it in the microwave.

I skipped and sang as we walked into the first animal shelter because I was so excited. Aside from dormitory and sorority house living, I had never lived without a pet. The idea that I'd be bringing home an adorable fur ball that very evening was almost too much. I was hyperfocused on selecting the perfect feline companion, completely ignoring Eric, because remember:

cat hater! Fuck him. But he was into it! All the kitties were so adorable. Well, not the twenty-five-pound diabetic cat that needed insulin shots twice a day. There was NO way that piggy kitty was going to be our number three! We were going for a low-maintenance pet. Eric encouraged me to consider visiting a few places before making a decision, and although I wanted a kitty NOW, I agreed. I was in love with every animal I laid my eyes on and realized that choosing just one would be tough. I agreed to visit a few shelters, looking at different kitties before making a decision. Off we went.

I was playing air guitar and drumming in the car on the way to our next destination, singing, dancing to the music while completely ignoring Eric. I was used to his constant sniffling and conk-honking nose blowing, and I was just so excited that I didn't notice A) that his face and neck were blowing up, or B) his now pink eyeballs were leaking like rusty old pipes, or C) his nose was the size of a grapefruit and was oozing thick globs of mucus. I was daydreaming about my kitty. I leaped out of the car at the next animal shelter and ran ahead like a toddler in a parking lot. Eat my dust—I'm getting me a kitty cat!

After a few minutes, I noticed Eric hadn't come inside. I supposed he was outside smoking a cig, listening to the game on the car radio. Most likely regretting both his decision to come with me AND his suggestion to look around a bit before choosing our third family member. Fine with me—I never wanted him to come along, anyway. He could stay outside! And so I excitedly carried on with my kitty-hunting adventure.

Honestly, each one was cuter than the last! I turned to say, "Look at this one, honeypot," and still, he was nowhere to be found. Now I wanted him, so where the fuck was he? I pulled myself away from sweet kitty heaven to look around for him. Aside from a tall man with leaky eyes whose face looked like a pillow on fire, I was alone. I quickly walked by the yucky man, in a rush to find my pot o' honey husband, and that's when that yucky man grabbed me by the arm. "Hey, Sweet-tits, where you going?"

Eric was yucky man! I had vowed to stay with him in sickness and in health, and he was sick. It would have been cruel to expect him to be constantly sick in order to make me happy. Bummer. I would not be getting a kitty.

At least not unless we decided to get a divorce, in which case the first thing I would do after kicking his ass out would be to get me a kitty cat.

I sighed and took his hand. We slowly walked back to the car and, since his eyes were almost completely swollen shut, I drove us home. There was no singing or car dancing or kitty cat daydreaming, only the rattling of phlegm and hacking cough of my puffy hubby. I couldn't pout. I was so grateful that he loved me enough to try—and deep down I think I knew it wouldn't work out. I just wanted it to so badly! I acknowledged our future as a pet-less couple and gave that slobbery, snot-filled sweetheart a big, fake smile. I'd rather have him than a cat (but in the spirit of full disclosure, if he got hit by a car, the first thing I'd do after burying him would be to get a cat or ten. I'd use the life insurance money; I know that's what he'd want). That's when he reminded me that we had another option. He could live with a dog, and actually he'd prefer a dog. Sure, it would be a bit harder to care for, but we would work it out.

YES! An adorable doggie dog! I smiled for real.

I smiled all week anticipating our return to the animal shelters and rescues to find our pooch. Finally the weekend came, and I happily hopped into the car, but not before loading Eric up with antihistamines. The first dog we honed in on was a spastic, black Labrador puppy, but the sweet face of a quiet beagle mix in the cage next to that yippy puppy caught our attention. She had that adorable, droopy, "feed me" hound dog look, and she was just sitting calmly watching us watching her. The name tag on her cage said that she was called Mona. How cute! Mona! What an original and old-fashioned name! It was love at first sight for both of us. Mona was so quiet and sweet, licking our hands as we reached down to pet her. There was no jumping or humping either! This dog was a well-trained lady! Not only did her name kick ass, her easy disposition would make her the perfect apartment dog. (The people at the shelter neglected to tell us that her easy calm was a result of all the pain meds she was on after getting her lady parts removed.) Without hesitation, we signed on the dotted line and became a family of three.

It wasn't long before we figured out why the people at the shelter had named her Mona. The moaning started seconds after we got her in the car. Moan, moan, moan, moan, moan . . . the moaning continued that night as she whined and moaned relentlessly at the back door, waiting for Eric to come in after raking leaves. Our furry four-legged child was attached, and didn't want either of us out of her sight. How sweet, we thought, she already adores us. It's a good thing we were ready and enthusiastic, because I'm pretty sure that hog of a diabetic cat we mocked on our kitty-hunting adventure would have been much lower maintenance than Mona the shelter mutt.

Her second day with us began with her hacking and coughing. Kennel cough, swell. A round of antibiotics was followed by relentless nesting behavior. She started tossing pillows off the couch, making a place to give birth to the puppies that we didn't know had been aborted at the animal shelter. Mona's milk came in, making her doggy nips leak, and the poor mutt had no idea what was happening to her. Moan, leak, moan, leak, moan! She continued to moan and whimper if either of us was out of her sight, unable to curl up for an uninterrupted snooze unless the two of us flanked her like bookends. And her incessant whining, moaning and barking made her exactly the opposite of the perfect apartment dog. Sweet mother of god, she was a fucking nightmare.

The family who lived above us had two small children who napped during the day. Mona's continuous whining and barking while we were at work made it impossible for the kids to sleep. If our hardwood floors could talk, they would tell the story of how Mona rammed her body against her crate so hard, so often, that by the time we arrived home after work, her crate would be clear across the room from where we'd left it. We weren't ready for *this*! Something had to be done. The vet recommended The Dog Whisperer.

The Dog Whisperer would be expensive, but being a double income, no kid family at the time, we could afford to hire this mysterious and talented "expert" pet psychic to help us help our anxious pup. He said he could help us communicate with Mona. After half an hour with her, the Dog Whisperer told us that our precious pup was bored. The two of them had "discussed" her need for more stimulation. We were to take her to training classes to socialize her, hide treats in the house for her to "hunt," walk her more often (because half an hour twice a day wasn't enough?), and her crate needed to be moved into our bedroom so that the familiar smell of her loving masters would provide her with calming comfort and increased opportunities for communication. Because apparently we weren't "listening" to Mona's efforts to express her feelings.

So that very Saturday, we moved her crate into our bedroom, hid treats, walked her three times and signed up for a dog-training class. We were willing to do whatever it took to help our girl and ourselves. When I arrived home from work on

Monday, Mona had used her body-thrusting powers to get her crate across the bedroom and managed to pull our brand-new, three-hundred-dollar down comforter through the bars of her crate and chew the living shit out of it. Yeah, she smelled us, all right. FUCK YOU, DOG WHISPERER!

And so it began, our new life with a neurotic dog. She needed medication for anxiety, wouldn't let us bathe her or cut her nails and couldn't seem to naturally pop her own anal glands (her constant ass dragging across the carpet clued us into this). And so each month we would take our trip to the vet to have her butt sacs expressed and nails trimmed and fork over more cash for her medication than we spent on both of our prescriptions put together. But we loved her. I think her issues made us love her more. She needed us and it felt good to be able to take such good care of her. Eventually Mona settled in and became a loving and faithful—albeit half-crazy—companion, snuggling with us on cold nights and greeting us with excitement and love whether we were gone four minutes or four hours.

Just when we felt like things would be okay, Mona had her first seizure. Many more were to follow. We had an epileptic dog. More medication! More money!

But we didn't even consider getting rid of her. We had chosen to adopt a furry baby, and although neither of us had ever imagined adopting a special needs dog, we were a *family* now. We didn't want to be the kind of people who would abandon an animal just because she had some "issues." Animal shelters and rescues are jammed to capacity because of those people, and people who just tire of the expense and hard work it takes to care for a pet properly.

Caring for such a challenging pet made me think about caring for a child. I thought about it constantly. Caring for a baby couldn't possibly be more difficult than caring for this high-maintenance pet! If I could "mother" Mona, why couldn't I mother a person? I adored the damn dog, despite the fact that she was an expensive mental case, so I was positive I could care for and love a flesh and blood, living, breathing, screaming shit-machine a million times more. And if the kid turned out to be just as fucked up as my fur-baby, who better to handle it than Eric and me? It was the *dog*—my amaze-balls mothering of the goddamn motherfucking dog—that made me think that I might just have what it took to mother a human. The nagging from our parents, a bunch of pep talks from my momma and my biological clock ticking like a time bomb probably had something to do with it, too (and we did have enough money, education, and five kid-free years of cavorting naked, even if those things didn't consciously factor into our decision).

With Mona, arguably the most insane animal I would ever own, I had done what I thought was impossible: risen above my selfish needs. I had been neither flaky nor irresponsible in caring for another. I was a devoted pet mom and believed I would be an equally magnificent mother to a human. I was obviously entertaining delusional thoughts, specifically delusions of grandeur. But it wasn't just me! Eric and I were experiencing folie à deux: shared insanity. He believed we could do anything together, that we'd be better than our own parents, better than any parents, ever, for that matter. We would be the best!

Today, as a result of this shared delusion, we are the parents of two kids. People tried to warn me, to prepare me, but despite all evidence to the contrary, I believed that I would be the one to rise above, all due to my special powers and abilities caring for a special needs pooch. Today I'm sure that taking care of a pack of epileptic dogs with severe separation anxiety would be easier than maintaining any semblance of sanity in my current environment. I wasn't ready for this. I'm still not ready for this.

Motherhood didn't cure my delusional thinking; it's only made it more intense and complex.

For example, sometimes I have paranoid delusions and think, "I know these little bastards are plotting against me," or "I think the neighbors are counting the wine bottles in my recycling bin and are considering calling Child Services." And there are delusions of guilt, such as, "I know I'm supposed to think this Christmas choir concert is adorable, but I think it's awful and I'm counting the minutes until I can get home and curl up with a good book. Oh, and god hates me more than anyone else on the planet because of my evil thoughts." The worst are the delusions of poverty: "Oh my god, if these kids don't stop needing so much stuff, we are going to end up living in my brother's garage, sleeping on blow-up mattresses and eating the crappy leftover shit from the food pantry for every meal." The scariest delusions, though, are my delusions of parasitosis. It's terrifying to spend entire afternoons searching every corner of the house and car for lice, tapeworms, ear mites and flesh-eating bacteria, and find nothing, even though I know it's all there hiding, waiting to infect and kill us all.

So, my friends, I leave you with what I do know. I do know that when a kid-less person tells you that they are ready to have a kid, you should agree with them. Ignore their rationalizations, and just agree. Nod your head in the affirmative and do not attempt to convince them otherwise. Their statement of intent means they are long past courting the insane idea of readiness; they have married that crazy bitch! They are in full-blown folie à deux, crazy just like you ~~were~~ are.

And besides, some of the evidence they're using to convince themselves of this readiness is the dozens of times they've witnessed your parenting mistakes and talked behind your back about how much better they will be at it than you are.

CONVERSATIONS with **CROTCHFRUIT**

TOY LOYALTY

CATE   If you guys get divorced, where would I live?

ME   Where would you want to live?

CATE   Wherever my toys are.

ME   You would have toys at both houses.

CATE   New toys?

ME   No, you'd keep the toys you have now. Some would be at Dad's place and some would be at my place.

CATE   My toys need to stay together.

ME   Well, Dad and I are staying together so you really don't have to worry about this.

CATE   Good, because I could never split up my toys.

MOMMA'S BOY MEETS DADDY'S GIRL:
Love, Marriage and Family Baggage

"Remember, as far as anyone knows,
we are a nice, normal family."

—Homer Simpson

THE STORY OF A DADDY'S GIRL

My father, Jack, could frequently be found pacing either in the kitchen or the driveway, chain-smoking while waiting for our family to get our shit together. Poor man just couldn't understand the dawdling and putzing around by his offspring and wife. He often referred to us as "monkeys trying to fuck a football." I, in particular, drove him crazy and was probably responsible for a good fifty percent of the stress in his life. Okay, maybe sixty-three percent, but that's all I'll admit to. Running late to whatever cheerleading or gymnastics meet, he would drive like a cabbie trying to navigate rush hour in downtown Chicago, cussing at other drivers and mumbling around the cigarette that was *always* hanging out of his mouth. There was usually some news station or sporting event blaring on the radio, which gave him the opportunity to express his "expert" opinions on the events of the day or the game. That was my dad. He was vulgar, impatient, annoying and hilarious. He adored bourbon, doughnuts, swearing, comfortable recliners, inappropriate jokes, sports, being on time and cigarettes—cannot forget the cigs. He was also completely devoted to his family. It took me far too long to embrace the reality that I am a mini version of him, because if I'm being honest, I didn't want to be.

We fought CONSTANTLY, giving each other lip, arguing

over the smallest detail. "It's cold in here, Dad. I'm miserable," I would complain.

"No, it's not. You're fine," he would say.

"OH MY GOD I'M NOT FINE! Just because you're not cold doesn't mean I'm not cold! I'm not you. I'M COLD!" I'd screech. And then he'd crack up, snorting his spitty laugh. But he still wouldn't turn down the air-conditioning.

I could not resist treating him like a hungry fish, throwing him the juiciest worm in order to get him on my hook. "Narcissist," I'd spit at him. "Bitch," he'd reply. As much as I sometimes hated it, *hated* that he didn't listen and did whatever the fuck he pleased whenever he pleased, I also secretly loved it and craved the challenges his presence in my life provided me almost daily. I loved trying to get my way and being the only one with the guts to push his buttons. And from the way he continually provoked me, I know he loved it too. It was constant. In our family, it was always the two of us, alternately loving and despising each other over the years while we engaged in a relentless, never-ending battle of wills. There was no question that we were related. Sure he had a male heir to the throne, but I was the female version of him, his mini-me. Annoying, vulgar and impatient times TWO. I'm surprised my mom didn't drink more.

When I was fourteen, he said that I wasn't allowed to go on dates (especially with boys who drove) until I was sixteen. Silently I thought, "Fuck that shit! I'll do as I please," but as impulsive and oppositional as I was at the time, I was also not stupid enough to say it out loud. Besides, I knew a better way to get me a car date with a foxy upperclassman. I told Dad that he could either give me permission to date (including boys with cars), or I'd just end up lying to him about where I was going. I gave him a choice, right? I felt that my honesty should be commended. Now it was his turn to NOT voice his silent thoughts, which I assume were similar to my "Fuck that shit," and after a slew of cuss-combos and empty threats about grounding me for the rest of my life, he consented to a compromise.

Every interaction involving his right as a parent to set limits, rules and consequences was met with my resistance, day after day, year after year, resulting in story after story to be told over the dinner table with laughter for decades to come. But there was *one* story in particular—you know, the story that your family tells over and over that makes you roll your eyes and slink a bit lower in your chair. THAT story. The one moment in time, a turning point, that defines you for life. My story, our story, THE STORY, was told by my dad no less than a hundred times, the level of embellishment and embarrassment increasing with each retelling. (He could hyperbole the fuck out of a good story. It's one of the traits I'm grateful to have inherited.) And each time I heard him tell THE STORY, I equally loved and hated him even more, if that was possible.

THE STORY took place when I was ten years old. I was a handful. I pretty much did whatever I wanted, regardless of the consequences. I ignored repeated requests to sit quietly or to stop crawling under the tables in restaurants; I'd escape to the bathrooms and unroll entire rolls of toilet paper so that I could take the cardboard rolls to my gerbil. I had to do *something* while I was waiting for my parents to smoke post-dinner cigs and drink bottomless cups of coffee. I touched everything, climbed on everything, talked to everyone and was oblivious to the idea of personal space. I don't know that I ignored my parents as much as I lacked the focus and impulse control to honor their requests. I think that is why nobody remembers exactly what I said that resulted in THE STORY forever known as "the face slap"; it could have been one of a hundred things, because I had a mouth on me from the time I uttered my first "Oh shit" when I was barely even two years old.

You have to understand that my parents did not spank us, hit us or emotionally wound us with angry, hateful words. As a family, we were too busy trying to make each other laugh by competing for the title of most clever or biggest smart-ass. The day my father slapped me in the face was the first and only time he ever laid a hand on me in anger. Dad's standard reaction to most of my tomfoolery was the face-palm/sigh/head shake from side to side, combined with him slowly dropping his chin to his chest.

People find it odd that neither of us can recall specifically what I said that led up to THE slap, but we both remember the strange aftermath. It was in the kitchen, afternoonish, and I was stupefied into silence as his huge hand made contact with my face. His gentle yet strong hand that carved pumpkins, made pancakes, tickled me and always held mine tightly as we crossed the street had *smacked* me! His perfectly well-groomed hand that wrote the fancy cursive that I couldn't forge on school notes, and played the most beautiful piano music, reached out to cause me pain.

I didn't need to be told to go up to my room. I was already at the top of the stairs by the time my dad started screaming, "Get out of my sight," and "Go to your room and do NOT come down until I tell you that you can!" I slammed the door and started kicking toys and clothes out of my way as I headed toward my bed so that I could fling myself onto it and perform a dramatic sob fest (for whoever was surely going to come immediately in order to provide me with the comfort and sympathy I clearly deserved after such a shocking experience). Don't get me wrong. I was truly upset and outraged, but I've always had a flair for the dramatic and you cannot take the drama out of the queen. You just can't.

Nobody came. Nobody. Yet even without an audience, I could NOT stop crying. My father had hit me. What an ASSHOLE!

After what felt like at least the length of a full episode of *The Love Boat*, I realized that not only was nobody coming to comfort me, but that my cheek hurt just as badly as my feelings. Did my dad actually *whack me across the face*? I looked up and saw the creepy Madame Alexander doll collection that I hated. All the beady-eyed dolls were staring at me. Even my stuffed animals seemed offensive and threatening. I had to get the hell out of my room—it didn't matter that nobody had rescued or released me at that point. This was too much quiet, stillness and creepiness. And then I had a thought: why was it so quiet? Had my family packed up and left me? I was still chewing on the idea that my brother had recently planted in my head about me being adopted. Maybe that was it! They left me because I wasn't really one of them! Had I finally made them mad enough to give up on me? Nooooooooooooooo!

I zoomed down the stairs without bothering to stop and do my usual backflip while holding on to the railing and whizzed around the corner—into my father's open arms. He smelled like Dial soap, cigarettes and bliss. The safest place in my world was with my father. He squeezed me tight, stroked my hair and kissed my head as I buried my face in his chest. He still loved me and he was still there! What a relief. I started crying again.

"How's my Nikki-babe?" he asked. Was he kidding? How was I? I was fucking devastated is how I fucking was! I had just spent a good hour wasting an excellent performance on creepy dolls and stuffed animals, all the while wondering if my family had packed up and left me. I sobbed as he shushed me and rocked me in his arms. He said, "Nikki, I am so sorry that I hit you. I am so sorry. I will never, ever do that again." I looked into his beautiful blue eyes and I knew that he meant it. His eyes didn't lie. My handsome, hot-tempered Irish father, who I worshipped and loathed equally, was the most reliable and loving man I had ever known (and still is), and he was asking me to forgive him.

Then he asked me if I was sorry and although I didn't know what I was sorry about (I was always apologizing for something inappropriate I said or did, even if I wasn't sure what it was), I nodded furiously, my puffy, tearstained face still buried in his chest. He took my face in his hands, looked me straight in the eye and said, "So, are you going to run your mouth and try to fight with me again?" And I said, "Yeah, Dad. I'm pretty sure I will."

And I did. Do it again, I mean. I was mouthy. I argued and smart-assed my way through high school. I stomped and pouted. He told me to wear a jacket on chilly nights. I refused and froze my ass off, but I never admitted it. He suggested that I save my birthday money for our upcoming vacation so that I would be able to buy some fun souvenirs; I spent it immediately on random crap, but didn't sulk or argue when I was refused extra money on our trip. He began to yell and argue less with me as the years passed, and I stopped living to piss him off.

However, because I was a fully formed asshole, I picked one last fight at the end of high school, a fight I knew he couldn't resist gloving up for. I wanted to go to beauty school, but he insisted that I try college for a year. He claimed that I was too smart to pass up the opportunity to get a degree, no matter what I wanted to do with it. I buckled, but I didn't want to give him the satisfaction of being right, so I screwed around for a few years before I figured out that he was not going to give up. His daughter *would* graduate from college.

So I did. And then I went on to earn two master's degrees. I lost the fight and then some.

Despite the fact that the man WAS always right, and he took every opportunity to drop the old "I told you so," I never admitted he was right about anything, EVER. But over the years I secretly began to listen to his advice. My dad had something to say about everything too! He really knew me, because after all I *was* like him.

The summer after I turned nineteen I decided that I needed to cut off all my long, blond hair. It was damaged from years of Sun In and chlorine, and frankly I just needed a change. I didn't tell anyone I was doing it, I just went out one day and got it chopped off. I was sitting at the kitchen table when my dad came home from work. He walked over slowly and sat down across from me, looking concerned and upset. I was afraid that he was going to deliver some bad news. His health had started to decline over the year I was away at school. I had noticed it immediately when I returned home for the summer. He looked at me somberly and said, "Are you a dyke? Is that what's going on here? Did you get all your hair cut off because that's your way of telling us you are a dyke now?"

I burst out laughing, so relieved he was just worried that I was a lesbian and not sick or dying. "No. Dad, I am not a dyke. My hair was just so damaged from bleach and swimming and I wanted to start over fresh! I like it short! I think it suits me."

The news didn't seem to relax him and he didn't start laughing along with me. "Well, I don't like it. You look like a fucking dyke."

Wow, he really hated my hair, and I started to get upset.

What an asshole, I thought. Why did he have to be so mean? "Well, Dad, I don't fucking care if you don't like my short dyke hair!"

Seeing I was hurt, he quickly made an effort to smooth things over. "Honey, I don't like your dyke hair, but I love you. And I would still love you if you were a dyke. Are you sure you aren't a dyke?" I assured him I was heterosexual and informed him I would be keeping my hair short regardless of his opinion.

I really did love my sassy pixie cut (and to this day I wear "dyke" hair) but even if I didn't, I'm sure I would have kept it short just because it bothered my dad. I saw my short hair as a victory, one that he had to acknowledge every time he looked at me. Was rubbing in the win passive aggressive and immature behavior? Hells yes, and super fun too!

The one time I let him flat-out win was when he asked me not to elope because he wanted to throw a big party for my wedding. After all, I was his only daughter. He said I wouldn't be sorry, that he would take care of it. He certainly took care of it.

I don't even want to know what it cost. I just showed up in the dress that I chose based on the brightness of my mother's smile when I was trying a bunch of them on at the bridal store. I didn't give a shit about the pomp and circumstance, but it was the least I could do after giving them twenty-three years of grief.

Then this weird thing happened. I was standing at the back of the church on my wedding day, holding my dad's arm, when he said to me, "Baby, if you changed your mind right now, I wouldn't be mad. We could just walk straight out the door. None of this matters if it's not what you want." Really? You wanted me to have a traditional wedding complete with confetti and shit and now you're encouraging me to act out a scene from *The Runaway Bride*?

What the fuck, Dad?

This time I did say what I was thinking. "What the fuck, Dad?" Because one of the *only* things my father and I didn't argue about was Eric. My father loved Eric like he was his own son. No hyperbole here: he ADORED Eric. But for years after my wedding, I often wondered why he made that offer, too freaked out to ask.

There were a few other surprises over the years. For example, it was a wee bit surprising that he was the one holding my hand during early labor with my firstborn (after getting bit on the neck, Eric was being all lunchy and wandery in order to avoid my accusatory and angry cuss-outs at even the slightest perceived infraction). He sang me some Elvis, smoothed my hair and squeezed my hands while I cried out in pain with each contraction. But what the heck, he had been there to support me throughout my entire life, the one who could always take a beating from me with a smile and beat me back without leaving a mark.

So it stands to reason that the day I found out his cancer had spread to his liver, and he was labeled "terminal," I immediately fell apart both emotionally and physically. I was unable to deny any longer that I would soon lose him. This really did surprise me, because I thought there was nothing stronger than my father, not even cancer. He was going to die. Goddammit! I couldn't bear the idea that my long-running war with my wonderful asshole of a father would actually come to an end. His cancer was aggressive and there was little time to waste. We had said so much over the years, we didn't need words to bring closure to our time together, but I did finally ask him why he had given me the option to change my mind and run away on my wedding day. Did he think I was making a mistake? His answer was simple. "I just wanted you to know that you had a way out if that's what you wanted. That your happiness was more important than the money we'd spent."

The day of the biopsy that sealed the death deal, my father, who was still digesting the bad news, took care of me. He hooked me up with some of his cancer stash (Valium and Xanax) as he tucked me into the bed I had slept in throughout my childhood. He hated to see me suffer. It was the first time he couldn't fix something for me. I thought it was the end of our fighting; in fact, we still had a couple of epic battles left.

We argued over cigarettes (he dropped them everyfuckingwhere because he was all doped out on morphine) and my decision not to have another baby (he thought it was stupid and selfish). He wanted to drive and my mom hid the keys. (Morphine and driving do NOT mix.) He called to tattle on her and get me to take his side. I told him not to be an asshole and of course he told me not to be such a bitch. The most ridiculous of our final battles was over his insistence that his fucking hospital bed be placed smack dab in the middle of the family room, blocking the view of the television for every seat in the room. TOTAL ASSHOLE. He died in that room two days after I told him he was a jackass for moving the bed in there. I know, you're thinking I'm a horrible person for doing that and you'd be right. Sort of. I mean it *was* kind of a dick move to set up his death camp in the center of the happiest place in the goddamn house. He even made death annoying.

The absence of his enthusiastic spirit and his overwhelming physical presence manifests itself as an awkward silence at even the loudest family gathering. Life is good and I am happy, yet every good in my life seems a bit less, because he is not here living it with me. I really miss calling him up and hearing his belly laugh on the other end of the line after telling him some filthy, hilarious and completely inappropriate joke. He was a character, a real piece of work, uniquely irritating and endearing to all who knew him. I spent years wishing that I could be something, ANYTHING else than to be so much like him. Now with each eye roll and huffy sigh I encounter in response to my shenanigans, I miss the wink of his eye or the squeeze of his hand, reassuring me that he understands what it's like to be the lovable family jerk.

And I really miss fighting with him: our competitive and never-ending attempts to prove each other wrong and push each other's buttons were truly vital to our relationship. It was through all these battles, disagreements and fiery, intense conversations that our mutual love and respect for each other grew into an important friendship.

The loneliest moment of my life was watching the freezing rain bounce off his casket as it was lowered into the ground. I feared that no one would ever really know or understand me again. And who would I argue with? Who would challenge me? *Nobody* but my dad ever had the balls to fight with me. I looked at the people surrounding the grave, with their quivering lips, tears and looks of disbelief that this absolute LIGHT could have gone out. I briefly felt a rush of love and understanding for them. Briefly, because even though I knew they would miss him too, with each new day, they would grieve less and continue to feel whole.

It was all I could do not to scream, "FUCK ALL OF YOU WHO HAVE NO IDEA WHAT LOSING THIS MAN MEANS TO ME!" It was a rare moment of restraint. I blame exhaustion and give both my parents props for raising me to be considerate despite my piece of work-ness and impulsive nature, because like my father, I usually had no problem telling people to fuck the fuck off, if that's what I wanted to say.

My restraint made me laugh. He would have been proud of me and right then I knew he was there with me, reassuring me of his ability to know just what I needed when I needed it. I knew that my dad was with me, in me, that all the years of hearing "She is definitely her father's daughter" now made me feel incredibly proud and comforted.

Yes, I am the female version of my asshole father. I'm loud, blunt and annoying. I pounce on my kids with slobbery kisses and hugs and fart in front of their friends. I'm overinvolved in their personal business, nosy and irritating. I nag them and fire off a barrage of bullshit on the regular. Both of my kids do a fantastic imitation of me and both of them are chips off the old block. We are always butting heads about something, but that's when we aren't having endless conversations about everything and anything, trying to one-up each other. I hope every day that the battles we fight will become part of the story of us, and they will understand them as further evidence of my love and respect for the people they are, separate from me yet with a very evident part of me in both of them.

I wish that my father were here to see it. If he were, I know that he would really enjoy telling them THE STORY—and listening to THE STORY that I will someday tell about each of my own kids, over and over and over, year after year after year.

I always bitched a blue streak about my father, even after I became a parent myself. It took losing him for me to realize not only how much I loved him, but also how important it is to embrace the part of myself that I had always tried so hard to deny, the part that was so much like him. His energy, his spirit, his foulmouthed, opinionated and combative nature were passed on to me and now seem to have somehow landed in my offspring. BOTH OF THEM, FOR FUCK SAKES! I've got my work cut out for me here, creating my own stories with my family. As my father asked me so many years ago, will I continue to run my mouth and pick fights (with my own kids, that is)? The answer, of course, is yeah, I probably will.

> Zach talking to a friend on the phone: "Dude, of course you can have dinner here and sleep over. (pause) Well, no, I haven't asked her, but seriously you know my mom—she loves this kind of crap." NO, I DON'T! BUT SERIOUSLY, NO, I DON'T LOVE THIS KIND OF CRAP!

SHUT THE FUCK UP, HONEY

I am a working mom, a wife, a daughter, a mother, a sister, a writer, a friend and a few more things I can't think of right now. I won't say I wear many hats, because I hate when busy women say that shit, but I have to admit that it's a damn good metaphor for my life. I'm as busy as a one-legged man in an ass-kicking contest, yet most of my busyness, responsibilities and roles are played out where I'm easily distracted and hat-free—my home. It's no big secret to anyone who knows me that even with a metric ton of ADHD medication coursing through my veins, a mote of dust flying past can turn me into a hot mess, wandering around aimlessly rearranging picture frames, fluffing up flat throw pillows and taking pictures of my dogs when they are sleeping and posting them on Twitter (because they are so fucking cute I CANNOT resist, and I especially like to tweet my dogs' feet). At times these odd distractions render me completely unable to focus on a task. I can't even *remember* the task I was focusing on before I became unfocused.

This is why I need people to leave me the fuck alone when I'm working. As a freelance writer, I get paid for what I produce, unlike people who get paid to show up even if they practically phone in their damn work. If I'm not left alone, I can't think, and if I can't think, I can't produce. So I need to be a-fucking-lone when I'm trying to work. And since I work from home, there is no one who needs to understand this more than my husband, yet as many times as I tell him to stop distracting me, the horny bastard will not leave me alone. I'm sidetracked by particles floating through sunbeams, so just imagine how difficult it is to work when he smacks me on top of the head with his penis and makes it "say" things to me in his penis voice like, "I'm cold. Can I warm up in your vagina?"

Seriously? SHUT THE FUCK UP!

I don't say that to him, though. I say it more like this: "Honey, please shut the fuck up and stop with the talking peen puppet or else I will have to chop it off and that will really get me off task as well as cost us a fortune in medical bills, because you will need to get plastic surgery to reattach the twig to your berries."

See? I'm loving and incredibly focused and responsible when it matters.

The thing is, he has an office—a *real* office, an hour away—and he's a focused workaholic. Lucky bastard doesn't have to deal with nearly the amount of distractions that I do on a daily basis at his place of employment. Unlike my husband, I am surrounded daily with demanding dogs, dirty dishes, dust, laundry and noisy kids (during the summer months), so it takes a lot of discipline (and medication) for me to stay fucking focused. So, even though I don't begrudge him the occasional day off or day working from home, I *cannot* have him disrupting my groove with his verbal and nonverbal requests for sex ALL FUCKING DAY.

I really DO have to work, at least part-time. We need the money. We also need to have meals and clean laundry and because I am at the house full-time, whether I'm working or not, the responsibility for the vast majority of tasks that must be done around the house falls to me. There are literally hundreds of time-consuming and disgusting chores, like cleaning out the bottom of trash cans after a bag leaks, removing the overripe fruit slime lining the bottom of the crisper drawers in the refrigerator, or scraping sticky mystery substances off of doorframes, that must be done in order to keep our home squalor-free. Is there a deadline for laundry? No. Am I earning a paycheck for picking up dog shit? No. But if I don't do these things, they aren't getting done. So, I do them, AND I work, and I don't appreciate anyone messing with my system. Every mom knows that time management is important when flexible hours present all kinds of excuses and distractions, and each distraction is better than the last. I'd choose sex over unloading the dishwasher any day. Who wouldn't? There are endless other activities I'd choose over housework. Let's see here: a nap, reading an entire book uninterrupted by children, going to the mall, and pretty much anything else that doesn't involve manual labor.

The thing is, I'm not a stay-at-home mom! I'm a mom who works and that work just happens to take place in my home. No production, no payment. It's that simple. So, I must be a master of time management. My husband air humping and being up my ass all day is a distraction and fucks with my mastery of this time. He finds it impossible to understand how much harder it is to work where you live, amid the constant lures of a dryer buzzer or the sound of the dishwasher finishing. I have learned to ignore those things and to NOT intermingle housework with work-work, but it's hard.

What makes him think I'm available to sex him up while I'm on the clock? There is absolutely no way in hell I would show up at his office during the day and start fucking with his flow! He would lose his mind. He's an accountant, so he needs efficiency, organization and structure. I can just imagine how he'd feel if I popped into his office one day and started rubbing my boobs all over his whiteboard, smearing his to-do list into a blurry mess and adding random numbers to his meticulously prepared spreadsheets. I have gobs of respect for him as a provider and as a professional, but I'd love to give him a taste of his own medicine one of these days and wreak havoc on his system!

I have a magnificent passive-aggressive fantasy. I see myself strutting into his office on a day when he's stressing BIG-TIME over a deadline or he's on an important conference call, and squirting whipped cream out of a can onto my nipples, grinding all over his desk and making loud licking and sucking noises with my fingers. "Baby, I brought you some lunch!" I'm telling you, he'd be pissed off. But the man has some mad focusing skills and I'd be willing to bet high dollar that he would stay on task and find me completely resistible. It makes me want to sock him in the nuts, but he'd probably stay focused despite the pain. He's that good.

I wouldn't punch him, though. I frequently imagine jacking him a good one, savoring the details right down to the look of utter flabbergastedness on his dimpled face. Of course, this wicked imagination is often what prevents me from focusing, so I guess it's not always *his* fault. Focus is my archnemesis. Focus mocks me. Focus is the itch that I just cannot seem to scratch sufficiently, so when he's around during the day and refuses to shut the fuck up, I can't focus at all on *my* system. Yes, I have a system too. I call it STFU and it guides me through the day.

S stands for Schedule. I look at the calendar and see what's popping for the day and then while I'm drinking my coffee, I make a schedule.

T stands for Time management. This is a key concept, because it's just too tempting to fart around and procrastinate in an unsupervised environment. Sure, I could watch Internet porn or bad daytime television while gabbing on the phone with my friends, but I don't. Not when I'm working.

F stands for FOCUS and FINISH. If I'm in the laundry room and I remember that I forgot to put the bills in the mailbox, I wait until I'm done with whatever laundry task I'm working on. If I don't focus, I'd never accomplish anything. I finish shit. Period! Medication makes that possible (ADHD, remember?).

U stands for Understanding. I try to be aware at all times of just how important both of my jobs are. I do my best to balance my time between hausfrau shit and freelance work. I know what I have to do and what kind of time I have to work with.

I'm not usually one to brag, but it's a fact that I'm fucking awesome. I rule. STFU is not only an acronym for my fantastic system of working and managing a home and family, but it's also what I want the husband fella to do during the hours that I'm working. I want him to SHUT THE FUCK UP and see our home as my office, because that's what it is!

I may seem harsh about the boundaries for all the aforementioned reasons, but as I mentioned, I have a lot working against me both internally and externally without him adding to my challenges. And then there is the problem of him being a total babe who I would rather have sweaty, acrobatic sex with than work. See? Just another big (and I do mean BIG—wink wink) reason that I have a strict system when working at home. Even if I have good intentions, straying from my system always ends badly, especially when I stray with him. I know, because one time, I strayed.

He was working from home that day, and actually going about his business, when my friend called to tell me that Oprah was doing a show about improving your sex life. I'm not an Oprah devotee, but I am a big fan of sex, and this friend and I had just recently had one of those intimate woman conversations about sex while drinking wine and bitching about our husbands. She insisted that I tune in. I usually have music or television on in the background while I'm working, and that is only just one of the many rad things about working from home. Loud music, hot and delicious lunch and walking around unshowered and in a stained T-shirt and panties with holes in them are just a few of the luxuries that come with a home office. Usually the noise doesn't affect my ability to focus. Oprah preaching in the background would be no different from anything else— just background noise, I told myself. WRONG. This particular day it distracted me. BIG-TIME.

So Oprah has this "sexpert" as a guest and the guy proposes an exercise where couples each create a diagram of their own bodies, front and back, and then rank their erogenous zones. Supposedly this "love map" exercise helps couples communicate their wants and needs without hurting each other's feelings or egos during the sex act. Right on, Oprah. I might have started watching her show on the regular if it hadn't gone off the air! Anyway, after over a decade of marriage I still had to remind my husband that I like to be touched in nongenital places during foreplay. This diagram thingamabob sounded awesome! I tossed my laptop aside (because all the sex talk was making me horny), grabbed a couple of pieces of paper and pens, and hauled my pants-less ass upstairs to where my husband was working. I told him all about the exercise and he agreed to do it with me. I knew his laser focus didn't apply to work when he wasn't at work and he NEVER turned me down for some nookie. Sweet! We were making love maps! MAPS OF LOVEY LOVE! Maybe it would result in having the best three minutes of my life (that's what my husband says all the time to lure me into his web of love)!

I carefully drew a silhouette of my front and back, taking special care to minimize my tits (hint, hint) and accentuate my neck. I love me some neck nuzzles. Number 1: NECK! I continued on with my diagram of foreplay, thinking about how maybe I'd been too hard on my horny honey. It made sense that he would want to hump my brains out when we had the house to ourselves, and it occurred to me that most people didn't get to have orgasms during their workday. I'd have to add orgasms to the list of benefits of working from home. I looked over and Eric seemed to be finished with his diagram/love map. I was already in just my panties and a T-shirt, and thinking about all the places on my body that were going to get some loving made me giggly. I was thinking that sex could totally be worked into the schedule on the days he worked from home. My imagination was out of control, as usual, and I wasn't even trying to rein it in.

I said, "You first," and he said, "No, you first," right back. How sweet and considerate! He wanted to know what I liked and since that's not his usual MO, I was all about guiding him through the map of love. He listened intently, nodding his head indicating that he understood what I was saying—and as usual I was saying a lot. No CliffsNotes here. I had the *War and Peace* version of the erotic love map, fueled by my dreamy, sexual fantasies.

I finished my presentation on foreplay and erogenous zones, eager to find out something new and different that I would soon do to please and tantalize my mate. I complain about him regularly, but I can't find fault with his sex appeal. He's a fox and that's a fact. I looked at Hottie McHusband, anticipating a meticulous diagram befitting an accountant. I was all ready to jump him but I controlled myself because he'd so generously let me present my love map first and I wanted to give him the same consideration.

He slowly turned his piece of paper around. I was only slightly amused and not at all surprised that all of the numbers, one through ten, were attached to a long arrow pointing to one spot on his diagram—the spot even a man of many words would most likely have marked as his number one erogenous zone. Yep, you guessed it. His peen was number one and two and three and four and all the way to TEN! That's all he wrote. So, without giving it a second thought, we went on to give each other what was not even close to the best three minutes of either of our lives, but it wasn't the worst either. BAZINGA!

And so after a good "pop" (another one of his euphemisms for sex), he shut the fuck up (just as I'm always asking him to do) and got right back to WORK! He was as hyperfocused as before I'd interrupted his work with my unfocused fuck-focused behavior. It was like he had just taken a break to sip some coffee and take a few bites of a sandwich between calculations. It's not like the sex was an earth-shattering, ten-course meal, but it wasn't merely a sack lunch either. I was awestruck at his level of discipline, concentration and complete detachment from the previous three (maybe five) minutes of devouring each other. It was the exact opposite for me. I was screwed, literally and figuratively. I knew that I wouldn't get a lick of work done that day, but I had learned a good lesson.

As I snuggled into the covers, I knew that straying from my system should and would have to be worked into the schedule on the days that my husband worked from home. It could actually be to my advantage, in fact. If he could take a work break for sex, he could take a time-out or two during the day for window washing and furniture vacuuming! After all, that's what he expected from me, right? Oh yeah, I could use this. The thoughts of having more help with household chores comforted me like a bedtime story, the happy images of Eric scrubbing floors and fishing out socks from behind the dryer soothing me to sleep. I took a guilt-free nappy for the rest of the afternoon. I wanted to get back on track, but I was just so sleepy and satisfied. I didn't even get up to make a sandwich and I ALWAYS like to have a little snack after I get my boots knocked (he calls it that, too). I felt like I had actually binged on a big, hearty dinner and had no control over falling into a carb-induced food coma.

One would think that a gal like me with a fierce need for conversation would require some chitchat and snuggling after, but I don't. Much like when I'm working, when I'm simmering in my after-sex fog, my honey of a husband knows I just want him to shut the fuck up.

JESUS JUDY

I was surprised to learn how much of motherhood is a muddle, leaving me mixed-up, confused and bungling. I doubt I could do any mothering at all if I didn't have my own mother still here helping me figure it all out. Part of the reason I was fearful of becoming a mother was because my own mom set the bar so fucking high, I didn't think I was up to the task. But little by little over the years, she cleared up some important aspects for me, revealing the story of her own misadventures in motherhood and muddling, which convinced me that I not only wanted to be a mother but also would adore it . . . despite my tendency to be a massive muddler of all things.

Speaking of muddling, my mom used to drink Old-Fashioneds. For those who have no idea what that is, here's one version of this delicious and seriously fun-to-drink cocktail: take a cube or two of sugar (a packet if that's all you got), add a few dashes of Angostura bitters and a splash of club soda (or water if you don't like the fizz), and muddle it. Some people add fruit like oranges or cherries and then muddle (not me—I say who gives a shit about nutrition when you're drinking?). Next you toss in some ice cubes, but not too many, and a few ounces of rye whiskey. Defuckinglicious.

Did you get a bit thrown by the muddle part? Muddling the

sugar, bitters and club soda (or fruit, which I already explained I don't agree with) just means mushing it up good, combining the flavors for a taste explosion! My dad occasionally added a splash of the juice from maraschino cherries. He fancied himself a great bartender and was always looking for new ways to zing up a cocktail, especially when he was making them for my momma, because he loved doing anything and everything special for her. He loved her madly.

I often felt muddled around my parents when they were playing bridge or bowling while boozy beverage drinking. What the hell were the grown-ups doing playing games, and how could they stomach that nasty stuff? Grown-ups weren't supposed to have fun; they were supposed to work and take care of children. I was especially muddled when it came to understanding my mother having fun—not because it was rare for her to have fun, but it was rare for her to have fun if that fun didn't revolve around ME!

Both my parents were somewhat mysterious to me when I was a child, but more so my mother. Where my father was extroverted and prone to jabbering too much, especially after a couple of Old-Fashioneds, my mother was quite the opposite. She had only one Old-Fashioned every night and it never loosened her lips. Not one bit. How did my mom tolerate any of our shit without drowning herself in Old-Fashioneds? That was another muddle.

Anyone who knew my father can hear him yelling, "Jesus, Judy!" Now, my mom does remind me of Jesus—I'm not kidding, she's that good—but that's not why my dad called her that. He just had a foul mouth and when he called for her, it was always "Jesus, Judy." When I was growing up, my good-natured, quiet, pretty, petite, well-dressed mom, who drove a yellow station wagon with a white dog in her lap and a cigarette held delicately between two long fingers, and could be found daily waiting outside the mall, school or gym, was known even to my friends as "Jesus Judy."

"What time is Jesus Judy getting here to fetch us from this cheerleading practice?" my pals would ask. Jesus Judy was always driving Miss Bitchy (me) and my friends all about town or to the mall to buy some Forenza sweaters or accessories from Claire's.

The neighbors always cracked up when they heard the yelling coming from our house. "Jesus Judy," my father bellowed over and over, because he was always freaking out over something and needed my mom's calming influence to give him some perspective. My mom was so chill. She would become so absorbed in gardening, needlepoint, reading, macramé, hooking a rug (so 1970s), cooking, laundry or whatever she was doing around the house that she often didn't answer him (or us) right away when we called. This drove him crazy. Who the hell knows why? The man had issues, and needed to know where everybody was at all times, especially his bride. So he screamed, "JESUS JUDY! WHERE THE HELL ARE YOU?" or "JESUS JUDY, DON'T SCARE ME LIKE THAT!" or "JESUS JUDY, CAN YOU HELP ME WITH THIS FUCKING *&^%%!" I think Jesus himself would have bitch slapped my dad once in a while, but not my mom. More patient than Jesus, she chose to run with and happily serve a crowd of idiots, as evidenced by her devotion to our family.

With a smile and a calm hand, once she heard the pleading call, my mother would come walking (never running) towards the source of the screaming and take care of whatever needed taking care of. And apparently nothing she was doing was more important than finding him some nail clippers so that he could trim his hangnail, or change the channel for him so that he didn't have to get up, or dig through the trash with him to find the partial denture he threw away for the fiftieth time, or scratch that place on his back that he just could *not* reach. The woman was a relentless giver.

I adored her for it. We all did. My mom is the person I always wanted to be. She handled my crazy father, my sensitive and brilliant brother and of course my hyperactive, freakish, loud, in-your-face 24/7 self with the grace of a taller and much prettier version of Mother Teresa if she chain-smoked cigarettes.

Here is a list of things my mother never did (not in order of importance, but in order of random remembering): yell (or even raise her voice), swear, hit, complain, punish, tease, spank, gossip, whine, cry, fart (at least not in front of us), pee or poop with the door open, serve store-bought cakes or cookies on birthdays or holidays, fight with my father, fight with her friends, argue with or be rude to service people, make excuses to get out of volunteering, snap at us when she was tired, forget birthdays, get mad when something spilled, get mad when something was broken, get mad when something happened that would make most normal people mad, stay in bed with a hangover or any illness, and last but not least, my mother never once spoke negatively about anyone. EVER. She just didn't say much at all.

She confounded me. I was muddled around her. How was she so calm, so sweet, so gentle—and so consistently? HOW? And why did I have to be like my foulmouthed freak show of a father? NOT FAIR!

My mom's parents were Swedish immigrants who met at a dance when they were teenagers. Her mother, one of six children, was clever and hilarious, but also bat-shit crazy and a royal pain in the ass. Her father, the youngest of ten, was a good ole boy who drank a ton of Schlitz and dreamed of owning his own tavern. He was lighthearted, joyful and beloved by all who knew him. Mom also had a sister who was older by eight years named Marilyn, who was loud, opinionated, driven, fun loving, and incredibly attentive and fiercely protective of my mother. Marilyn had named my mother after Judy Garland (totally not Jesus-like AT ALL).

The family was full of characters! I think that's why my mom was NOT a character. There was no room for another big personality in the tiny house across the street from Winnemac Park. So, she escaped into books, skipping third grade and then graduating a year early from Amundsen High School. That's where she met and fell in love with my father. It doesn't take a Freudian analysis to figure out why she was attracted to him. We all gravitate toward what we know.

My beautiful, elegant, brilliant mother left college—Northwestern University, for god's sake—to marry my father. Given her generation, her decision wasn't met with shock or disappointment at all! As a matter of fact, her parents were happy and relieved that she was going to settle down. And so was my mom. Jesus Judy knew exactly what she wanted. She wanted to marry her blue-eyed, dimple-cheeked, charming high school sweetheart, make a home and make babies. And she did just that. It muddled the fuck out of my mind as I grew up, as I could not understand her choice. And even when I did ask questions (which was constantly because I never shut up and still don't), she either gave minimal information or turned it back to me.

But honestly I didn't consider her life much at all if it didn't relate to mine somehow. I was busy being a kid and she was busy making sure everything about my childhood was good, sacrificing her own comfort and needs for her entire family.

My mom is *not* a baby boomer. Born to Depression-era,

immigrant parents, she was raised to be seen and not heard and to embrace the traditional female role of housewife and mother. She did all these things very well. Too well, in fact, because it wasn't until shit hit the fan in a massive, wall-splattering way that I was able to see her as anything but a figure to facilitate my needs. And she will tell you herself that she saw herself the very same way up until the shit-hitting-fan incident brought us to a new and very different reality.

Long story short, I was a wild child, taking breaks (yeah, plural) from college and basically acting like a fucking lunatic— all the time. I was like that character in an after-school special into whom everyone wants to shake some sense because she is obviously a hot mess and will either A) die in a dramatic accident as a result of drunk driving or B) clean up her act and go on to become president of a Fortune 500 company or a neurosurgeon and live happily ever after while a song by Elton John plays in the background and people laugh in slow motion.

My parents were completely uncool with my wild thing phase and let me know about it. If they were going to pay for school and I was to live under their roof, there would be rules. I would need to stop the partying, start working and studying more, take care of myself and get back on track. It was really the first time they were harsh with me; this was some tough love coming at me. I needed to prepare myself to leave the nest. They were willing to teach me to fly first and had demonstrated this by helping me financially and emotionally, but they wouldn't tolerate me shitting all over that nest in the meantime.

FUCK YOU BOTH, I thought. I'll do as I please.

My mother, as usual, was the parent who knew what I was thinking, but as NOT usual, was the one to speak up about it. Um, **"NO,"** she said aloud in response to my unspoken yet clearly understood thoughts on how the shit was going to fly.

Honestly, I was too shocked and surprised to do anything but listen. Was my mom really laying the smack down? The words began to flow.

"You can no longer just do as you please. Not if you want to live here. Nicole, we will not stand by while you waste your life. Clean up your act. Your father and I want to pay for your college education and your wedding, not your funeral. We realize that you are an adult and can make your own choices, but you are making choices that we cannot support. If you continue to do so, you will have to leave."

It was something like that. She probably said it with less verbiage and more ka-pow fantastic-ness. My mom has a gift for articulation and efficiency. I had a gift for muddling. I had muddled my way into a period of dumb-fuckery that she just could not stand by and witness any longer.

Awkward silence. What the WHAT? My mother had never been the one to throw down the gauntlet or make idle threats. That was my father's job. If he had said these words, I don't think I would have even reacted, but my mother? My ally? My soft place to fall always? It was my turn to say NO, but I said something else.

"I HATE YOU!" I screeched, red faced and with clenched fist and a few foot stomps. The quote is verbatim; I'm not sure about the face, fists or feet, but there are good odds that I'm right on with that too.

I said it. Out LOUD! That hateful bullshit sprayed out of my mouth toward my mom like it was thrust from a whirling fan. We were covered in it and it was the most horrible and disgusting mess we had ever been in together, not counting the hundreds of real-life shits of mine she cleaned up when I was in diapers or sick as a child (because now that I'm a mom myself, I know what a huge part of motherhood actual shit is). Even as the words were coming out of my mouth, I was regretting them. What had I just said?

I had never told either of my parents that I hated them. I had thought it a million times about my father, because he was like me, and therefore drove me NUTS, but NOT my mother. Not even one time in twenty-one years had I even really been angry with her. She was always fair and levelheaded when my fiery temper flared up, even when she was the target of my rage, or when I was making bad decisions and getting in trouble, which was ALL THE TIME.

So back to the hateful words I regret to this day, "I HATE YOU!" I had just told my mother that I hated her. I DID NOT HATE HER—I LOVED HER. I loved her more than anything in the world. And I was so ashamed. What it must have cost her to talk to me the way she did that day, how much she was hurting to see me screw up my life and how painful it would have been for her to let me go! Her life revolved around her family; we were her purpose, her passion, her LIFE! She was willing to risk losing me, and god knows that could have happened, because I was functioning at lobotomy level in my early twenties, a complete blockheaded idiot with no sense of direction.

I remained very unpopular with both my parents for a short time, but not because I didn't change my ways. I did— immediately, in fact—but it took time for me to earn back the warmth and ease of the relationship with my mother that I had always taken for granted. Neither of my parents acted or said anything close to hateful towards me in the wake of my tantrum. You see, what I didn't know then, but I know *now*, is that it's in the valleys that a mother's love really grows.

The good times in mothering are like being on a mountain-top, where there is beauty and awe and a sense of accomplishment. Sometimes you fly so high that at the oxygen-deprived heights, you are dizzy, happy and dreamy. But you can't stay up forever. Motherhood is about raising wild little animals known as children and children are messy little wormy things who poop and bite. Eventually we all have to come down from the mountain, back to the fertile valleys, where the animal shit mixes with the soil and worms to make for some good crop growing. Nobody tells you how dark and smelly and scary it can get in those valleys, though. Especially an experienced mother; she won't tell you, because she knows it won't matter anyway.

A mother's love only gets stronger while her newborn sucks away at nipples that are cracked and burning, devoted to making a go at breast-feeding. It grows while she burns with fever in the middle of the night, bending over to pick up the bottle her baby has thrown on the floor for the twentieth time because he is equally sick, exhausted and frustrated that breathing and eating are painful. A mother gives, knowing that kids will take everything until she thinks she has no more to offer and even then is surprised at the endless supply of everything she dreamed possible for them, regardless of what she gets in return. And that is exactly how it's supposed to be—at least in the beginning and for a good few decades thereafter.

And although every parent can tell you this, you won't be able to understand it until you are in it. Being pregnant, the first words, first steps, snuggles, declarations of love, Mother's Day necklaces made of pasta, award ceremonies, uncontrollable laughter and gestures of genuine appreciation for your efforts— these things are mountaintop experiences! But they don't exist without shitty diapers, puke in your mouth, sleepless nights, broken bones, broken hearts, struggles over homework and practicing, slammed doors, angry words, tantrums and tears. That's all just shit right there. SHIT. And that shit is your life.

Like a turd hitting the fan, motherhood touches everything. Nothing in your life is the same after you become a mother. Not your marriage, your friendships, your career, your ass, your breasts, your mind or your heart.

And even if somebody does tell you, you will understand it as much as a newborn baby understands the literal meaning of the lullabies you sing to her (or him), which is good because otherwise nobody would have kids. (Nobody in their right mind, anyway.) You must experience it.

Kids will grow so fast, and it feels like it can't possibly be real when they start giving back to you in ways you never imagined as they become adults—as they become your friends. At the age of twenty-one, I became friends with my mom. All her giving paid off, as I fucking figured it out—finally! But that giving, those strong boundaries and relentless strength, almost tricked me into thinking that it was impossible for me to consider being a mother myself. (Seriously, the story does eventually end and I do have a point, but my journey to motherhood, like the journey through motherhood, is really, really LONG).

At twenty-one, I had a new friend in my mother, and I had come to terms with being more like my freak-spaz father than saintly like her. I knew I would never be as good as my mom and that was okay. However, in coming to terms with that, I also felt that I didn't have what it took to be a parent. Nope. There was no way I could be a wife, mother, hell, even a friend like she was. I believed that I would never have children.

I told her these things some years after I was married and the pressure on Eric and me to have kids was increasing. I told her because she needed to know the depths of my regret and the appreciation I had for her sacrifice. I didn't hate her. I adored her and respected her and cherished her. I wanted to give her grand-babies, but I felt ill equipped and inferior compared to the example she had set.

And that's when she gave me her secrets. I started a new list. A list of things my mother actually DID do but since they were none of my beeswax before I became an adult, she hid from me. OH MY GOD, my mother was not a saint. This list helped me to see that the perfect mother does not exist. Even my own mom is sometimes a HOT. DAMN. MESS.

The list of things that make Judy *not* like Jesus at all:

1) She never enjoyed housework, cooking or any of the chores that nobody ever helped her with, aside from the gardening, which she loves to this day. She also had many a moment of loathing for motherhood. Who the fuck didn't? The pressure she had to keep things perfect was frustrating, my brother and I were pains in the ass and sometimes she felt suffocated by the demands of our family. She might have made it look easy, but it was hard. She did all sorts of crap with a scowl, feeling maxed out and unappreciated. Some nights she had two Old-Fashioneds. Or three. Sometimes she was depressed. She had no idea what she was doing and still doesn't. She often feels like a failure. Like she can't possibly ever be good enough.

2) My dad did piss her off, and they did argue, just not in front of my brother and me. Once I was grown, that changed. I got hysterical when she told me that if he could, my father would probably grow ovaries and have a period just so he could say that his cramps were

worse than her cramps. She was so right. He would have! I. PEED. MY. PANTS. (And this was before I had two kids that stomped the shit out of my bladder.)

3) She did not like everyone. Matter of fact, there was a list of people who made her want to skin kittens. The reason she didn't gossip is because she really didn't care enough to do so.

4) She farted all the time. Just never in the car or on our heads like my dad did. She liked to fart (and pee and poop and bathe) in private, thankyouverymuch.

5) She thought I was the most wonderful person in the world. She wished she could be more like me, outgoing, confident, friendly and driven. Seeing me succeed thrilled her. She would not be disappointed in me if I chose to have a career instead of babies. But she wanted me to experience the joy of motherhood. She believed I would be amaze-balls as a parent and thought I was way smarter and cooler than she ever dreamed she could be.

WOW!

More than once since then I've uttered "Jesus Judy," and laughed my face off, thinking of the way my mother tricked me—without trying to, of course, but nonetheless, she tricked me! When I was growing up, my friends would complain about their mothers a LOT. I mean all the time! Some of my friends had nitpicky mothers who always had something to say about their schoolwork, weight, friends, clothes, boyfriends or taste in music. My mom didn't. If she didn't like my outfit or boyfriend, she never said so. She let me choose the radio station sometimes, and other times she said, "My turn!"

and we sang along to The Carpenters' "Top of the World" together. She held my hand and skipped with me every time I
asked her to, no matter where we were. We did cartwheels together IN THE MALL. If she commented on my appearance,
it was a compliment, never a critique. And despite the plethora
of demands on her time, energy and finances, she never once
hinted of frustration or unhappiness, bitterness or resentment
over her life or acted put out by the needs of anyone in our family. THIS STUNS ME!

Now that I'm a parent, I know how fucking hard all this is.
My mom says that she cannot imagine the stress that women of
my generation experience, because we are expected to be more
than just full-time, stay-at-home mothers. With so many choices
and options, it's understandable that women today expect more
from their partners and more from their children. She shrugs off
my adoration and compliments, saying that had she been faced
with the complexity of roles and stresses that women face today,
she can't say she would have handled it as well without more
than one drink per night.

"Tell me about it, sister!" I respond, usually over lunch or
dinner where we are drinking wine and waxing massively philosophical and intimate, sharing all the details of our lives—
fears, hopes, dreams, joys, disappointments and whatever else
we feel like talking about, depending on how buzzed we are.
We do this because now we are the best of friends.

My mom tells me that it amazes her to see how much I play
with my kids, how much effort I put into my education, and
how often I hold my husband accountable for his own dumb-
fuckery. She has known most of my friends since before they
had boobies and babysits my kids so that I can socialize with
them and maintain our support system. She says she admires me
for knowing what's not important, like how much I weigh, the

cleanliness of my house, the car I drive or what anyone fucking thinks about me other than the kind of person I am. She says that in her day, there was a lot of pressure to put on airs and keep up appearances, and that NOT talking about things was actually pretty tough sometimes.

Had she not befriended me, I would be childless and you would maybe be reading some book I wrote about how I know everything about parenting, not because I had kids, but because I was a Licensed Clinical Professional Counselor and I'd seen it all done wrong and knew how to do it right—IF ONLY THOSE DAMN PARENTS WOULD LISTEN TO ME! I know I'd have written a book, regardless. But I digress, as usual.

Trouble is, all the stuff and fluff in the parenting books and magazines is basically bullshit if you use the information without understanding why you are using it and who you are using it with. What I am in awe of when I speak of my mother is not how clean her house was (although it always was) or how she never farted or complained or yelled or gossiped or got snotty with my dad (at least in front of us). I am in awe of how she recognized and embraced me as an individual, guiding me but not pushing me, accepting the idea that her role wasn't to tell me how to be or think or act. Her role was to guide and observe as we flew through the peaks and valleys together, and she knew this! She never tried to be my friend or advisor or mentor or idol; she was my PARENT. She was my parent until I was old enough for her to be my friend. She knew when that was, and when the time came to change from parent to friend, she was the friend who encouraged me and inspired me by revealing the truth about motherhood. The truth is that nobody is perfect. There is no perfect mother. That she wasn't perfect and I wouldn't be either. Nobody really knows what the fuck they are doing, and everybody is really just winging it, do-ing the best they can with what they've got.

The truth is that we are all just muddling through this thing. Parenting is a bittersweet treat, like an Old-Fashioned that incorporates deliciousness and danger in one stiff drink. Muddling through by definition is this: "to achieve a certain degree of success but without much skill, polish or experience or direction."

Jesus Judy—I mean, MOM—I think that sounds about right. Don't you?

SAY THAT TO A JACKASS AND HE'LL KICK YOUR BRAINS OUT

Many of my most precious memories include my grandmother Adelaide Twilia Kane, or "Buddy" as everyone called her. Snuggled up on the davenport with her, eating Andes mints out of a Waterford crystal candy dish, watching *The Lawrence Welk Show* is my absolute favorite one. But make no mistake, she wasn't a fragile blue hair who sat on the sofa crocheting and telling stories nobody gave a shit about. She was four feet ten inches of polyester-clad, brooch-wearing, cookie-baking, pocketbook-swinging force of fucking nature. Even as a small child, I knew she was a force of nature, a tornado I chased in order to be caught up in the exciting chaos she created. I want to be a grandma like Buddy. I want to be snuggled up on a fluffy sectional with my own grandchildren someday, watching *The Justin Bieber Variety Show* while eating banana Laffy Taffy. I want it so badly that after twenty years and dozens of failed attempts, I finally quit smoking.

Remember when all the cool kids smoked cigarettes? Me either. I was born in 1970, just around the time the warning on the pack went from "Caution—cigarette smoking may be hazardous to your health" to "THIS SHIT WILL FUCKING KILL YOU, MOTHERFUCKER." Kidding. It actually said,

"Warning: the Surgeon General has determined that cigarette smoking IS dangerous to your health." But in 1969 when I was in my momma's belly, it was still only MAY be hazardous, and my mom's doctor told her to just cut down on the cancer sticks during pregnancy. So, because I bathed in a bath of nicotine from the moment I was conceived, I think it was inevitable that I became a smoker.

Buddy quit the year before I was born. Why, you might ask, did she lay down the smokes after forty years, never to spark up again? I'll give you a direct quote—and I know this is exactifuckingly the way she said it because she told me a minimum of six hundred times: "I quit when I had the Asian flu and I was too sick to smoke. I was so sick I would have had to get better to DIE! Only a jackass would start up again."

I swore I would never smoke. I promised her, crossed my heart, hoped to die, stick a needle in my eye that I would never, ever let a cigarette cross my lips and I meant it! I was as committed to not smoking as she was, and a big reason for her commitment was her love for me; she wanted to set a good example and live a long life having fun with me. It pissed me off that my parents continued to smoke, and although my grandma wasn't happy either, she saw it as an opportunity to reinforce the dangers of addiction to me. "Anyone who would start smoking, knowing what we know now, is just a jackass," she would say.

I became a pint-sized anti-smoking activist. To my parents, I was more like a tiny, towheaded terrorist constantly on the attack, begging, pleading and sometimes taking it to tears if I thought it would get either one of them to stub out a lit stick. I *hated* growing up in a cloud of smoke, and I complained relentlessly about it. I threw cigs in the toilet, cartons of them in the fireplace, hid them and tossed them in the trash. I kept up this annoying behavior right up to the day I took my first hit from a Marlboro Red while standing on a rock under the Riverwalk Bridge in the middle of the DuPage River. I took a drag because everyone else was doing it, knowing how stupid it was. Everyone but me coughed, hacked and spit. I loved it. I loved the smell, the taste, the feeling. It was like coming home. I very quickly became what I loathed: a smoker. That year, a new warning was added to cigarette packages. It said flat-out that cigarettes caused lung cancer. I wasn't worried.

I was fifteen and invincible, so I figured I'd quit smoking long before I became a victim of the big C. I hated being a smoker, but I loved smoking. I was disgusted with myself and I hid my habit. I didn't want my parents to find out; I especially didn't want Buddy to know I had broken my promise to her, that I was a jackass, plain and simple. I was her pride and joy who could do no wrong, but I knew I wouldn't be if she found out I had embraced the idiocy of smoking.

Buddy had my dad when she was thirty, which was considered "advanced maternal age" in 1940. She and my grandfather (an Irish Catholic she had insisted she wouldn't marry if he were "dripping in diamonds") had been married for almost ten years when my father was born. Before that she had suffered numerous miscarriages, and a "nervous breakdown" that landed her in sunny California to recover for a year. (What constituted a "nervous breakdown," I still do not know, but I'd like to live in California for a year, so I hope to have one someday.)

You can imagine why my father's birth was celebrated as something that can only be compared to the second coming of Jesus Christ. He was her little prince, her one and only miracle, and she doted on him as if her life depended on it, and I swear to you it actually DID. The woman was born to mother.

Fate didn't give Buddy more babies or breakdowns, but it

did give her a fertile daughter-in-law whose second pregnancy made her very nervous (but not enough to break down, which confuses me still. How nervous do you have to be before you actually break down?). She voiced her concern that she might not be able to love another grandbaby as much as she loved my brother, the mini-version of my father, who had also been celebrated in a grand Jesus-like way. Was there room in her heart? How could a mother love the second child as much as the first? Buddy had no experience with this.

This baffled her until she laid eyes on me and fell. In. Love. I was hers, a real-live dress-up doll. And she was mine! I loved her even more than she loved me, though if she were here, she'd surely argue the point. My grandpa always said, "I don't argue, Buddy does." Most people knew better than to argue with Buddy. Of course *I* could argue with her and get away with it, because she was *that* nuts about me.

Throughout my childhood, I frequently escaped my smoke-polluted house to spend the weekend being smothered by her smog-free attention. I wanted to be with her all the time, but not because she had a ready supply of nontoxic air! Buddy was fun personified, and well into her eighties she kept up with me both mentally and physically. We would spend countless hours baking cookies and cinnamon rolls. I loved holding her soft, wrinkly hands and stroking the raised strawberry birthmark in the middle of her palm during long, boring church services. A favorite activity at her house was rummaging through her costume jewelry, old photos and scarves while she sewed clothes for my Barbie dolls. I could talk for hours on end and she was the one person who never tried to bribe me into silence. The rest of my family offered me quarters for five minutes of quiet, but Buddy didn't. Nobody embraced my Nikki-ness the way she did.

I wasn't sure what it would mean to our relationship if she found out I had started smoking. I hated lying to her, but I could not tell her the truth. She wasn't a potty mouth, so when she called someone a jackass, you knew she had absolutely no respect for him or her.

She loathed Cubs commentator Steve Stone. JACKASS!

Her sister-in-law's husband, Allen? JACKASS!

The guy who left his laundry in the washer in her apartment building all wet when he went to work? JACKASS! (And that particular jackass regularly received a wet blob of special delivery plopped on his doormat with a message from Buddy!)

My father's insistence that she move in with him and my mom after she slipped on the ice taking her garbage out, breaking her arm and ankle and lying on her ass in a snowdrift for an hour before being found made him the biggest jackass of all time, and that was saying something. Her pride and joy, her only child, was taking away her independence. I was a teenager when this happened, at the height of my belief in the jackassness of my father. I really enjoyed hearing her call him a jackass.

When she moved in I quickly realized that I needed to either quit the cigs or get really good at hiding my filthy habit. I'd always smoked in the house. Really, how would anyone know, with my parents puffing away 24/7?

"I can't believe YOU of all people turned out to be a JACKASS!" I imagined her saying upon finding out that I was a smoker. It's hard to say which of us would be more heartbroken. Of course, with her way of knowing and seeing everything, especially when it came to everything about ME, the big bust-o-rama came pretty quickly.

It was the summer before I went away to college. I was eighteen years old and enjoying a bubbly bath and a cig (and some bourbon in my Diet Coke can, if I'm being honest) when she walked into the bathroom. It was dark, because I was having a soak by candlelight with my Sony Walkman and listening to Peter Cetera. She flipped on the light and BOOM—there I was blowing smoke rings to the tune of *The Karate Kid* theme song. I felt twice the amount of naked when I looked at her big blue eyes, bulging from years of thyroid problems, sure that her super-sleuth senses also smelled the sweet scent of my booze-laced diet beverage. We stared at each other in silence for I don't know HOW long, but it felt endless. Then she abruptly turned around, flipped off the lights and walked out. And that was it. I immediately began working on my defense, apology and string of excuses while soaking in the dark.

At first I blamed my parents. How could I NOT become a smoker? I was an addict moments after conception, I suggested. Resistance was futile! I could no more resist smoking than I could change my blue eyes to brown!

"You want sympathy?" she replied. "Look in the dictionary under 'symp' 'cause you aren't going to find it with me, girlie."

Next I blamed the power of addiction. I said I had just been curious, but now I couldn't possibly break the habit.

"If you said that to a jackass, he'd kick your brains out," she barked. I wallowed in guilt, knowing she was right, hating myself for hurting her, and wishing not only that I had never started smoking, but that I could find the willpower to quit the way she did.

But what the hell did I know about deprivation? Growing up, I never wanted for anything materially. I always went to sleep in a soft bed with a full belly. I had access to top-notch medical care and education. Buddy's father died in 1921, when she was eleven years old. In the blink of an eye, the days of waiting for him to come home to light the candles on the Christmas tree were gone. Heck, the days of having a Christmas tree were gone, because she moved into the kitchen with her mother and sister, sleeping on cots so they could generate income by renting the rest of the rooms in the house to boarders. My grandma was lucky to get to the tenth grade before dropping out to help support the family. Off to work Buddy went, saving a little money for Tuesday's Ladies Day at Wrigley Field where she could escape into the world of her beloved Cubs. I knew her story and her struggles and this made me feel like more of a jackass. If she could be strong despite her difficult early circumstances, how could I be so weak and ungrateful? I REALLY WAS A JACKASS!

But Buddy never made me feel any less loved or valued because of my smoking, even though she didn't approve. I never stopped feeling guilty for disappointing her, and never more so than when she was diagnosed with emphysema in the early 1990s. Emphysema is a really ugly, painful and scary way to die. Buddy died in 2003. I was thirty-three years old. I know how lucky I am to have had so many years with a grandmother like her. She was bold, brilliant and the best role model a girl could wish for. Her bravery and steadfast commitment to loving others inspires me to this day.

Her death prompted me to put real effort into quitting. I HAD to quit smoking! How would I live to become a fantastic grandma like Buddy if I kept sucking down toxins and tar? At first it was hard to imagine my three-year-old son, who was still sporadically shitting in his Spider-Man underpants, having kids of his own someday, but I made myself do it. Not only did I NOT want my own kid to see what a jackass I was for smoking. I wanted HIS kids to have the remarkable experience of being raised in a multigenerational family, smothered with a never-ending supply of love and attention from their grandma Nikki. At the risk of sounding like a conceited bastard, I tell you right now that I'm going to be a fucking AWESOME nana; it's just a fact. How could I be anything but amaze-balls after being raised by Buddy?

So I quit. I did it.

It was FUCKING HARD! I still crave those poison darts of tobacco, but I resist the temptation.

And as my kids grow, I still try to imagine what kind of parents they will become. I pray every day that both of them end up with at least one stubborn, sneaky little shit that makes them want to bang their head against the wall every single day. I dream of someday swinging by their homes for a visit and listening to my grown children tell me how much they now appreciate and understand just how hard it is to be a parent and how damn grateful they are to me. Yep, that's when they will finally understand why I dropped so many f-bombs, drank jugs of wine and hid from them in the laundry room. And quitting smoking makes it more plausible that I'll be around to scoop up my naughty little grandbabies for fun-filled weekends at my house, snuggled up together watching the Biebs play the accordion, belting out "Baby" accompanied by the background vocals of former Disney Channel stars while we eat gobs of junky food and candy. This happy dream is what keeps me cig-free.

SAYONARA TO SUPER-TWAT AND MY HUSBAND'S NUTS

"I think I lost my mucus plug," I hollered from the bathroom to my husband, who was still in bed.

"Where did you last see it?" he grunted.

I looked closely at the hunk of nasty discharge on the wad of toilet paper, holding it up to the light and examining it carefully as if there was actually anything to indicate that it was indeed the famous plug of snot that was known to forewarn that a pregnant lady was thisclose to going into labor.

"It looks like a piece of lemon Jell-O dipped in snot. Want to see it?"

"Yes, please, and if you took a dump make sure not to flush so I can see that too," he mumbled.

"I HEARD THAT!" I screamed. I figured the gelatinous glob probably was my mucus plug, but I couldn't be sure. What if it was just an extra gloppy hunk of the usual pregnancy slime? I wanted a second opinion. If I had to look at a chunk of slimy snot that came out of my vag, so did he. It was the least he could do, considering he didn't have to be pregnant or give birth. "You better get in here and take a look at this!"

And he did. Because he was afraid of what might happen if he didn't.

With both my pregnancies, I went back and forth between giddy and Godzilla in the blink of an eye, but it wasn't my mood swings that propelled my husband's buns out of bed. It was the knowledge that if he didn't humor my request, he was risking actual bodily harm. He learned during my pregnancy with our first child that the slightest provocation could catapult me in to violence. Having a baby in my belly made me nuts. Speaking of nuts . . .

I managed not to lose my mind the first time around, but just barely. So, when my second pregnancy required me to be on strict bed rest for fourteen weeks and the isolation and boredom were pulverizing what little sanity I had left, his way of helping me stay out of the loony bin was volunteering to get his nuts cut after the baby was born. He reasoned that once he was neutered, we would never again suffer through one of my multiple personality–plagued pregnancies. No baby batter = no babies! HOLLA! I've heard it's rare for a man to show enthusiasm about getting a vasectomy, and my friends say I'm lucky he was such a good sport about it, but they don't know the depths of his fear. Luck, my ASS! I scare the shit out of him when I'm pregnant. He knew that if I became pregnant a third time, he was courting permanent injury and possibly even homicide at the hands of Super-twat, my pregnancy alter ego.

It didn't start out so badly. With each planned and prayed-for pregnancy we were both stoked, but Eric's immediate enthusiasm and interest in all things baby the first time around took me by surprise. I'm talking uncharacteristically outgoing and chatty and willing to talk about girly stuff like nursing bras and maternity pants. It was totally bizarre to listen to my introverted math nerd of a husband ramble on about breast-feeding like he was talking about the Cubs. He didn't even want to wait until after the first trimester to announce the bun in my oven. I was fine with that. What I wasn't fine with was him telling everyone that "we" were pregnant.

I could tolerate almost anything else he wanted to say about me being pregnant, but the "we" thing ignited the smoldering pregnancy psychosis within me. I immediately made it clear that he was no longer allowed to say that "we" were pregnant. I was pregnant! Me. His sperm came OUT of him and into ME. His part was done in ten minutes (if that).

Whoa, when did I get so bitter? This Super-twat side of me was freaking scary. I tried to fight her vicious influence, but didn't realize the depths of her power until I saw how she bitch slapped some of the joy out of my husband. It was only my first trimester and I had already turned into a caricature of a pregnant woman in a bad romantic comedy. My poor husband was stuck playing the role usually occupied by Hugh Grant, the conflicted, bumbling daddy under constant attack by his erratic (yet skinny aside from a giant baby bump) wife. Before I was even into elastic waistbands, I was talking crazy and jumping down his throat just because HE really wasn't WE and part of me wished he was. If I wasn't puking in a bucket I was demanding vats of Stouffer's creamed spinach. Poor fella didn't stand a chance against his baby momma's powerful personality plus pregnancy hormones.

Save your pity, though. He had ways to cope with my temporary psychosis: beer and his buddies. I would have coped better too if I'd been playing darts at the bar with my friends while watching sports and tossing back a five-dollar bucket of brewskis a few nights a week instead of sitting home alone hurling and crying over diaper commercials. Even when he was home, he had Miller Lite to smooth over the sharp edges of my alter ego's tongue-lashings in response to his well-meant but useless efforts to be supportive—and I needed a LOT of support. I was urping in my mouth or in the toilet every four seconds and exhausted from weeks of burning stomach acid making fifty round trips a day from my lips to my gut. My moods were swinging so fast and hard that even Superman wouldn't have been able to avoid getting throat throttled. From the get-go, my body and mind had difficulty tolerating the company of my little uterine parasite. But I wasn't ungrateful. I really wanted to be a mother and knew that all the discomfort would be worth it once I wrapped my arms around my little baby. I was in love with him already.

In the meantime, my BIG baby's behavior was fueling the Super-twat fire. Not even five minutes after the hurling stopped in my second trimester, I started swelling up and sobbing more regularly. And I was lonely. All my friends were at least an hour away and Eric was either at work, at graduate school or out with his pals. I was working a lot myself and although I could have gone out with the gang too, I didn't have the energy. The idea of spending the evening comparing myself to some sweet, young thing with a tight ass and watching everyone tie on a happy buzz while I downed club soda and bar pretzels was about as appealing as the vomit soup I had finally stopped spewing. Another reason I stayed home most of the time was because even I didn't want to be around me. With Super-twat, the miserable pregnant jerk, running rampant at home, it seemed unfair to begrudge my husband socialization time with his bubbly buddies. After all, after the baby arrived, he sure as hell wasn't going to be gallivanting off to the bar after work; he would be on daddy duty. I figured it was best to let him get it out of his system.

Then came one night I just couldn't bear to wallow in my misery alone. That was when my baby daddy finally began to understand how terrifyingly dangerous a pregnant woman can be . . . and explains why he became so eager to get his nuts cut.

Anyone who's had a head cold when pregnant knows that it's a special kind of hell, since you cannot take any medication stronger than a baby laxative to relieve your symptoms. I had been battling a head cold for weeks, and on top of that shit luck, I was having a particularly freaked-out, feeling-fat-as-fuck day. I asked Eric to *please* come straight home from work, completely forgetting that we had been invited to a birthday party. Well, even if I hadn't been carrying the plague, I knew that I was in no mood to celebrate anything. I had just hit a number on the scale that made me run into my bedroom, dig out my string bikini and sit rocking in the corner, sobbing, sure that my body would never again rock the shit out of that sexy thing on a sandy beach. It wasn't a good idea for me to be alone, but even a short appearance at the party was out of the question. I was toxic. So, I did the right thing and encouraged Eric to pop into the party and convey our best wishes before coming home to simmer in the cesspool of Super-twat. And so he did.

When he strolled in the door SIX HOURS LATER, completely hammered, I had tossed the bikini aside and was sobbing into my sweatshirt. It was the only thing within reach to soak up the endless river of snot and tears that had been flowing out of my face.

"We are FUCKING out of Kleenex!" I yelled at him as he stumbled into the room and zigzagged his way into a sloppy

SAYONARA TO SUPER-TWAT | 173

flop onto the sofa next to me. His eyes were glazed over and he stunk like stale beer and smoke. Not punching him took every ounce of my self-control, but I couldn't help but shove him away from me as hard as I could with my exhausted and increasingly chubby arms. "GET AWAY FROM ME!" Even sloshed, he was smart enough to move away from the mood swing. It's a good thing too, because although he may be a foot taller and a hundred pounds heavier than me, his high blood alcohol level didn't stand a chance against my baby incubator-fueled rage.

I was just about to wrap my swollen fingers around his neck when he stood up and walked out of the room with that same drunk-ass sway that had brought him in. My mouth was still hung open in the "Did he really just leave me here and go pass out in the bedroom?" position when he reappeared with a roll of toilet paper in his hand. "Use this," he slurred as he gently set it on the sofa next to the foot-high pile of snotty tissues I had built over the course of the day. He didn't risk coming too close this time, knowing he ran the risk of being smacked with either a mood swing or a hand.

Then, out of thin air, Super-twat vanished and Sweet-tits (that's what he calls me when I'm being nice) appeared. Warm fuzzies and overwhelming attraction to him washed over me along with love and gratitude. Suddenly it seemed sort of funny that he was sloppy smashed, and I felt glad that he'd had fun. He deserved a night of laughter with friends after so many nights at home with his miserable, moody baby momma. How I loved him. We were having a baby! "Come 'ere and gimme some love," I whimpered.

Even though my arms felt like anvils, I reached up and wiggled my fingers in the air, signaling for him to come back to me.

My spirits were low and I needed to be kissed and comforted by my big bear of a baby daddy.

Sadly, Papa Bear still lacked experience dealing with unpredictable pregnant women. This made him think that not only did I want a bear hug but some kind of supportive messaging. Looking me straight in the eyes, or at least trying to, he started the tanked-up talk that set my mood a-swinging once again.

"Listen, baby, I read something in *People* magazine about what you're going through, in this article about Marie Osmond . . ." He trailed off, pausing to see if I was listening and possibly to make sure that I was still in Sugar-tits mode. "You shouldn't feel bad about being crazy as fuck all the time, because after the baby comes, you'll get back to normal. And you won't stay fat forever either—"

I think he was going to keep talking, but I can't be sure since that's when he got himself HIT!

Note that technically I didn't hit him. I picked up the empty Kleenex box and whipped it at his head as hard as I possibly could, so the Kleenex box hit him, not me. Then I got up and got the HELL out of there before I started heaving lamps and coffee table books at his face. It was my first and last physical attack on another human being. And it was literally the only time I felt complete relaxation and release during my first pregnancy (because I was also constipated the entire fucking time). GODDAMMIT IT WAS AWESOME!

I felt only a teeny bit of shame the next day to see the physical evidence of my tantrum on his forehead. My entire body was affected by pregnancy, so it seemed only fair that he should suffer some physical discomfort as well. For the remainder of my pregnancy he did not mention any member of the Osmond family, mental illness or the size of any part of my body. I'm not sure he even made eye contact with me without first making sure he had quick access to something he could use as a shield in case I decided to fling something else at him.

For the next few months I didn't so much as lob anything in his general direction. I was either sleeping or too busy shoving Peanut Butter Crunch in my face to notice him—unless I needed him to refill my cereal bowl, because I couldn't get up off the sofa without great effort. Labor and delivery went pretty smoothly aside from the few times I screamed in his face, the one time I bit his neck (but I didn't break the skin) and the fact that he almost missed the birth of his firstborn because he went home to let the dog out. At some time over the next three years we both managed to minimize the extent of my pregnancy psychosis and romanticized the idea of adding another member to our family. All I could seem to recall about the whole thing was the fact that my epidural and accompanying narcotics were EPIC and I got a lady boner listening to the sexy-voiced South African anesthesiologist!

When women who have been through labor tell you that you forget the pain, it's not entirely true, yet it's not a lie either; the memories definitely become fuzzy, and the urge to breed is simply more powerful than the prospect of actual childbirth. It took three years for me to forget, but once the memory of the first go-round was fuzzy enough, I actually wanted to do it again—all of it. The pregnancy, puking, my ass expanding at the speed of light, the pain of childbirth and sleepless nights all seemed as if they were just memories from a chick flick I had watched years ago (starring Hugh Grant as the bumbling daddy, of course).

So we did IT again, and IT worked. I got pregnant with #2. Blah blah bed rest and blah blah Super-twat, who reared her ugly head sporadically throughout the months I was growing our daughter inside my possessed and puffed-up body.

As it turned out, the ginormous glob of goop I demanded that my husband inspect *was* my mucus plug, and the next day we were doing loop-the-loops around the hospital together, trying to speed up our baby girl's arrival. This time I screamed at him only once and that was because he was too busy trying to get comfortable on the bed after he had ditched me for an hour to go out to grab lunch. My contractions were coming two minutes apart, and I *still* didn't have the good drugs pumping through my veins. In hindsight, the big guy realizes how lucky he was that everyfuckingthing in that hospital room was bolted to the wall, because what I really wanted to do in between each excruciatingly potent, stabbing labor pain was chuck a heavy object at his head! I would have eventually found something, too, if the anesthesiologist hadn't come in to shoot me up with sweet, sweet spinal block sauce. Saved by the syringe!

I'm really glad I didn't pitch something at his head that would have potentially hurt him, because having his face to look at when our daughter came into the world was one of the most precious experiences of my life. He was beaming as the doctor put her wiggly, slippery body on my chest so that I could see her perfection up close. (He was much less traumatized the second time around.)

Maybe my friends are right. It is quite lucky for me that I married and mated with such a good man. Over the years he's demonstrated mad dad skills with both our children and perfected the tone and timing of each "Yes, dear" to practically every request I make of him. I suppose he would have said, "Yes, dear," had I asked him to put his testicles out of commission too, but it was all his idea. He knew that WE might not survive another pregnancy. And I knew that I had been wrong about him not being part of the WE all along. In our little family, HE has become the person that WE (especially ME) could never survive without. He really was a good sport and still is. So, I do realize how lucky I am.

And he's lucky the nut cut took! Can you imagine the damage I could do to him hurling all the kid shit WE have accumulated over the years?

SEX, LIES AND FUN DIP

CATE   Who do you love best, Zach or Dad?

ME   Oh, honey, I love them both. I don't love one more than the other.

CATE   Yes, you do. Everybody loves someone most. I love you most.

ME   Thank you. I love you so much. I adore you.

CATE   I know because you tell me, like, a hundred times a day.

ME   I do that because I want to balance out the nagging and complaining with love words.

CATE   So, do you love me most?

ME   Honey, it's not that simple. You and Zach are my kids and Dad is my husband. I love you all and I love you all in very different ways. This is a very hard to explain.

CATE   What if you HAD to choose because somebody had to get killed?

ME   Why would somebody have to get
        killed?

CATE   Because there is a war and somebody
        has to die.

ME   I'd choose me to die. I'd want you guys
        to live. I love you more than I love
        myself.

CATE   Maybe you love Dad more than you love
        yourself because he milked you and
        put the babies inside of you.

ME   Dad didn't "milk" me. That's not how it
        works.

CATE   Oh, yeah, that's right. Zach and I
        milked you. You don't give boob milk to
        grown-ups.

ME   No, no, you don't. Only babies drink
        milk from their mother's boobs.

CATE   So, if he didn't milk you, what did he
        do to make you a baby in your tummy?
        I want to have a baby in *my* tummy.

ME   Don't tell anyone, but I love YOU the
        most.

CATE   I KNEW IT! I KNEW IT! Can I have a
        Fun Dip?

ME   Yes, and you don't even have to brush
        your teeth after you eat it.

CATE   This is why I love you the most.

KIDS ARE PEOPLE TOO:
Caring for Children Without Crushing Their Souls

....

"The mother's heart is the child's schoolroom."

—H. W. Beecher

....

PIG BITCH HAS A SLEEPOVER

"Mom, what if we pooped out our eyes and looked at stuff with our butt hole?" Cate asked me at dinner, spilling half-chewed pasta out of her mouth and flinging the stuff in her bowl around with her slimy, cheese-covered fingers.

Oh shit, I laughed nervously, this wasn't good. Not good at all. This was bad.

Potentially fatal, even. The precious me time I had planned once I got Cate tucked into bed could be snuffed out if I wasn't careful with my words and gentle with my response to her dinnertime slobbery.

Incoherent and incessant babbling is always a sign that she's exhausted and is about to either A) have a Chernobyl-esque meltdown or B) burst into flames from a fever that comes out of nowhere, ensuring MANY meltdowns until she recovers. It was the end of a busy day and we had jam-packed it with adventures. The end was in sight. I just had to do everything in my power to prevent "A" (I hadn't seen any sign that "B" was skulking around), get her cleaned up and put her to bed in the next hour so that I could chill the fuck OUT. Like I said, it had been a hell of a day!

And OH MY GOD she was filthy! Summertime filthy, and even non-moms know what that means: head-to-toe grime from a long day of sweating in the sun, digging in the dirt, jamming sugary treats in your face and wiping the crumbs and juice on the nearest and least schmutzy spot.

A dozen S.O.S. scouring pads and a fire hose on full blast wouldn't scratch the surface of the dirt on her tiny body. Maybe a presoaped loofah would do the trick—IF she didn't have *severe* sensory issues. My daughter couldn't even bear a washrag much of the time; if I started on other grooming issues, like toothbrushing and nail clipping, I'd need a few more pages and a box (or six) of wine to write it without sobbing all over the keyboard. How was I going to get her clean without scrubbing her into hysterics?

As horrible as she looked, I couldn't take my eyes off her. My adorably derelict daughter, who regardless of her level of filth makes me want to hug her with every breath! Her mop of wavy hair was matted and clumpy and her nostrils were encrusted with boogers. I tried not to notice the dirt wedged under her fingernails while I watched her eat and listened to her blab about "what-ifs," and although I wanted to tell her to stop talking with her mouth full *and* to use her utensils, I stopped myself. The layer of sludge covering her body and her query about leaky poo eyes reminded me that I needed to save my strength for the inevitable post-dinner face-off over BATH TIME! I shifted my parenting style from strict and structured to wimpy and accommodating. I really needed her cooperation and I was not going to get it if I started picking at her about table manners.

I took a deep breath and closed my eyes. Dealing with dinnertime slop was really nothing compared to the bath-time battles I had with this kid. If I were to start nagging her when she was hungry and tired, it would result in her labile mood shifting rapidly and without warning. I needed my sweet little scuzz-bucket to continue jabbering joyfully in order to prevent an epic battle over bath and bedtime. So, I took some deep breaths and counted backwards from ten until the urge to bitch at her passed.

Every parent knows you have to pick your battles—and that overtired kids are like time bombs, just waiting to explode. Because I wanted desperately to melt into mommy time as soon as humanly possible, I was taking every precaution not to set her little ticker off. I'm not known to be an inflexible and perfectionist parent, but my kid was just too grimy to plop into bed without a bath, even by crack whore standards, so I kept my mouth shut as I watched food tumble out of hers.

"What if dogs pooped on the toilet and we pooped in the backyard and the dogs had to clean up OUR poop?" she giggled. "I wish I could eat while I poop so I'd not be so bored in the potty. Can I do that, Mom?" She didn't giggle when she asked me that last question. She was dead fucking serious; the kid doesn't have a sarcastic bone in her body. I don't know anyone who hates the bathroom more than my daughter. But that's another story. And it's not in this book. Anyway . . .

She was all about the poop, and in our house, poop talk at mealtime is a big no-no.

Picking battles is tough in general, but when you have a kid with special needs, like my daughter, it's even tougher to know what battles to pick! I frequently struggle to decipher which behavior is pure and simple kid stuff and what is related to her challenges. I'll probably have that one completely figured out NEVER but there are times when a mom does just know.

Unfortunately, when it comes to my darling daughter I could be right one minute and all sorts of wrong the very next. Her nervous system is a hot mess of unpredictability, a wind changing direction so rapidly that it sweeps up everything into its path and sends it flying through the air, landing in unfamiliar territory.

And it is NOT her fault.

Much like the weather, she cannot control the hypersensitivity of her body and brain and so I remind myself on the daily that if I think it's hard for me to live with her unpredictable moods and behavior, it must be a gazillion times harder for her. She's the one who has to live with the uncertainty and fear on her skin and in her soul. The bitch of being a girl with developmental and neurological problems is that those problems make people wonder if you are, indeed, just being a bitch, which I know sometimes she really and truly is! She takes after me, of course. I am one fierce bitch.

But not this particular night. I was trying not to be a bitch while watching her gorge like a midget Henry VIII, ripping through her food with her unwashed hands, talking about poop and not wearing any pants under her colorful dress-up skirt (since she had peed through them just before dinner and was "airing out her junk"). Gross. She was at maximum disgustingness. The whole scene was uncivilized and unsanitary. Medieval Scotsmen would be offended by her lack of manners, although that's hard to say for a fact since I don't even know any Scottish people. But I've seen *Braveheart*. It was that bad.

When I was pregnant with Cate, I had to endure three months of strict bed rest, trying to give my girl the best chance at being completely cooked. Going into labor at twenty-six weeks, when her lungs, eyes and so many other important parts were NOT quite done, could have been fatal! It was scary and overwhelming and many times I thought I'd lose her. I tried to remember this whenever I found myself getting set off by random kid crap that I knew I should be grateful for even experiencing. But still, looking at her this night, I wasn't thinking that way. I was irritated and exhausted and totally fucking DONE. I had to continue to count silently in my head, the rhythm of the numbers soothing me. Ten, nine, eight, seven . . .

The counting helped. I was feeling calm and confident that I would successfully maintain the kind of neutral and tension-free attitude toward her disgusting behavior that would allow me to get her nasty little miracle of an ass clean afterwards. I visualized myself as the picture of enough self-control and even-tempered discipline to make June Cleaver look like she could use an hour in a backwards jacket and a shot of vitamin V. No matter what it took, I would use all of my good-mom skills to facilitate a clash-free conversation about manners, as well as my unpopular position on my post-dinner plans for her.

Using my most tenderhearted "indoor" voice, I gently re-minded her for what must have been the six hundred ninety-ninth time in her short life that poop/pee talk belonged in the bathroom and not at the dinner table, and then, trying to stay positive, quickly began to jabber away about how much FUN I'd had with her that day. She agreed, singling out the late af-ternoon visit from the ice cream man, which reminded me of the star-spangled Popsicle with her name on it waiting in the freezer for dessert. Thank you, Ice Cream Man, for ringing your jingle bells just before dinner so that my ravenous daughter could sprint out the door half-naked chasing you around the cul-de-sac, totally losing her marbles over your tantalizing truck of treats, begging and pleading for one, and then whining be-cause I wouldn't let her eat it before dinner.

Thanks. A. Lot. Asshole. I hated that motherfucker. One of these days I'd tell him so, I thought. Maybe I'd . . . OH MY GOD, I was imagining that I was the one chasing the truck, but instead of waving money around, I was waving a baseball bat and screaming obscenities! Whoops, what happened to my calm and serene creative visualization of me out-momming June Cleaver? June wouldn't be caught dead even letting her kids have ice cream out of a truck. She would churn that shit herself and Ward would be all like, "June, this ice cream might be too hard for the Beaver." My thoughts were now completely going to crazy town. God, I was so exhausted. I looked at my daughter's drooping eyelids as her head rested on the table between bites. She was sleepy too.

But not too tired to remember that she had an exciting dessert chilling in the freezer and my promise that she could have it after dinner.

"I'll die if I don't eat my Popsicle. I'll DIE! You said I could have it if I ate all my dinner. I NEED it. It's MINE. I love it. Someone will steal it if I don't eat it. Mooooooooooooooooooom!" she whined, ramping up the drama while slinking down in her chair so that her skirt hiked up, giving me a full view of her privates.

Really? She needs it? She'll die? "A" for effort, and "V" for vagina. I wished I had a vitamin V. But I did have wine chilling in the fridge, and any hopes of sipping that sweet nectar in silence rested wholly on my ability to keep it together until Cate was snoring like a geriatric pug.

"Well, that would be terrible! I'd miss you. I promise you can have your treat, but I really don't want to see your vagina at dinner, so please sit up straight and finish eating. Then you may have your Popsicle."

She calmed down quickly. A promise is a promise. I visualized her eating the Popsicle, and I realized that the mess I was looking at was soon to become a lot more colorful! The layer of oil surrounding her mouth would be a neon shade of blue. And red. I had to get her clean or hit rock bottom in terms of the level of revolting I was willing to accept, regardless of her sensory issues. Most of the time, I did pretty damn well letting my mess-pot of a kid go un-scrubbed and understanding her disdain for anything pants related. Having a clear understanding of her sensory issues made this necessary and although sometimes the sight of her rat's nest hair and naked butt day in and day out made me feel trembly and stabby on the inside, outwardly I usually held it together. Even before she was born, I had really lowered my standards when it came to what constituted "clean enough," because as a mom working full-time outside of the house, I just had to learn to prioritize. But this night, a battle *would* be picked. Cate's current filthiness was far below even the lowest I'd ever sunk. I figured that a sweet treat combined with her exhaustion would make her too happy and tired to fight too hard at bath time.

I patted myself on the back for exercising such tremendous self-control. I was just as tired, if not more so, from towing her around all day in the 100 degree heat. I dug into my own food, starving and spaced out, wondering if I could even stay awake for some "me" time. I tried to get lost in the fantasy that in an hour, I would have my full-bellied, squeaky-clean little girl tucked tightly into bed like a burrito, sound asleep and drooling all over her freshly cleaned pillowcase. I'd feel refreshed once I had successfully conquered the bath and bedtime tasks, because I typically did seem to catch my second wind when I didn't have kids mauling all over me, draining my energy.

It wasn't like me to expect a relatively stress-free transition; I had too many battle scars to remind me of this fact. And I wasn't bitching AT ALL about the mess or her manners. The heat had really drained me. I figured the food would power me up for the potential battle and slugged down some water too. I knew I should hydrate before having a glass of wine (or three) on such a hot day and I needed to perk the fuck up. Maybe I was delusional from dehydration, thinking things would go smoothly later if I kept my cool now. Or maybe I was actually doing some of this parenting shit right, you know, learning from my past mistakes.

Maybe.

I was too tired to think it through so I lost myself in make-believe mommy musings and continued to shovel food into my mouth. Tonight it was just the two of us—the boys were out of town—and I was going to do everything in my power to whittle that number down to ONE conscious person within the hour. That one conscious person would of course be ME and I'd be enjoying a Reese Witherspoon film festival on DVD, drinking wine buck-naked on my king-sized bed all . . . by . . . my . . . self.

FOR THE WIN!

Not one minute after I allowed myself this blissful fantasy, my food-lubed little one announced that she was not going to bathe or brush her teeth because she was too tired. She continued to use her dirty fingers to shove handfuls of curly pasta in her mouth. Confident that I would agree with her plans to remain a stinky sow, she wiped her hands on the tabletop, leaving greasy butter smears, and delivered another humdinger about her plans for the evening. "I'm sleeping in your bed tonight, too. We are having a girl's night, Mom. With popcorn and a movie!"

"No," I told her, firmly but as friendly as I could. "After you have your Popsicle, it's bath and bedtime. Today was all about YOU and tonight is all about ME. Mommy needs some alone time."

Fuck that, was what I was really thinking. The only thing getting me through dinner at this point was the knowledge that I would soon be enjoying a huge amount of personal fucking space, a chick flick and cheap wine. I kept eye contact. She needed to know that I meant business. *She* was glaring back at me, ready to rumble, her big brown eyes boring holes into my skull. I had done so well up to that point, literally doing everything strictly according to my own personal therapist-mom code of conduct with a side of awesome. This grown-up and handling-shit-like-a-pro behavior was not my usual MO at all, let alone at dinnertime. I had not only anticipated her button-pushing, bossy-pants behavior, but I had taken great pains to go above and beyond what I would usually tolerate at the dinner table in order to prevent myself from provoking an argument. I wasn't going to be intimidated by the stink eye of my scuzzy daughter.

She started running her mouth, alternately begging for a sleepover and insisting that I was the meanest mom in the world. Rolling out of her mouth with the food were reasons she absolutely could not muster up the strength to bathe, brush her teeth or GOD FORBID sleep in her room alone when her dad and brother weren't home.

"Somebody might break in and kidnap me. I need to be with you. I DON'T WANT TO BE KIDNAPPED! THIS IS THE WORST DAY OF MY LIFE," she hollered, her chin covered with noodle slime.

I just couldn't fight it anymore. Tired Potty-Mouthed Momma kicked in hard. My mind was counting to ten silently, but it was too late. My mouth was already moving. And I did NOT use my indoor voice.

"NOBODY IS GOING TO KIDNAP YOU! You WILL shower tonight and you WILL sleep in your own bed, but first you will finish your dinner and use your manners, young lady! I just cannot watch you eating like a little pig! ICK!" I barked out, half-horrified, half-satisfied that I could release the tension that had built up over the past half hour trying not to go ape-shit on her about her manners, or lack thereof.

I was overwhelmed with sudden fatigue and frustrated at myself for losing my shit after I had worked so hard to hold it together. I knew that I had just delivered a fatal blow, killing my chances for alone time.

With each word that came out of my piehole, my daughter looked more incredulous. I couldn't blame her for being shocked. She didn't have time to duck when the mood swing came hurtling in her direction. Ugh, so much for a smooth and cooperative evening ending with my snuggly, clean child snoozing in her own bed, and me, horizontal and buzzed, saying, "Bend and snap," along with Elle Woods. I had blown it and I braced for the worst. My shameful loss of self-control would inevitably cause a corresponding blowup by my sensitive girl . . . or so I thought. In fact, she was speechless, standing next to the kitchen table with her head cocked to the side looking like a confused puppy. I wondered why she wasn't fighting back.

She climbed up on my lap and put her slippery hands on my cheeks. With a quivering lower lip she asked, "Why did you just call me a 'Pig Bitch'? That's not nice." Then she started to cry.

Wait, did she seriously think I'd said "bitch" rather than "ick"? Crap. Bitch is one of the many bad words I ~~occasionally~~ frequently let fly; why *wouldn't* she hear pig bitch? It all made perfect sense.

And so I leaped up with her in my arms and ran to the freezer to retrieve the only thing that could possibly save me. THANK YOU, ICE CREAM MAN! I didn't mean it when I said you're a fucking, sadistic bastard opportunist who hates his mother and that's why you torture mothers of the world by driving your piece-of-shit truck around at dinnertime.

I was now totally committed to giving in to my demanding

daughter. Do you blame me? I mean she was exhausted AND believed that her soul-crushing, foulmouthed hypocrite of a mother had called her a "pig bitch." I felt dirtier than she looked and smelled. She was really hurt.

I thrust that multicolored monstrosity into her gunky little fist and squeezed her as tight as I possibly could, planting a million smooches on her slick cheeks. And then I did what any other parent in the face of overwhelming failure and potentially bankrupting future therapy bills. I carried her up the stairs while she sucked down an ice-cold serving of red dye #1, 2, 3 and blue #4, 6, and 10, and plopped her in my bed, where she sat half stunned, working on that Popsicle like it was her *job*! Then I snuggled her up next to me and read her a long book without skipping *any* words or pages as she faded in and out of sleep, dripping the colors of her patriotic Popsicle all over my sheets in MY bed.

So basically what I learned that night was that I wasn't anywhere close to getting the smelly, snoring pile of dirt sleeping beside me to do things my way. I'm a pig bitch who has a long way to go before I figure this shit out. But in the meantime, I'm keeping Popsicles in the freezer.

INSIDE THE MIND OF MY CHILD

On the way home from basketball practice, realize that you will be driving past your favorite restaurant. Whine loudly about how weak you are from hunger and wish aloud that your family wasn't so poor because you really want to eat dinner at Larry's Diner. Wait until you see your mom's eyes in the rearview mirror and then stick out your lower lip, shrug your shoulders and sigh loudly. Act humble and surprised when your mom says your family isn't too poor to go out to dinner and that it's really a good idea, since it's getting so late and everyone is hungry. Sigh in the most ostentatious way and offer to give all the money from your piggy bank because you really want to contribute just in case she's just saying that so you won't worry about grown-up stuff, knowing your offer will be rejected. Think how much it would suck if your mom took you up on your fake proposal, because you are saving your money for a new DS game. Hope she forgets on her own but quickly distract her by professing your gratitude for having such a cool mom and add that EVERYBODY says so. Start a sing-along. Squeal when you realize you are in the parking lot of Larry's Diner and nobody has mentioned your payment proposition. Tell yourself to remember the sing-along distraction trick for another time.

Tattle on your sister for unbuckling her seat belt before the vehicle stops even though you did the same thing. Shove sister out of the way trying to be the first out of the minivan, knowing she is too busy getting reprimanded for taking off her seat belt to tattle on you for shoving her. Ignore her cries and haul ass to the front door without looking for cars in the parking lot, causing mother to freak out and threaten consequences she will never follow through on. Know that she is distracted by the gigantic and totally overblown fit pitched by sister in response to the seat belt debacle and will quickly forget that you were responsible for the meltdown as long as you hold the door for her like a gentleman. As she walks through the door carrying your sister, give her your most adoring grin and wink at her. Once inside the restaurant, wish aloud to no one in particular that it would be extra fun to be able to choose where you want to sit. Act surprised that the hostess hears you and asks you if you want to pick where you want to sit. Mention loudly that she must be incredibly smart to know so much about kids.

Get excited about getting the booth you wanted and briefly be distracted by the bald woman at the next table. Stare at her until you feel yourself being yanked by the arm to what you have declared to be the "best seat in the house." Wonder out loud why she doesn't have hair. Get shushed by your mom and told that the lady could possibly have cancer and has lost her hair from treatment. Hope out loud that you don't get cancer. Hear sister ask what cancer is and yell at her for making a comment about bald "cancer lady." Point out that sister embarrasses you *all* the time by asking so many stupid questions. Ask why Larry's is called a DINER instead of a restaurant. Proclaim diners to be superior to restaurants because people are much friendlier and customers don't have to take off their hats during the meal. Point out specific examples of other customers, thereby defending your right to wear your skater hat knowing that your mom isn't going to argue when she is surrounded by hat-wearing customers. Complain about getting crayons and a kid's menu until your mom hands you the grown-up menu. Flip immediately to the drink section claiming that you are dangerously close to being dehydrated and hope that one of the "bellboys" will bring some water. When your mom corrects you and tells you that they are called "busboys," ignore her. Claim that they should be called bellboys and that tables should have bells to ring so that thirsty customers can easily get their attention. When your comment is ignored, flop your head down on the table for dramatic effect. Maybe that will get the bellboy's attention, even if your mom is continuing to ignore your brilliance. Lift head up to see if your attention-seeking gesture worked, just as the bellboy finishes pouring your glass of water. Decide that you are going to call him the bellboy until your mom acknowledges your clever idea. Say, "Thanks for the water, Bell Boy," and chug it down as fast as you can. Think to yourself that you might have actually died from dehydration if you were still in the car driving home. Ask your mom if you can drink her water as well, informing her that her decision to take you to Larry's Diner probably saved your life. Thank her for saving your life. Tell her that she is the best mom in the world and that EVERYBODY thinks so. Assume you have adequately butt-kissed enough to start thinking about how you will get her to let you order pop AND an expensive steak. Silently formulate a subtle plan.

Step one: break into a restrained but recognizable pout because you just WISH you could actually choose something other than milk for a change. Suggest that you are lactose intolerant. Avoid eye contact, and continue subtle sadness until your mom tells you that you can choose whatever you want to drink. Decide on heavily caffeinated pop, knowing that although your mom would normally not allow it, she's exceptionally accommodating this evening. When drink choice is denied, decide it's worth a shot to attempt the same sad face, shrug and sigh combo you worked in the minivan. Accept defeat gracefully knowing that an argument has the potential to turn your mom from accommodating to angry, and that could jeopardize your chance for a pricey steak.

Step two: dramatically sigh and wish aloud that the steak wasn't SO expensive. Claim that you have enough in your piggy bank to pay for it yourself. Wish you had your bank with you. Act surprised when mom tells you to go ahead and order the steak and of course, you don't have to pay her back for it. Think how great it would have been if you had gotten her on board with the pop AND the steak, but appreciate the meat win. Be briefly annoyed that you feel sneaky and a tad guilty, because your humble, sacrificing act worked and your mom didn't even realize you were playing her.

Go with the T-bone, even though you don't know the difference between a T-bone steak and a filet, other than the fact that it costs more money. Act grateful and adorable and get up to hug mom knowing that the hugs will increase your chances of upgrading to something from the dessert case as well as easing your guilt about your extreme manipulative behavior. Suck down your entire glass of caffeine-less pop and let out a loud belch. Look sorry and say "excuse me" but secretly ponder if you can get away with doing it again after your next drink and louder the next time. Inform your mother that pop without caffeine has more bubbles and makes you burp more.

Be amazed when waitress delivers a second beverage just as you are finishing your first and apologize for your burp. Tell her that you don't usually have bad manners; however, the pop they serve is extra bubbly and delicious so you couldn't help yourself.

Tell her that people can die if they hold in burps and farts. Ask her if she is psychic because of her incredible timing with the drink delivery. Look at the waitress's name tag and read her name aloud. Tell her "Janet" suits her. Wink at her and declare her to be the best waitress in the world and that you know this to be true because you've had a lot of experience with bad service "in your day." Giggle when she says "taters" instead of potatoes. Roll your eyes and shrink down into the booth acting embarrassed that sister spills gallon-sized ziplock bag of crayons on the floor. Point out more of her shortcomings, provoking another emotional volcano that requires significant intervention from mother. Smile at Janet, shrug your shoulders and sigh in response to your sister's dramatics. Look around to see if anyone else is watching. Worry aloud that your sister is upsetting the other people in the restaurant. Apologize to Janet. Know that Janet thinks you are the good kid in your family and obviously your sister is the bad one. Act humble when Janet pats you on the head and calls you a "sweet boy."

Feel smug and reassured that you are, indeed, the better kid and that once again your mom is too distracted and busy calming down her bad kid to remember that you provoked that kid into her latest meltdown. Wink at the waitress and say, "Thank you, Janet," in your most polite and delightful voice as you receive your chicken and dumpling soup. Proclaim it to be the most delicious soup that you have EVER had. Ask her to ask the cook for the recipe. Compare consistency of dumplings to worm skin. Slurp soup. Remind mom to tip waitress in cash so that she doesn't have to claim it on her taxes because that is what your dad always does in restaurants. Wonder what taxes are. Wish aloud that you could have the remote control in order to change the channel of the television behind the bar. Notice the lack of response to your latest hint and repeat loudly to no one in particular that it would be really nice if *someone* would change the channel on the television set. Consider increasing the volume of your opinion when Janet approaches the table with your T-bone. Assume she brought your dinner first because you are her favorite. Give her another wink as she puts the plate down in front of you, warning that it is hot and she wants you to be careful. Feel surprised at how much she cares about you, considering that you just met. Notice that she doesn't warn your sister or your mother when she brings their plates, confirming your assumption that a dessert upgrade is going to be as easy as taking candy from a baby. Janet probably wishes she could adopt you.

Point out that the bone looks like the letter "T." Look at Janet for acknowledgment of your intelligent observation. Realize that the steak is going to be difficult to cut with that bone all up in it. Sigh. Repeat the lip/shrug/sigh thing while simultaneously alleging that you are so starving and weak that you can't even cut your steak. Again declare your mom to be the best in the world when she offers to cut the steak for you. Wink at her and warn that the plate is hot before she lifts it up to help you out. Janet may not like your mom enough to warn her, but you do. Besides, if her fingers get burned, then you will end up having to cut your own meat. Remind her that EVERYBODY thinks she is cool because of stuff like this.

Impatiently watch mom cut steak and start stabling the cut pieces with your fork and shoving them into your mouth before she even finishes. Declare steak to be the best you have ever had, yet leave room for the soon-to-be-upgraded dessert. Groan loudly about being as "full as a tick." Ask if you can wander to dessert case to pick out the goodie that comes with your meal. Wait until Janet the waitress is in earshot to wonder aloud why the desserts included with the full dinner don't include the dessert YOU want. Once you have her undivided attention, implement the amazingly effective lip/shrug/sigh combo. Act surprised when she agrees with you and tells you that she'll just give you the double chocolate cake at no extra charge. Say, "Really? Are you sure? No, I can't," at least three times so that she thinks you are humbled by her generosity and your good fortune. After all, you already know that acting grateful works to ensure future things to be grateful for. Wink at Mom and wave. Notice she's making the face that means that the lip/shrug/sigh combo is starting to lose its magic. Consider if you are laying it on too thick with all the winking, pouting, shrugging and complimenting. Return to the table and play a game of tic-tac-toe with your sister to smooth things over and distract your mom from whatever she was mad at you for. Let your sister win three times in a row, ensuring that your loving big brother gesture sinks in. Squeal when chocolate cake is delivered to the table and pronounce it to be the biggest piece of cake you have ever SEEN!

With each bite of cake utter, "Mmmmmmmmmm . . . oh my god, this is so good," because it shows gratitude and reinforces the chance of upgraded dessert on next visit to the diner: "Well, last time, our waitress, Janet, did it so I just assumed . . ." Believe that there is absolutely no way Janet could possibly forget what a unique and special kid you are. Think how she probably never had as good a customer as you. She will probably be talking about it when she gets home and her husband asks her about work. "Well, there was this one little boy who was incredible— INCREDIBLE and thoughtful—but his sister was just horrible." Remind your mom about tipping her in cash just as she is approaching the table to bring the to-go boxes. Fumble around with the cake, deliberating whether eating the entire piece will be worth the inevitable butt-fire diarrhea you get whenever you eat too much chocolate. Decide to bring half of the cake home, so that you can use it to taunt your sister, who has finished her dessert and will have nothing to eat later at home. Begin loading up your leftovers.

Accidentally drop the majority of your leftover pasta on the floor while putting it in the to-go box. Blame sister because she was showing waitress her jazz dance with her pants off and this completely distracted you. Act remorseful and humiliated at the mess by smacking your forehead and calling yourself a klutz. Offer to clean up the mess, but pause long enough to allow Janet to tell you not to worry about it. Ask her if she is sure about this at least three times, and stand up the third time so it looks like you are really willing to get down on the floor and start picking up the scattered noodles. Wink at her when she assures you that she will take care of it. Count money on table repeatedly and loudly, making sure Janet knows that you are making sure that your mom leaves her a good tip. Ask for a calculator to calculate the percentage like your dad does whenever you go to a restaurant with him. Tell your mother that you are only trying to help since she is always saying that she isn't much of a "math person." Notice she has that annoyed look that usually means you've made her mad. Do the lip/shrug/sigh combo, hoping your helpless and humble gesture calms her down. Realize the combo is no longer having any effect whatsoever. Offer to carry the take-out bags of food and revert to what you know works every time: gratitude. Tell her three times how much you love going to Larry's Diner and thank her for taking you out to dinner even though paying for your expensive steak might make it harder to pay the mortgage. Wonder what a mortgage actually is. Humbly offer the money in your piggy bank again. When she smiles and kisses you on the head, know that your money is safe AND you've still "got it" when it comes to charming your mom. Hold the door for her for good measure when leaving the restaurant and start running across the parking lot so that you can be the first one in the minivan.

Realize that she might yell at you for running in the parking lot and slow to a walk. Exclaim the night to be the best you have had all year. Laugh because it is only the end of January, knowing that you are clever and hilarious. Believe that mother and sister should have also laughed. Repeat your joke and ask aloud if they get the joke. Notice the two of them ignoring you while they discuss which CD to listen to on the drive home. Realize that your sister didn't get upset about you beating her to the minivan, because she outsmarted you by asking first to choose the music. Realize you will have to tolerate "Barbie Girl" for the next ten minutes. Remind your sister that you have something that she does not: leftover dessert. Remind her numerous times on the drive home until you have provoked her into another hissy fit. When your mom turns around to see why your sister is screaming, try the combo just one more time, showing her that you are sad for your sister, but confused as to why she is upset. Ask if you can have a turn to choose a song, enticing more screams from sister. Feel vindicated. She needs to know that you will do whatever it takes to have the upper hand.

As the screaming dies down, remember you have many DVR'd television shows that you have yet to watch. Knowing that your sister likes to let the dog out of her crate and give her treats when arriving home, consider making a beeline for the dog's crate and letting her out, fully aware that this could either incite another meltdown and allow you first dibs on the television OR be the diabolical deed that finally does you in. Decide to risk it and nonchalantly speed walk into the house and to the dog crate. Briefly experience a touch of panic as your sister erupts like a street corner fire hydrant until the phone rings, distracting your mom from the drama. YES! Flip on the television while your mom starts gabbing away and your sister continues to screech about how much she hates you. Since you are stuffed like a Thanksgiving turkey, you are totally in the mood to zone out with some cartoons before you have to brush your teeth and get ready for bed. Maybe you'll even digest enough to throw down a couple more bites of that cake before bedtime?

Of course that would probably inflame an already hot situation, because even when you turn up the volume full blast, your sister's rant about what a horrible person you are is impossible to ignore. Decide to save the dessert for the next day and give your sister the remote control. You are too exhausted from such a busy day to choose a show, anyway.

NICK THE IMAGINARY DICK

"**C**an you **pleeeeease** help me find my fling-a-longer?" Zach begged me. He was red faced and sweaty, zipping from room to room in his Spider-Man underpants and utilizing the wood floors to get a good, fast slide. "Nick is freaking out!"

I had no idea what he was talking about and that was unusual. Before I ended up on strict bed rest a mere twenty-six weeks into my second pregnancy I would have known EXACTLY what the fuck a fling-a-longer was, AND where the hell to find it. Damn complications of pregnancy forced me to the outskirts of my son's life for months and that's when his imaginary friend, Nick, showed up from Cheeseland. That imaginary MENACE became a positively evil influence on my precious, innocent, cape-wearing, superhero-loving, god-fearing preschooler.

Nick spoke Cheese language and had a baby sister named Sarah, who he occasionally brought with him on his visits from Cheeseland. You cannot possibly imagine what a *dick* Nick was. I say this knowing full well that calling a child a dick is truly crossing the line of what's appropriate, even for me, but in my defense, Nick was merely an imaginary child dick. He existed only in the mind of my four-year-old son, yet I had moments when I wondered if the spirit of some dead sociopath had latched itself to my vulnerable preschooler while I was under strict doctor's orders to surf the sofa 24/7. I couldn't think of any other explanation as to how my little guy could manifest the personality of such a total and complete jackass. I even began to wonder about Nick's mom, because who the hell would let her four-year-old son bring his infant sister on a playdate to another land? Sleep deprivation, stress and discomfort were clearly taking its toll on my once sharp psyche. I was contemplating the competency of my son's imaginary friend's parent.

As bizarre as the situation was, Nick kept Zach busy and happy and for that I was initially grateful. I didn't understand Cheese language, and my brain was suffering from pregnancy-induced stupidity, so even when I attempted to figure out what the fuck Nick was saying, I failed. There was also the problem of me being stuck on the couch, clueless as to what a bossy and demanding little shit he really was when they were playing out of earshot. I did know to expect some weirdness, though, because Zach's first imaginary friend, Molly, was a bit odd. She had first appeared two years earlier, when I went to South Carolina for a four-day bachelorette weekend. That high-maintenance illusion of a buddy was always hiding and making us scramble last minute to find her because she was scared to be left alone in the house when we were gone. Every time I tracked her down, she would convince Zach that they were hungry or had to pee or find a lost toy or . . . you get it, right? Anything to make getting out the door a nuisance. Molly was a monster! She also was constantly taking off her seat belt and so I was frequently pulling over the car to buckle that little pisser back in. After I threatened to slam on the brakes and send her through the windshield, she stopped asking to go places with us and then her brother Max took her place. He was generally much less of a problem, but never remembered to clean up the Rescue Heroes and sometimes he shit in the bathtub.

Zach got tired of cleaning up after Max and sent him away. I hoped that was the end of the imaginary assholes, but then Nick showed up. I suspected that he would quickly go where all the other fantasy fuckers went once my hyper-imaginative kid had played out whatever developmental complex he was dealing with—like the arrival of crotchfruit number two. How wrong I was!

As a matter of fact, Nick's presence and influence over Zach actually increased as I wandered in a postpartum haze wearing oversized T-shirts with milk stains, offering my family nothing but cold cereal, frozen pizza and Chinese takeout for the better part of two months. "Whatcha doing, Little Man?" I'd often ask Zach as he was dragging his jam-packed Buzz Lightyear suitcase down the stairs to his playroom while I was nursing my newborn baby girl. "Well, I'm just getting supplies for me and Nick, that's all," he'd answer, not even bothering to give me one of his chubby-cheeked, drooly grins. I was so psychotically exhausted, I wanted to give Nick an imaginary hug for being such a good companion to my little guy. That feeling was short-lived. Nick started working my nerves about six seconds after my daughter started sleeping through the night and I began to see, hear and think in complete sentences again.

Nick was demanding, had zero manners and acted like a jealous boyfriend. He didn't want Zach to have his buddies over for playdates and he never even touched the food or drink that I set out for him when he joined us for meals (or bothered to bring his dishes to the sink). Really, was there NOTHING that cheesehead liked to eat? I had gone through the trouble to make a plate for him and I spent a good lot of time "rocking" his sister to sleep as well. "I have a newborn of my own, ya know," I'd tell him. "You need to leave Sarah at home." But still he kept bringing her on his visits, insisting that I care for her. My own son couldn't give a rip-shit about *his* baby sister, but he would hyperfocus on the safety of Sarah the pretend baby. Sarah spent most of her visits in the swing. She really was a good baby, quiet and polite, unlike her jackass, bossy-pants brother, Nick.

Grrrrr . . . that NICK! Sometimes he wouldn't even let me play with my own son, claiming that my grown-upness would make whatever game or activity the two of them were playing much less fun. While I was growing a human, that little opportunist took over my role as keeper of weapons, flashlights and overall fun-ness. After recovering from months of strict bed rest and childbirth, I was eager to play! I wanted to get down on the floor and build gigantic Lego towers and to use every pillow and blanket in the house to make epic forts to protect us from all the bad guys! I'm not ashamed to say that I'm THE greatest fort-building, shadow puppet–making mom-superhero with mind-reading powers and know more about guns than the average Marine Corps recruit. At least I was before Nick came along. Over and over I was politely turned down as I tried to get in on what I assumed was to be a bad-guys-busting, make-believe-filled afternoon making shadow puppets with flashlights in my son's play tent. Once or twice I demanded entrance, but Nick said that my "butt was too fat from having the baby." I told you he was mannerless and mean-spirited, but Zach defended him, saying that Nick was merely repeating what I was saying no less than ten times a day. Well played, Zach. Well played.

It was a sweltering summer day when I realized that Nick needed to be forced back to Cheeseland for good. I was upstairs nursing the baby to sleep when I heard Zach screaming down-stairs. Panicked, I raced down the stairs with the baby still attached to my boob. Poor baby girl was startled into a pattern of hiccups alternating with vise-grip chomps and was now wide awake, giving me the stink eye. Petrified, I was expecting to see my son lying on the floor with a gaping wound gushing blood. Instead he was jumping up and down, pointing to the television yelling, "Mom—Mom—Mom! Nutrisystem is how you can get rid of that fat on your butt from the baby! Nick wanted you to see it!"

No fucking way.

Way. And before I could even consider an alternative, words started shooting out of my mouth like fireworks on the Fourth of July.

"Have you forgotten that when I am putting the baby to bed you are not to disturb me unless you are seriously injured, bleeding, close to dead or something is on fire? You need to sit YOUR ass down right now and I will be back to deal with you when I get your sister settled!"

My throat hurt from screaming. I literally screeched as if a masked character in a bad 1970s horror movie was coming after me with an ax. I had sweat dripping into my eyes, and I noticed that there were tears rolling out of his. Yes, fucking way. Yes, he did call me downstairs to make sure that I saw a commercial for weight loss. I considered the number of times that I had mentioned the sixty pounds I had gained on bed rest and realized that the hyper-observant little guy was only trying to help. Or was he? Fucking Nick was in on this, so I couldn't be sure.

Oh my god, I was going insane. Had I really considered blaming this on an imaginary preschooler? Thank god the verbal fireworks had included a time-out so that I could get some oxytocin in my brain and distance from my boy.

I trudged my fat postpartum ass back upstairs to finish draining my massive mammary into my sleepy and thankfully nonspeaking (yet) daughter, thinking about how to handle the problem of Nick. That's when the two of them decided to run away! They didn't run too far the first time. I found them wandering around the backyard with a Spider-Man backpack full of supplies, including the contents of my wallet and two melted Popsicles. It was the second time that had me panicked! After searching for twenty minutes, I was about to call the police. Then they appeared out of nowhere, talking about how Nick's mom let them jump off the roof with umbrellas in Cheeseland. I didn't know whether to hug him or repeat the ugly scream. Cheeseland this and Cheeseland that—I couldn't stand one more complaint about how deprived my kid was because he didn't have a Game Boy like his friend Nick and Nick had a trampoline in HIS backyard and Nick had a television in HIS room and Nick could eat Fun Dip for breakfast. Nick, Nick, Nick! I don't even know why Nick came around if his crib was so goddamn superior to ours. How was I going to get rid of this bad influence? I was exhausted from panicking and sprinting around looking for my runaway four-year-old, so I sent them both away to play. I needed QUIET and I needed time to think about how I was going to annihilate this made-up motherfucking monster. But there is no rest for the wicked. I had not even managed to decide where I was going to sit quietly to do my thinking when I heard my kid barking at me.

"Mom, we are STARVING! Can we eat lunch in the tent?" Zach hollered up from the basement playroom. I suppose all the running away made him hungry, but it had been only a little over an hour since breakfast. It wasn't time for lunch so I offered the gruesome twosome an alternative. "How 'bout a snack? I'll pop some popcorn and we can all watch a video!" I was thrilled at my idea because I needed to make up for my screechy terribleness. Look at me snapping back and getting all fun again, moving towards forgiveness and understanding about his morning shenanigans! I would even turn up the fun with some fucking Fun Dip! I was mulling this over when Zach gave another holler from his play cave. "No, thanks. We just want to play down here, but Nick is in the mood for chicken."

Nick is in the MOOD for chicken? What, no Fun Dip?

"Oh, and he wants chicken legs, not nuggets. A LOT of chicken legs. Like ten. And baked, not fried," Zach clarified, as if he was just ordering around some schlub waitress in a restaurant. I took a deep breath. Chicken? I wasn't going to turn on the oven in 100 degree weather and make chicken for a snack. It was too much weirdness in one snack request, not to mention that I was already trying not to be hopping mad at him for his awful behavior earlier. Add to the weird the fact that I had never made Zach baked chicken legs. Not once had I served the kid chicken legs aside from the Kentucky Fried kind in a fast food joint on the way to Grandma's house in Indiana. In his four short years on planet Earth, I had never made him baked chicken legs, nor had he asked for them. I didn't even bake fucking cookies; I bought them. Always. Then there was his lack of interest in watching a video. Again, never, ever had he turned down an opportunity to veg out in front of the boob tube shoveling his favorite snack into his face. I was feeling stabby and still so sweaty that I sat down on the kitchen floor and put my head between my knees.

It was so stinking HOT and the heat only increased my irritability and exhaustion. The fact that I was leaking sweat from every pore in my body also pissed me off. I couldn't cool down and imagining the seventy-four ways I wanted to throttle Nick was adding fuel to the fire. The therapist in me knew that Nick was most likely NOT the spirit of some sociopath parasite sucking on my son's soul. My kid had no choice but to compensate for my long absence from his play life. I was stuck for months lying on my side, turning into a much larger and inaccessible version of his once favorite and most reliable human object. He was not only pissed—he was bored, confused by all the changes, and smart enough to know how to push my buttons. But the ten baked chicken legs were the last straw. What was he going to request for snack tomorrow, a turkey dinner with all the fixings? Maybe wicked Nick would suggest they hitchhike to Chuck E. Cheese's. I stood up, wiped myself dry with a dirty kitchen towel and began to formulate a plan.

That day I set my sights on sending Nick back to Cheeseland for good. "It's ON, you fictional freak," I smugly and silently vowed. "I will fucking DESTROY you!" Cheese boy would be no match for Momma. I was vertical again, invading the people and space around me, spreading my can-do attitude and actions. It was time to take back what was mine. And it wasn't just the loss of my status as weapon master and queen of all things fantastic and imaginary that I wanted back; that poisonous pretend preschooler was manipulating my son's mind. Inspired by the bursts of nursing mommy hormones and energized by my sudden awareness that I was no longer stranded-on-a-sofa helpless, I committed myself to defeating this dastardly DICK of a kid. I had to be ME again. The key to getting rid of Nasty Nick was not just to out-fun him, but to stop letting him boss me around on my own turf! THERE WOULD BE NO BAKED CHICKEN LEGS FOR SNACK TODAY OR ANY OTHER DAY FOR THAT MATTER! So I hollered right back, "It's popcorn and a movie today, pal, and you can tell Nick that Sarah is crying for her mommy and they both need to go home."

We settled in that day for a video/snack/snuggle session without Nick and I spent the time alternately sniffing the sweet smell of my son beside me and plotting against his invisible BFF. Monday we'd go swimming, Tuesday to the zoo, Wednesday Nick would have to tolerate a previously scheduled playdate, and Sarah couldn't come over because I was coming down with a cold (I made sure to cough on and off throughout the movie in order to support my fib). I told Nick that child care was gonna cost his mom, big-time, and that he should tell her as much. I kept us busy and out of the house as much as possible, considering I had a newborn and it was 500 degrees in the shade. Bribery was part of my strategy to exile Nick. We went to the movies, on playdates, to the carousel at the mall, and the Build-A-Bear Workshop. I endured the fresh hell of Chuck E. Cheese's, numerous times in fact, in order to distract my kid from calling on his shitty little BFF. There just wasn't enough money to include Nick and Sarah in our adventures. Zach understood. Nick was busy anyway lately, he informed me.

When Zach said Nick was going to Hawaii for a vacation so we probably wouldn't see him for a few weeks, I knew that I was winning more battles than I was losing. "That is good news," I answered, "because we are going to Indiana for a week before school starts and there is absolutely no room for Nick at Aunt Krista's house." Zach agreed that the timing really was perfect, especially since Nick was shy around strangers and he was excited to spend some alone time with his cousin, Bailey.

The visit with family flew by, and between shopping for school supplies, swimming lessons and an overall EPIC amount of previously planned entertaining and exciting activities to keep him busy, Zach hardly had time to miss Nick while he was in Hawaii. We didn't hear from him once for the entire two weeks! Like Max and Molly before him, Nick figured out pretty fast that if Momma ain't happy, nobody is getting baked chicken.

Or Fun Dip.

I was feeling more like my old self every day, realizing how stressful it truly was for my entire family to experience me as a helpless, horizontal incubator for months on end. Nick's appearance and disappearance made sense, but I'd be lying if I said it didn't creep me the fuck out that my kid had created such a jerky imaginary pal in response to the stress this time around. I wasn't convinced that Nick's absence was permanent either, as Zach's imaginary friends had been coming and going for years. Time would tell and I knew that structure and stability were more important than ever. We were *all* getting used to the new normal; we were now a family of four. Work, school and activities kept us all busy as the leaves began to turn, signaling fall. I no longer had to juggle an infant and a hyper-imaginative preschooler and his unstable alter ego by myself for the entire day.

I didn't ask about Nick. I hoped with my evening prayers that he had slipped Zach's mind and made sure he had plenty of things to do and people to see so that he would no longer need an imaginary friend in his life. After four years of me being the center of my universe, it was no surprise Zach didn't appreciate sharing my attention. Nick helped him say what he didn't fully understand himself; he was struggling with the changes and he was taking it out on me. He began to recognize his anger and share it with me more directly when he could, and I thought this was a sure sign that we had seen the last of that sneaky snake Nick. Big E and I realized that even though we felt that our baby girl had made our life complete, her arrival had completely disrupted the life of our son, who would have much preferred a trampoline or a television in his room. We tried to remember that when he was acting up. In particular, I tried to anticipate times when he might feel slighted by all the attention given to the baby, because I was still harboring delusions that I had actually gotten control of the situation. Dangerous delusions that left the door wide open for Nick's return.

And return he did. Nick rode in on a rhinovirus just before my husband was riding out of town for a week on a business trip. He showed up with a mega-fuck-ton of attitude, as he knew that I would be worthless in my compromised condition. Actually I was less than worthless: burning with a fever, a thick river of golden snot running endlessly down my lips and chin and an equally miserable four-month-old who wanted nothing but milk of mom 24/7. I was putting a Pop-Tart in the toaster for Zach's dinner, hoping my weak and dehydrated muscles had the strength to lift up the container of milk to pour him a glass, when I heard what sounded like a pack of wild dogs thundering down the stairs. Nick and Zach had decided that there were just too many supplies to carry to the playroom so they'd thrown EVERYFUCKINGTOY Zach owned down the stairs!

NO, NO, NO, NO, NO, NOT NOW, not when Daddy was out of town and I barely had the strength to remain upright. Nick could NOT have returned at a worse moment.

"Can you make Nick a Pop-Tart too? He's STARVING!"

I yanked out the tissue that I had jammed up my nose and called my kid over for a chat. I told him that I would not be making a Pop-Tart for Nick and that until he picked up every last toy that he had thrown down the basement stairs, *he* wouldn't be eating one either. I told him that with his daddy out of town, he was supposed to be the man of the house and that I was really counting on him to help me while I was sick. I laid it on thick, telling him that his dad would be terribly disappointed to hear that he had dropped the ball in his absence. I ended my performance by asking him for a hug. He pounced on me like a cat on a mouse, wrapped his chubby little arms around my neck and squeezed so hard that tears started rolling down my face. "Don't cry, Mommy," he said. "I'll be the man of the house!" I wasn't really crying at that point. I was just so sick that snot was even leaking out of my eyes, but damn, who knew tears were just as effective as fun?

GUILT. It was the only weapon in my arsenal that I could wield in my condition. I figured it would be as effective as throwing a thimble of water on a burning high-rise, but I couldn't go down without a fight. I would FIGHT! I decided to ham it up. "Okay, honey, I won't cry anymore. You made me feel all better and now I feel really safe with you as the man of the house." And just like that, he cleaned up the toys, ate his shitty dinner without complaint and brushed his teeth and got into bed without being asked. Even Nick was cooperating. Sweet, sweet guilt, how I planned to tuck it away for future use, and how nicely it blended with some ego-stroking! As I tucked Zach in I mustered up the last of my tolerance for bullshit and asked why Nick had not picked out a book yet, because they usually each got to pick one before bed and there was just one book sitting in his lap.

Zach lowered his eyes briefly before speaking. "Nick's dead."

Maybe I'd heard him wrong; after all I was a walking, talking toxic waste dump, leaking phlegm and scorching with fever. Hell, I didn't even know if I was really awake. "Did you say *dead* or read?" I asked, hoping it was the former and not something about how Nick had already read a book. BE DEAD BE DEAD BE DEAD, was all I could think. And that's when the pint-sized man of the house, wearing his Incredible Hulk pajamas, covered in Magic Marker because he had drawn scars all over his face and arms (so that he could look like a pirate) informed me that he had *accidentally killed Nick in a scuffle over toothpaste.*

TOOTHPASTE!

What the what? I needed a blow by blow of the crime. Nick wanted to squirt toothpaste all over the sink and make a mess but Zach wouldn't let him and Nick was trying to push him off the step stool, so Zach pushed him back. Nick fell down and hit his head, but people from Cheeseland don't bleed when they die—they just turn into a pile of ashes. So, Zach put the ashes in the backyard under the tree where Snowball the dog was buried. "Oh, buddy, I am so sorry!" I lied, but what was I going to do, start throwing air punches and congratulate my kid on his first imaginary homicide? "Are you okay? Do you want to talk about it?" I asked, trying to assess his mood and repress my smile.

"Nope," he answered with a goofy baby-tooth grin as his arms shot forward holding the book *Curious George Goes to the Hospital.* "I want to read about George!" And so we didn't talk about the murder, or as I like to call it, accidental death of Nick. The way I see it, it was really more like manslaughter. Instead we snuggled up together and laughed at the story of how our favorite monkey got himself into mischief, AGAIN! Once Zach was sound asleep, I crept outside to pay my respects to Nick. I hated his imaginary guts, but I felt the need for some closure. It has been said that in life, there is no gain without pain. Zach was struggling under so much change in his little life and he needed help shouldering the pain; I am grateful to Nick for this. But not so grateful that I didn't include a big "fuck you" in the short eulogy I delivered while kicking his ashes into the furious night wind.

WHAT THE FUCK?

A few years ago, I wrote a somewhat sanitized version of how things went down the day I told my son how babies are made, which was included in the anthology, *Fifty Shades of Funny: Hook-ups, Break-ups and Crack-ups.* I wanted the story to seem a little less traumatic than the reality because someday he might actually read it and I didn't want to live in fear that it'll cause some sort of PTSD meltdown/flashback. I still remember how I felt hearing my parents use the word "penetration" and how desperately I wanted to get beamed up to the starship *Enterprise* as my father drew smiling sperms on a napkin at the dinner table. I was catatonic for hours afterward. (I *still* need to pop a benzo when I think about my parents having sex.)

Anyway, the details in all their spooge-worthy glory were dished out over some tasty doughnuts while I was driving him somewhere in the minivan. I told him only because he asked how the mother of Michael Jackson's children couldn't know for sure if he was really their father because "Don't all girls know whose sperm they're eating?"

What the fuck?

Fuck you very much, *Headline News* or whatever dozens of shows, magazines and media sources were relentlessly exploring the sexual mysteries of my son's favorite singer. (Unless you were living in isolation, the question of the paternity of MJ's kids was practically unavoidable during the weeks following his untimely and dramatic death.)

I took a pause to cram another doughnut in my mouth before I launched into the baby-making information. "Remember that babies aren't in the stomach. They are in the uterus, you know, between the pee and poop holes there's a hole that leads to the uterus. Three holes, like a bowling ball, but they are in a straight line." I had explained this to him when he asked how his baby sister was going to get OUT of me a few years earlier, but I figured a refresher course was necessary. That part went okay. It was when I gave him the blow by blow of exactly *how* the sperm manages to get to the egg that he became mortified. After learning that his father's penis went *in* my vagina, the poor kid looked like someone just ran over his dog after breaking all his toys and force-feeding him a dog poo smoothie. He was disgusted! And it was *hilarious*. He sat in complete silence for a good long time, but when he finally started to laugh nervously and could manage to look at me again, I knew it was all good in the 'hood so I ate another doughnut, because doughnuts are fucking awesome.

Anyway, I wrote the story, and as I worked on it and edited the snot out of it, I relived the day numerous times. It really got me thinking about my son, and how for many years I feared that he wouldn't be the kind of kid who could have a laugh about things at all. He is still a serious and sensitive guy, and to know him is to be confounded by him, but he's nowhere near as stoic and weird as he was the first five years of his life.

THANK GOD, because those first few years were stressful. I think I said "What the fuck" no less than a hundred times a day, every single day, both out loud and to myself. Mothering was mysterious, as it was my first crack at it, but mothering *my* kid was a complete mind-fuck. He wasn't like any kid I had ever met or read about. He basically skipped the irrational, tantrum-throwing toddler behavior that so many of my friends were battling with their little ones. My kid listened. He was logical, rational and cooperative. It. Freaked. Me. Out. If you had told me then that he would grow out of his fastidiousness and become like a regular jerk of a kid, I wouldn't have believed you. I was too much of a mess with worry. You would be, too, if your toddler acted like a know-it-all vice cop with no sense of humor.

I can't prove it, but I think that the souls of a Marine Corps sergeant and a persnickety old man spent a good deal of time weaving in and out of Zach's psyche, fighting for dominance. That, along with his own unique temperament, made for a whole lotta what the fucks. On the one hand he was super sensitive, but on the other hand, not much for freaking out, melting down or overreacting like other people in the under-five club. He didn't throw shit fits—*ever*. He just needed people to follow the rules and for life to make sense. "Is that too much to ask?" he'd say, and I'd tell him all the time that honestly, it really *was* too much to ask. I'd tell him, "Life's like a box of chocolates. You never know what you're gonna get." Of course he replied, "Yes, I do. I buy the box with the ones I like, not the ones I don't."

Touché! Also: what the fuck, dude?

From the get-go, the kid had an uncanny ability to absorb and understand the nuances of body language and emotion that is rare even for most adults. How many other three-year-old boys do you know who could look at Murray the red Wiggle and say, "That Murray has sad eyes. I wonder why Murray has the blues? He has sad eyes with secrets," while dancing in front of the television to "Fruit Salad, Yummy Yummy"? None? Me either.

What the fuck?

At that point I might have said it out loud. Or not. It was stressful so I blocked some of it out. I'm sure I was thinking it, though. My kid needed to lighten up.

But he didn't. He grew more sensitive and serious and by preschool he seemed more like a middle-aged spiritual advisor than a child! From a developmental standpoint, it would have been more appropriate for him to be a punk-ass kid, working full-time to establish a sense of power by being defiant and annoying; instead he was busy spewing thought-provoking comments and being cooperative. He had exactly two time-outs during his second year of life before he learned that he didn't like time-outs so he stopped being a shithead. Just . . . like . . . that. And it wasn't just that the rules had to be followed to the letter. He needed everything just so. I called him "Mr. Spock" or "The Professor," because every last fucking thing had to be perfectly logical and supported by empirical data before he would buy into it. Santa Claus? Bullshit. He called me out on that when he was in kindergarten. If I left the light on in the bathroom or forgot to lock the door, he made sure to let me know about it. "Excuse me, Mom, leaving lights on isn't good for the environment," or "Excuse me, Mom, but that applesauce cup should go in the recycling bin."

What the fuck, Al Gore? I just wanted him to lighten up.

But he didn't. He was blunt, like most little kids, but his serious nature made the unfiltered kid stuff seem less funny to people who didn't know him very well. Sometimes it came off as rude. One time when I was pregnant with my daughter, and he was sitting in the grocery cart, he saw a particularly large woman bending over to pick up a lemon she'd dropped on the floor. He cocked his head to the side and said, LOUDLY, "Mom, I don't know if that lady is pregnant or just fat. It's hard to tell. You have fat on your belly, but it's a baby and you don't have fat on your bottom. That's how I know you aren't just a fat lady. That lady has a very fat bottom, and I just wonder if that fat on her belly is a baby or just a big pile of fat. Her belly is HUGE, but so is her butt."

What the fuck? That was beyond the unfiltered "kids say the darnedest things" type of comment, especially considering he was three years old at the time.

"Shhhhhhh," I told him, doing my best impression of a bank robbery getaway driver, speeding away from the scene of the crime, trying not to burst into tears from a combination of horror and amusement.

He was always up my ass about my chronic lateness. "Excuse me, Mom, it's ten thirty-five and you said we were leaving at ten thirty. This is a *very* big problem."

Say it with me now: what the fuck?

"It ain't no thing," I'd say, trying to get him to relax. But it was a thing to him. We were late. He did not lighten up, but he didn't melt down either. As always, the little guy had me perplexed. Should I be doing something about this? Raising an adult inhabiting the body of a toddler was nothing short of bewildering. I couldn't figure out why he couldn't just relax and go with the flow. My husband and I were the exact opposite of our son. How did two laid-back, chronically late former pot-heads manage to create such a punctilious and humorless human? I was constantly yet subtly working to get Zach to throw all caution to the wind and get groovy with life. He'd get silly with me, don't get me wrong. We had parades in full costume, splashed in puddles, ate snacks in a tent while watching a movie and painted ourselves from head to toe. He had no problem slopping around with his food or busting out moves to The Wiggles, but when it came to the rules, there was no wiggle room. NONE.

I was starting to worry that something was seriously wrong with my kid.

Then I got the phone call from school.

I knew he wasn't in trouble; from day one, a phone call from the day care center or school meant he was sick . . . and I mean *really* sick. For him to complain he'd have to have a hallucination-provoking fever and a complete inability to move his legs. He *hated* to give in to sickness! He wanted to go and play and learn and do and see and being sick didn't jibe with his plans for world domination.

So when the caller ID on the phone indicated his kindergarten was calling, I figured he was speaking in tongues while bursting into flames and that we were most likely looking at a week of steroids, antibiotics and/or nebulizer treatments. There was no way it was a discipline call. My little guy didn't break any rules—any time—anywhere! He even tattled on himself because the guilt of knowing he did anything wrong drove him crazy. One time he cried because he didn't wash his hands after using the shitter.

You know what I'm going to say, right? What the fuck? Lighten up. It's only E. coli.

The voice on the other end of the line was unfamiliar. She identified herself as Mrs. Sweetness, the substitute teacher. "Mrs. Knepper, Zach is pretty upset and says he would really like to talk to you." Upset? Well, this wasn't good news, but it also wasn't the plague. Nope, he wasn't being rushed by ambulance to the ER with a bad case of flesh-eating bacteria, so I figured it was a shart pants emergency (you know, thinking you are going to fart, but you actually end up shitting in your pants). I could deal with upset. I was used to upset. And skid marks? Well, let's just say his rules were less strict when it came to wiping his ass. "Please put him on," I asked Mrs. Sweetness, hoping to find out what the fuck was happening to upset my kid so much that he was calling home.

"Mom, it's me, Zach." His little voice trembled over the speakerphone. I melted into a pile of goo just hearing him identify himself, as if I didn't know who was calling. His squeaky baby voice often made the articulate and thoughtful things he was saying sound weird. Now he sounded terrible and I was no longer relaxed.

I leaped up from the sofa, ready to haul ass to the school and see what was making Professor Sergeant Spock so upset. This was NOT like him. "Baby, what is it?" I begged, my own voice oozing with concern. "Tell me what is going on. Are you okay?" He started to cry so I didn't understand what he said at first. Maybe something about a bully? I heard the words "concentrate," and "ugly," and "scared me." I encouraged him to take a few deep breaths to calm down so that he could just tell me what was going on, all the while jumping out of my skin and grinding my teeth in anticipation. He tried again and this time he succeeded.

"Mom, I need you to come and pick me up from school. I can't concentrate today because the substitute teacher is just so ugly."

WHAT THE FUCK?

I have never been so completely and totally unprepared for anything in my entire life. Even from him! I didn't know whether to laugh or cry. I was on speakerphone and it really wouldn't be appropriate to laugh *or* cry for any number of reasons I won't even bother to list because if you have ever found yourself experiencing overwhelming emotional relief upon hearing that a loved one is safe after fearing he is not, you know what all of those reasons are.

At the risk of being accused of fishing for a compliment, I tell you in all honesty that I am significantly below-average looking. I do have a healthy head of hair (neglected but healthy) and a charming personality, but I'm not a looker by any means. I am remarkably unremarkable. I couldn't imagine what the teacher must look like to freak my kid out, considering he spent a good portion of every day looking at my big nose and acne scars close up.

With absolutely no trace of weirdness or anger in her voice, Mrs. Sweetness started to laugh and patiently explained that he might be scared because she was missing a hand. It was an injury from long ago and often frightened little kids. That WAS it. At least part of it. Zach started to cry harder. According to the rules as he understood them, all people had two hands and this lady did not. The only person he'd ever heard of without two hands was Captain Hook. So, she was probably a pirate and he could be forced to walk the plank at any minute. As he told me later, he didn't "like the look of her *at all*."

This actually made perfect sense when I thought about it. For the first time, his regular teacher was not in the class-room. He was late to school that day (my fault) and when he opened his folder, his homework wasn't there (again, my fault) and he had to move his clothespin to "yellow," the warning color, for repeated talking (his fault). One or two of these things might not have mattered, as he was really getting the hang of being a kid, but this was just too much rule-breaking change at once!

Then he lost his shit completely when he realized that he'd called the teacher ugly, no matter how hard Mrs. Sweetness tried to convince him that it was understandable and that her feelings weren't hurt. She suggested that I come and pick him up. He just could not seem to regroup.

P.S. When I arrived, I noticed that his cheeks were flushed and he seemed a bit dazed. I got him home and took his temperature. It was 102. So, on top of everything else, he *was* sick!

Now, here's the biggest "what the fuck" of all. After that day, he was more playful, relaxed and silly. He left turds in the toilet, threw out stuff that clearly belonged in the recycle bin, forgot to turn off the lights and turned into a dawdling procrastinator. He made selfish choices and had moments where he was oblivious to the needs and feelings of others—just like a normal kid! It was amaze-balls; a fucking miracle, as far as I was concerned. The relief was nothing short of overwhelming. I had worried that I was to blame for his high anxiety and weirdness; that I had one really fucked-up little human on my hands. I admit it. I was terrified.

What the fuck was I thinking?

Well, I was thinking and worrying what most parents think and worry about, which is basically, "Am I totally fucking this shit up?" And I think that a parent who *isn't* asking him- or herself some form of that question might want to look into whether he or she has a mental disorder that blocks normal human thoughts and emotions, because being a parent is a total mind-fuck.

The good news is that it becomes less so as kids grow and you learn to let go of the worry and accept your own limitations and imperfections. It's truly the key to not losing your marbles completely. I know this is true, because once I did it, once I started saying stuff like, "I'm okay with not knowing what the fuck is going on all the time and not worrying about shit that I can't do shit about," I stopped entertaining insane thoughts about how my kid was going to end up on the clock tower with an AK-47, screaming, "This is all my mother's fault!"

At twelve, my kid is now scarily like his parents with his sarcastic sense of humor and craving for chaos. I think he might rival me in his ability to ride the wave and go with the flow, rarely getting upset or angry long enough to act on it (unless his sister provokes him, then all bets are off). He jabbers on like a typical boy about things appropriate for his age. He's a skateboarder, the ultimate anti-establishment, rebellious sort who laughs at the dangerous wipeouts featured in the "Hall of Meat" in *Thrasher Magazine*.

What the fuck?

He tells me what songs and bands are "sick" (that means cool) and tries to get me worked up by saying he thinks the Jonas Brothers are a bunch of pussies because he knows how much I love me some Jonas. He calls Justin Bieber a lesbian because he knows I have Bieber Fever. He makes practically everything revolve around turds, farts, video games and whatever pop culture phenomenon is all the rage at the moment. I have to ask him sixteen times to clean his room and even then, he does a half-assed job, but I prefer that! He could have ended up like Felix Unger, painstakingly straightening the books on his bookshelves and vacuuming out his sock drawer every week. The only thing that really bothers him is when I refuse to put on a bra when his friends come over. That's normal, right?

I don't know any parents who don't question themselves almost constantly about what they could do better or different. I did plenty of freaking out when Zach was the most uptight child I'd ever known, maybe even the most uptight *person* I'd ever known. There was so much "What the fuck" back then. I *still* look at him on a daily basis wondering what the fuck I'm doing and what the fuck he thinks about it all, but today I don't worry so much because, seriously? FUCK IT.

I just feel so horrible that you learn nothing at school day after day. Of course I feel even worse for your teacher, because now I have to call the principal and rat her out for letting a roomful of brilliant minds rot while she's doing zip, zero and zilch. And so guilty that I haven't called and insisted that something be done about this sooner. I hope you'll forgive me. What? Oh, you *are* learning stuff? That's fascinating. And truly a relief since the holidays are just around the corner and it would be so sad if your teacher got fired and had to move her family into their car and I was feeling like such a bad parent and . . . what? You need it quiet so you can do your homework? All righty then!

THE BEST DEFENSE
IS A GOOD OFFENSE

Old adages and old wives' tales have long been used to advise or guide. Personally, I've found the old wives' tales to be useless and ridiculous. That the gender of an unborn baby can be determined by the direction a wedding ring on a string swings over a pregnant belly is about as believable as early withdrawal as an effective form of birth control. Old adages, on the other hand, tend to come in handy, and are based on essential truths. Old adages are like condoms: consistently reliable as long as used correctly. I have one favorite parenting adage in particular that I use to guide and advise me: the best defense is a good offense.

AFUCKINGMEN.

Sports and war aphorisms are dependable and simple, their truth reinforced each time they guide a team to a win or a combat unit in battle. Parenting, of course, has elements of both war and athletic competitions. There are endless battles to fight and games to play. Preparing for them takes discipline and practice. Teamwork is essential. Strategy is superior to brute force.

A popular bit of sports-themed advice to first-time parents is "Use man-to-man defense." In other words, when possible, take turns! One-on-one increases the chances of success. Eric and I used this technique. We took turns caring for our super-colicky firstborn, "covering our opponent" until we were desperate for a break. For six months, we were in a perpetual state of man-to-man defense, practicing our teamwork—lots of passing and assists!

When we started talking about having a second kid, friends of ours who had experienced going from one child to two all said the same thing: get ready to transition. No more man-to-man. You guys will need to use a zone defense. Once we had two kids, if either of us was going to get a break at all, we'd have to learn to cover a zone instead of just one player at a time. We'd still be taking turns, letting each other escape with friends or just get the hell out of the house to run an errand, but we'd be up against two challengers: two opponents with no understanding of battle safety or the rules of the game. Two kids crawling, climbing or running in two different directions, one towards a steep flight of stairs, and the other up a wobbly bookshelf in his or her bedroom. The only way to prevent a dangerous situation would be to cover the zone, not just the man.

Oh! I hadn't thought of that. I always appreciated experienced parents' advice. Information from a professional mom, a veteran if you will, is the opposite of an old wives' tale and should never be ignored or ridiculed. So, when other friends said, "Going from zero to one kid is a battle, but going from one kid to two kids is like going to war," I took it seriously, because everybody knows that war is hell.

In fact, I felt like we'd already been through a war with one kid. At least, I had. For three years, I'd been the first-string quarterback and MVP (most valuable parent). I was man-to-man with our little man, who was not only colicky but chronically ill with upper-respiratory infections. *I* called the majority of the plays, and *I* took the hardest hits after already fighting the difficult battles of pregnancy, nursing and sleepless nights alone. It was tough, and Eric and I fought more in the first year of parenthood than we did in the previous six years of our marriage. It took us a long time to learn how to work as a team and we both bear scars from the battles. Benjamin Franklin famously said, "Keep your eyes wide open before marriage, half shut afterwards." Ah, more truth!

What were we fighting about? I have always believed that Eric can do each and every parenting task as well as I can, and some better. He just didn't choose to very often. He would help me when I asked him to, but I had to ask. I always had to ask. It frustrated me that he just assumed it was my job to do the majority of the caregiving and I bitched about it incessantly.

"Words, words, words, why do I always have to, words, you never, words, how the hell do you sleep through the crying, words," is what I think he heard during those first few years. If we were to grow our family, I knew I would be the one taking the metaphorical bullet for the next nine months, but I could NOT do for two kids what I did for one. Eric would need to step up his game, add some weapons to his parenting arsenal and commit to increased practice. Not only would he need to be more active as a parent; he would need to be more proactive. He agreed. Eric really wanted another kid. He said a lot of words. Words, words, words and more words, and I trusted him and believed his words. He promised to be at the top of his game.

Neither of us considered the idea that I'd actually spend a good portion of my second pregnancy in a time-out. At twenty-six weeks along, I was put on strict bed rest. I was in and out of the hospital. Baby number two wasn't even born and she was proving to be just as worthy an adversary. Eric had to take care of all three of us. He was the lone zone defender of our team for the next three and a half months.

Ironically, the baby who seemed hell-bent on coming into the world early would spend the next two years of her life doing everything else late. She was late reaching every developmental milestone. Cate refused to drink from a bottle or a cup, demanding the boob for every feeding well past her first birthday. Solid food? No, thanks. Sitting up? What's the rush? Crawling? Never. Cate never crawled. When she was fifteen months old, she considered walking and took her first steps, only to decide that walking really wasn't for her after all. She would not try again for another three months. When she did decide it was go time, she also decided that she would never fucking stop. She was the Forrest Gump of toddlers. Wherever she went, she was running! If she wasn't running, it was because she was sleeping. And whether she was running or sleeping, she was the epitome of Freud's theory of oral fixation. Her mouth was always full. Instead of most solid foods, she preferred either my boob, one of her ninety-three pacifiers, or filthy, toxic, sharp and dangerous objects she had the knack for finding. Naps and clothes were met with the same enthusiasm as you and I might have for being hit on the head with bricks. Cate made sure her daddy kept his word!

Another helpful adage when parenting more than one child is "divide and conquer." Each parent takes one kid. An experienced parent will tell you that once you've survived the madness of zone defense, going back to man-to-man is like having a break. This is true in many situations, with all different types of kids. Unfortunately, in our particular situation, with our particular kid, the divide-and-conquer adage does not apply.

Cate is a zone all on her own.

Because of this, Eric and I decided that our best defense against Cate, a skilled and powerful opponent, would be to build up our offense. We baby-proofed the living FUCK out of our house and decided to significantly decrease the boundaries of Cate's zone. Keeping the naked danger magnet safe was a full-time job, and she wasn't our only lunatic offspring who needed care and keeping. Zach needed us too. It frustrated him when Calamity Cate was constantly on the move and I had to chase her instead of pay attention to him. So, converting the dining room into a playroom became the new game plan! We all hoped that having her in close proximity to all of us in a baby-safe environment would significantly reduce the number of chase-and-rescue-Cate missions.

The first step was to paint the dining room. Eric and I promptly had a big fight over who would paint and who would be in charge of the crotchfruit that day. Neither of us wanted to be in charge of the kids. Painting would be a break! In fairness, we were both exhausted. Like most families with young children, we were on the go all the time, rarely got a minute to relax, and aside from brief phone conversations (that were mostly about the kids), we had little time for just the two of us and what time we had was often interrupted by a needy kid. We were ripe to fight and fight we did!

I was pissed when I lost the coin toss deciding who would paint, and not just because it would have meant a break. I have always been organized slash borderline OCD when it comes to home-improvement projects. The reason is simple: it makes cleanup easy, and since I'm the one who cleans everyfucking-thing up, I like to make it easy on myself. Eric is *not* organized. His painting process makes me cringe. Drop cloth? Fuck that. He doesn't put down the drop cloth, use painter's tape or wipe down the straight edges. Painting supplies are scattered, misplaced and messed up and sometimes it takes him a week to completely clean up after himself. For years I was able to keep my eyes, ears and mouth shut, not picking at him or complaining and just being grateful for his efforts. All that changed once we had kids. I had to keep my kids safe; therefore, Eric got an earful from me on the regular about how his clusterfucky style and slobbish home-improvement habits created a dangerous environment. Eric is just as good a parent as I am, but it must be said that I am more vigilant when it comes to safety.

I would have preferred to get the kids out of the house on painting day, but it was freezing cold, so playing outside wasn't an option, and we had zero dollars to take them to an amusement venue. Besides, I couldn't handle zone defense in a crowded public place.

So, stuck with a playing field littered with ladders, paint and scattered tools, I needed a perfectly executed game plan. I hauled both kids upstairs, hoping for the best. Game on, motherfucker!

We were upstairs all of five minutes before Zach declared that he was "starving" and "dying of thirst." Of course he was. I was so focused on defense that I had forgotten to create a good offense. It was lunchtime and I had neglected to feed the kiddos. I trudged downstairs to whip up a little something for them to eat. On the way down I called out to Eric, "I forgot to feed the kids lunch. I need you to watch for them while I make stuff!" I hustled to the kitchen, knowing I had to be quick about it. "Yup, just hurry it up," he said. "I want to knock this out before the game starts." Oh yeah, the Bears were playing! He'd definitely want me on kid duty during the game, which meant bedtime would be mine all mine to read a book and drink wine! I was going to drink a lot of wine and I could not wait for some me time. GO TEAM GO! Yes, I would do my part and show some meal-making hustle.

I got down to business making minimally messy kid fare, since we wouldn't be eating at the kitchen table. "Mooooooooom!"

Zach bellowed from upstairs. "Can I have chocolate milk please!!!" I was just on my way back upstairs when the dog started having a seizure. I dropped the lunch tray on the kitchen counter and ran to her, trying to guide her into the kitchen as her legs buckled and her eyes rolled. "Shhhh . . . it's okay, girl," I crooned, laying her down on the floor and stroking her as she jerked and shook, urinating all over the floor (which is why we always tried to get her into the kitchen and off the carpet). I called out to Eric, letting him know the game was in time-out. I had to take care of Mona. One of us always comforted her, making sure she was safe, and then without fail, as the shaking stopped and she started to come around, she would erupt with a post-seizure puke, so there would be quite a bit of cleanup involved. It would be a long time-out.

As soon as it was over and Mona was stable, I cleaned up the pee and puke, retrieved the lunch tray and headed upstairs. As I passed the dining room I paused to tell Eric that he was off duty. That's when I realized he was never ON duty! Our naked daughter was standing on the bottom step of the ladder, sucking on one dripping paintbrush and dipping another one into the open can of paint. Thick, white paint was dripping out of her mouth. She looked at the tray I was carrying and then at my face. I could tell she was upset; she flipped the paintbrush out of her mouth and pointed to the tray with it.

"MUUUUUUOOOUMM WHHEESSS MUH CHOOOKLOOOOT MUUUKKK?"

What? What was she saying? She stepped off the ladder and started running towards me, still trying to tell me something. "Whess muh choooklooooot muuuuk?" Globs of paint were falling out of her mouth onto the carpet, which of course was NOT covered with a drop cloth. "Holy shit, Eric! I thought you were watching the fucking kids!" I screamed, running back into the kitchen to put down the lunch tray and grab some towels. "Cate's got a mouthful of fucking primer! FUCK!" I was yelling my face off and dropping f-bombs like a World War II fighter pilot. "Why weren't you watching her? Oh my GOD!"

I went on and on as I tried to pry the paintbrushes out of her fists. She started flailing and screaming, not wanting to let go. There was so much paint in her mouth. The stuff just kept spilling out as she yelled at me, pointing to the tray in the kitchen. Holy fuckbags, I had no idea how much she had actually swallowed. I was sweating profusely, panicking and hollering at Eric to call the poison control number. Goddammit all to motherfucking asshat fucknuts! I was shaking as hard as Mona during her seizure. Oh god, where was Zach? Who knows what he had gotten into during all this unsupervised time? "ZACH!" I called out for him. "I'm in here, Mom!" came a voice from the kitchen.

I looked in the kitchen and Zach was sitting on the counter, sucking down his chocolate milk through a silly straw and throwing Cheetos to the dogs, snickering as they caught them midair. Eric had cracked open a beer and was applauding the dogs for their good catches. Cate was kicking me so hard trying to escape from my arms that I thought I felt a rib crack. I released her and she sprinted to the kitchen toward her daddy, still clutching both paintbrushes in her paint-covered hands, using one of them to point to something on the counter. I felt woozy, like none of it could be real.

She flung herself into Eric's legs. He hoisted her up and asked her what she wanted. Cate's tongue and lips (and face and hands and torso) were coated with paint, but her mouth was empty enough for her to speak clearly. The counter was covered with craft supplies, dirty dishes, and unopened mail. Zach had shoved the mess aside in order to make himself a space to sit and eat. What the hell did she want now? Cheetos? The paint was more nutritious.

"Mom forgot MY chocolate milk!" Cate cried, pointing at her Disney Princess sippy cup, sitting on the counter amidst the mounds of crap. "She didn't bring *my* chocolate milk!" Eric handed her the cup and she started sucking down the milk, presumably to wash down the rest of the primer, but also because she had finally gotten her mitts on what she wanted from the time she saw that it was missing from the tray that I was bringing upstairs at the time I busted her guzzling paint. Calamity Cate was correct. I was in such a hurry and so distracted by Mona's seizure, I had neglected to put her chocolate milk cup on the tray. Some might say that she was so hungry and thirsty, she had no choice but to suck down some paint, but some would be wrong. If Cate had been near the dog's puke instead of the paint, my poster child for oral fixation would have sampled that instead.

"I'm calling poison control. We should take her to the emergency room! She could die from lead poisoning!" I cried, grabbing Cate out of Eric's arms. I was getting ready to resume screaming at him. How could he let this happen? Did I have to have eyes everywhere? Wasn't it enough that I was home with the kids 24/7, rarely getting a break? Could he not take *a few minutes* to keep an eye on the kids while I was making them food and taking care of our fucking epileptic dog? "Nic, the paint is water-based. Look at her! She's fine! There's no way she had enough for it to kill her or even poison her. Maybe she'll end up yakking it up later, but I've seen her eat worse. Remember when she ate poop out of her training potty?"

Yes, I remembered. That happened on my watch. Shit.

I handed Cate back to Eric. "Fine, then *you* hold her. I've already cleaned up puke today. The next one's on YOU!" I looked at the clock. It was still lunchtime, and I was hungry. I went to the fridge and pulled out a bottle of wine. Momma would be having a liquid lunch. Everyone else was having a drink anyway and because I love old adages, I decided to let another favorite guide me that afternoon: if you can't beat 'em, join 'em.

BUBBLE GUM AND
BAD INFLUENCES

Recently Cate was jumping rope with her little buddy Mavis (not her real name). "Ice cream soda with a cherry on top, how many boyfriends do you GOT?" Cate called out in her sweet, singsong voice and proceeded to count jumps/boyfriends: "One, two, three . . ."

Hmmm . . . that was a jump rope rhyme I'd never heard. I didn't much like the boyfriend-counting reference in that particular song. I knew she wasn't currently a big fan of boys, but I didn't want her thinking it was normal to have enough boyfriends that they needed to be counted. The jump rope songs of my childhood were silly and innocent. I was under the impression the songs were supposed to help kids with their gross motor and counting skills, not to prepare them for a future collecting boy toys.

Oh my god, I was overthinking it. It's just a fucking jump rope chant, nothing to get upset about, I told myself. Why was I thinking about the future, letting my worries distract me from the joy of watching her be all adorable-like? Probably because one of my current worries was about how early young girls are sexualized these days.

I sat in the grass sucking on what might have been my

twenty-second grape Popsicle (I had stopped counting after twelve so I couldn't be sure), contemplating my tendency to overreact. As usual, I had to resist letting my psychology professional paranoia flare up every time either one of my kids said something that reminded me how hard it was to protect their innocence in a media-saturated, sex-focused world. Enjoy the moment, be a mom, and stop overanalyzing, I told myself. Stop being a therapist, assessing and interpreting words as if every interaction is a counseling session, and enjoy watching your baby girl and her friend play. At seven years old, she wasn't really a baby anymore, but she was MY baby. Maybe that's why thinking about her having even one boyfriend, let alone a bunch of them, raised my blood pressure a bit.

Although I was glad to be getting quicker and better at recognizing my paranoid thoughts and shutting them down, it still bothered me that I allowed myself to get all jammed up with concern over a couple of Brownies from Troop 184 singing about having multiple boyfriends in a silly jump rope song! I still had to work hard to consciously turn that contemplation shit OFF.

And I did. I worked at it! But old habits die hard: even after almost eight years since actively working as a therapist, I had difficulty remembering that it's really only a tiny number of grade school kids who are sexually active or even sexually aware. In fact, my professional experience with sexualized kids contributed heavily to my decision to be a stay-at-home mom after my daughter was born. I had become jaded and suspicious of people based on what I had seen and heard from children over the years. It scared me, made me sad and angry. It changed my worldview completely, and not in the "change is good" kind of way. I was scarred for life.

It's fair to say that I was, am, and will always be stuck in a state of hypervigilance when it comes to my kids, and this hypervigilance is a major problem at times. I'm oversensitive and borderline paranoid, as evidenced by my reaction to a jump rope song about boyfriends. You'd have thought my daughter was a teenager who had just confessed to being a pregnant super-slut with a bad case of the clap who could only guess the identity of her baby's daddy, instead of a grade school virgin who had just celebrated her seventh birthday and believed all boys, including Justin Bieber, to be "yucky." So, you can see that saying my tendency to overreact is a major problem is not, I repeat NOT, overstating my anxiety, although the problem has lessened as the years pass.

That being said, when it came to protecting my kids from being exposed to things or people that would harm them, I didn't fuck around. My goal has always been to give my kids a long and trauma-free childhood. This is the major reason I continued to be at home with my children long after they both could have easily handled the change and I could find a safe and trusted caregiver. Still, it was not an easy choice. I missed my career. I really missed the regular adult interaction. And I desperately missed the paycheck. But I was also having a blast being home and had developed a knack for stall tactics when it came to finding a full-time job outside of the house once again.

And so, on that sunshiny day of job-search-stalling and jump-rope-watching fun, I shook off the worry and relaxed as my daughter's dirty duet partner launched into a round of "Bubble gum, bubble gum in a dish, how many pieces do you wish?" My daughter joined in immediately.

PHEW! Thank you, wee Mavis (*not* her real name)! Much better. Counting bubble gum sounded much more appropriate from a couple of grade school girls.

They continued singing a variety of adorable and familiar

242 | NICOLE KNEPPER

songs and jumping rope with squeals of delight. Little girls are fascinating creatures, so innocent and full of whimsical energy and fun! Of course I realize that sometimes they can be whiny, bossy, bitchy and moody, but mostly they are too busy being creative, using their unbelievable imaginations to make life interesting and awesome.

It was an exceptionally beautiful summer day—not a cloud in the sky, with a light breeze that was just enough to keep us cool and comfortable outside despite the bright sun and what my daughter called, "the hot, hot heat." I was caught up in the moment, watching the girls and listening to their silly conversations and pretend play. The exuberance was contagious. Listening to them dissolve into giggles made me feel like serotonin had replaced the blood supply throughout my entire body. I was at risk of dying from an overdose of happiness. It took me back to a time when I giggled and squealed in the sunshine with my friends, jumping rope for hours without tripping over the rope repeatedly because my arthritic knee went out or having to stop to put on another bra in order to contain my now gigantic and floppy jugs.

I remembered the song about the bubble gum well and sang along. How many hundreds of times had I giggled and squealed and jumped while calling out that chant?

I relaxed in the shade reading and bingeing on purple Popsicles, while they spent the afternoon letting their Popsicles melt all over their faces, playing on the swing set, running through the sprinkler and jumping rope. "Watch me, Mom!" my daughter would shriek over and over, flashing her jack-o'-lantern grin. I felt my heart flutter, not even a bit irritated by the never-ending demands of both girls to be watched and applauded for their efforts. After many years wrestling with frustration and grief over what I thought to be the loss of my career and identity, I had finally learned how to appreciate and enjoy how special and important it was for me to be able to be with my daughter on a full-time basis for as long as I had. Work would always be there for me, but Cate's childhood would be over before I knew it.

I had finally come to understand and actually believe that my mother was telling the truth when she told my brother and me that she loved us "the same amount, but in different ways," and why she had chosen full-time motherhood over a career. I loved my daughter as desperately as I loved my son, yet it was impossible to compare or explain the complexity and distinction of my feelings for each of them. Any parent with more than one kid knows exactly what I mean and why the decision to work outside the home or not—if it is a decision rather than a necessity—is based on very individualized and personal circumstances.

I went back to work six months after the birth of my son. It was right for us at the time. I was losing my shit at home, alone with a colicky baby and severe postpartum depression. I missed work, as I was not yet burned out by years of counseling traumatized children. I still liked people, trusted most of them and managed to sleep at night despite the sadness of my job. Returning to work after my daughter was born four years later wasn't an option. By then, I had become burnt out and bitter. My soul was charred to a crisp. I needed a break from the sadness and a chance to heal. I was exhausted and angry, a distrustful people-hater. I was in a dark place and refused to trust anyone with the care and keeping of my kids. Being with them full-time seemed like a great way to get some perspective and restore my faith in humanity. I didn't know how long of a break I would take, but I can tell you that I did not intend to be a stay-at-home mom for the next seven years.

But even after seven years, I still wasn't completely ready to trust another person enough to leave my young children with them for ten hours a day while I threw myself back into the rat race. I wasn't charred any longer, but I was still a bit crispy and very suspicious. Since we needed two incomes, working part-time from home as a writer and a mental health consultant was a step towards easing back into full-time work. It was a shift in the direction of my career and certainly required me to leave my kids on occasion, but that was a compromise I was willing to make. My kids were only with people we knew well and trusted implicitly and only for short periods of time. Kind of ironic, though, that just as I had learned to embrace being at home, it had become crucial for me to generate income. We needed more money.

I vowed to enjoy the time I had left having the best of both worlds working part-time from home. Watching my bare-foot daughter sing and jump rope with her wavy, brown hair blowing in the wind was without question THE best of the best. Despite that silly boyfriend song, I felt more than a wee bit cocky about my success keeping my children safe and trauma-free for so many years.

Sure, I knew it wouldn't last forever, that my daughter had the personality of a potential stubborn, smart-ass, boy-crazy teenager, but I also believed that my vigilance was helping to stretch out her innocence, to prevent her from becoming aware of grown-up things before her body and mind were ready to handle them. I was proud of this and grateful for the oppor-tunity.

"Watch me, Mom," she called out, "listen to my song," as she started to jump rope and sing.

"Hey, girlfriend, you want to have fun? Here comes Justin with his pants undone!"

WHAT?

Did she just say what I think she said?

No.

I must have heard it wrong.

More no.

There is NO WAY she just sang about having fun with a boy who had his pants undone.

No. Fucking. Way.

She kept singing as her friend joined in. I leaned forward to listen more carefully.

"He is really, really dirty and can do the splits . . ." they sang together. Yeah, that part was clear as a bell. That Justin kid with his pants undone is dirty and can do the splits? Damn right he's dirty. I think this was the point in the song where catatonia began setting in.

"Close your eyes, guuuuuuuurl (she drew it out nice and long), count to ten. If you mess up, you'll have to marry him! One, two, three . . ."

Had I not been gagging on inhaled grape ice, I would have passed out. Not only was the jump rope song totally inappropriate, but it didn't even rhyme for god sakes! This also upset me!

They continued counting to ten. They giggled, squealed, counted and jumped, not noticing my statuelike stillness and mouth hanging wide open in between desperate gasps for air.

Did I really just hear a couple of second graders chant a little ditty about having to marry a dirty exhibitionist named Justin because she got knocked up after ten seconds of unprotected sex?

I definitely did *not* sing that one when I was a kid.

They sang another round. I was still frozen (except for the gagging and coughing fits), listening again to make sure I hadn't mangled the words in my jaded, perved-out mind the first time around. I had not.

"Cate, where did you hear that?" I managed to blurt out while trying to contain a nervous laugh. I do that: laugh when I'm confused or scared. I can't be sure if it was thirty seconds or thirty minutes later that I was finally able to break out of my paralysis and organize my senses enough to ask her that simple question. I do know the girls had already launched into another song, and although I was still in shock and can't be one hundred percent sure, I think it was about dog poop.

Maybe there would be a time when I thought this was hilarious, but as I looked at Cate and Mavis (not her real name!) with their bathing suits and Popsicle-stained hands I felt horrified. They were singing about sex as innocently as they sang about bubble gum and ice cream. Did they have any idea what the words meant? The paranoid, distrustful therapist in me began to panic. Had somebody asked either one of them to have some fun while his pants were undone?

I felt the acidic tidal wave of purple hurl from the two dozen grape Popsicles I'd hogged down rising up my esophagus.

I took a deep breath and buried my face in my hands. After the urge to puke felt manageable and I got control of my nervous giggles, I asked them to stop jumping and counting so that I could talk to them.

"Girls, that song about Justin with his pants undone is very inappropriate," I calmly explained to them. "What you are talking about in the song is . . . well, it's . . . um . . . do you understand what you are singing?"

No response. They were standing on the sidewalk holding their jump ropes in silence.

Okay . . . I guess I wasn't clear. What should I say next? How could I rephrase the question?

What the fuck? In all my years working with kids professionally, I'd never been this tongue-tied when discussing sexuality. I urped up another wave of grape hurl into my mouth and swallowed it before it could escape. My throat was burning, my heart was pounding and my mind was racing.

I didn't know what to do, what to say, how to even begin to handle the situation. This wasn't a sexually knowledgeable kid I was working with. My naïve little girl's innocence was teetering in the balance. Luckily Cate broke the silence.

"Julia (not her real name) taught me that song, Mom. Why is it inappropriate?" She was clueless, confused by my overreaction, her big, brown eyes unblinkingly focused on mine.

I had to remain calm. Not only didn't I know how to explain but my mind had already leaped ahead to something that worried me just as much as what I'd heard: I was going to have to tell Julia's (not her real name) mother about the song, and explain the incident to Mavis's parents (not her real name either). Her conservative, strict parents were already wary of my laid-back parenting style.

I wanted to scream some bad words, because a good yelling of the words "horseshit" or "rat farts" never fails to help me burn off some frustration and collect my thoughts. I felt like a horseshit rat fart, too. Had I failed to protect my daughter? Had she lost her innocence under my watch?

"MOM!" Cate squeaked, yanking on my shorts and snapping me out of my fog. "Mom, why is that song inappropriate?" Yeah, Mom, answer the fucking question, MOM! What's so inappropriate about the song? Why didn't I want them to sing about a dirty child molester while jumping rope?

"Girls," I began, knowing I could no longer stall or avoid the inevitable, "it is not appropriate to sing about a boy asking a girl to have fun with his pants undone. Even if it's the girl's

248 | NICOLE KNEPPER

boyfriend it is not okay. First of all, when two people decide to hug and kiss and touch, it should be a private thing and . . ."

You see where I was totally screwed, right? I took a few deep breaths before continuing. Holding back another wave of burning vomit gave me a moment to think and that's when I realized I was going about this the wrong way. Distracting them was my only chance at buying some time to work it through. I was sweating profusely, both from the heat and the panic I was experiencing.

"Listen, girls, how about if we talk about this later and sing the good song about gum? You know what song I'm talking about, right? The bubble gum song! That's VERY appropriate and so fun, right? And we can all sing it together! Bubble gum is so awesome. What kind of bubble gum would you want in your dish? Do you guys want some bubble gum? Let's go inside and get some bubble gum. Do you want to learn how to blow bubbles?" I babbled on excitedly with a fake smile plastered on my face while grabbing them both by their little hands and dragging them into the house. That's right, Momma, talk about bubble gum! Keep talking.

Their vacant stares were replaced by toothy grins at the prospect of gum! Good stall, I thought to myself, you got this, guuuuuuuurl! I just did NOT want to talk about the song at all. As long as I could keep avoiding it, I would. I snickered to myself, thinking that my performance was worthy of some kind of acting award. Maybe not an Oscar, but certainly an MTV award for best performance in a dramedy. I believed that my distraction technique had done the trick. There would be no more talk of Justin with his pants undone for the time being. At least I thought there wouldn't be, but then good old Mavis (not her real name) came up with her own award-worthy distraction. It reminded me of Kanye West dissing Taylor Swift while she was *onstage* receiving a VH-1 or VMA or whatever award, claiming that Beyoncé deserved it more. I could just hear her words. "Mrs. Knepper, I know you think bubble gum and your ego had us all riveted and fascinated, and I'm gonna let you finish, but first let me say that Justin gave a performance full of mystery and intrigue that made yours seem weak by comparison."

No, she didn't say that. What she did say was this:

"Hey, Cate, didn't Julia learn that song on the American Girl Web site?"

I just barely resisted the urge to laugh, but only because I was hotter than hell and still experiencing waves of barf that needed to be restrained and contained until I could reach an appropriate vomit receptacle.

I was prepared to offer up all sorts of junk food and fun activities in order to distract the girls. Pizza, popcorn, ice cream, lemonade slushies, arts and crafts or a movie! I figured they had to be hungry and ready to chill out anyway. I know I was. We had been outside for hours in the heat, jumping around, eating nothing but Popsicles, but before I could suggest it, Cate was already addressing the allegedly slutty songstresses of American Girl. I bit my lip and swallowed grape puke as many times as I could. Was anything going to work with these two? If I puked purple Popsicle juice on their feet I bet they would be distracted.

"Yep," said my daughter, "she did. But we don't even like American Girl, right, Mom, 'cause it's a racket and a rip-off!"

That's my girl, I thought as I grinned! I felt proud that she understood why spending ten gazillion dollars on clothes and a bedroom set for a goddamn doll she wouldn't care about in a few years' time was NOT a good idea. It made me feel a little less pukey and upset. But she wasn't done talking.

"My mom says those fat bitches are worse than criminals, and that they crush dreams of poor kids whose parents can't even afford to feed them, so they can never have special dolls. My mom says they should be ashamed of themselves. But the fat American Girl bitches aren't as bad as those people watching all that humping and stuff on YouTube, right, Mom? Right? Right, Mom? Mom? MOM?"

(Just for the record, I NEVER called the American Girl people fat bitches. Greedy opportunist motherfuckers, maybe, but definitely not fat bitches.)

That's when I puked for real. It was a boiling hot, deep purple force of nature and smelled like sugarcoated shame. Was this how Milli Vanilli felt when everyone found out they were lying shit-bags? I fancied myself as a gatekeeper of my daughter's innocence, yet in reality I was more like a gateway drug.

"Right you are, kiddo," I managed to whisper when I finished barfing, and despite the boiling bile still dripping out of my nostrils, I could no longer hold back my giggles. The time to laugh about the whole thing had arrived MUCH sooner than I had anticipated.

My laugh quickly turned into a cry, still gagging on the occasional wave of stomach acid trying to escape, and tears were rolling down my cheeks. The whole thing wasn't just funny; it was ironic, ridiculous and chock-full of mind-fuckery. I'd eaten slices of humble pie before, but this was like eating the whole goddamn thing at one sitting. This time, I had made the pie, served it and eaten it all by myself. There was absolutely no one else to blame. It was a defining moment for me. My girl needed as much protection from me as she did from Justin with his pants undone or those fat bitch American Girl people (allegedly) teaching little miss Julia dirty songs online.

It was the moment I realized one of the best ways I could protect my daughter would be to get my filthy mouth and mind away from her, to get a job, full-time, OUT of the house. I

BUBBLE GUM AND BAD INFLUENCES | 251

started looking for a job like it *was* my job and scouring the Internet for a stranger I could pay to care for my kids while I worked. I mean there's really no reason to worry. From what I hear the nanny Web sites do background checks on those child-care professionals so you don't end up hiring some perverted bastard—right?

The girl kid is whining about her spelling packet. "Why do I have to learn to spell the words 'fatigue' and 'argue,' Mom? I'll never use them in real life." I just nod in agreement. I'm too fatigued to argue with her.

JESUS, GEORGE
WASHINGTON, IPODS
AND ICE CREAM

CATE   Who was in charge before God?

ME   Nobody.

CATE   Somebody had to be in charge.

ME   Yes, I suppose so. I've never thought about that.

CATE   You should. I think it was probably Jesus or his sister.

ME   Did Jesus have a sister?

CATE   He did.

ME   Who told you that?

CATE   You learn that in God school.

ME   What is God school?

CATE   It's where you go get communion, learn about Jesus, and get money from your family for an iPod.

ME   Do you mean religious education?

CATE   That's what you call it! I need religious education and communion so that I can get an iPod.

ME   Religious education isn't something you do so that you can get money for an iPod. You do that so that you can learn about God and Jesus. And not everybody gets enough money for an iPod for his or her first communion. And we aren't Catholic. Catholics go all out for the first communion. It's a more low-key type of thing in our religion. Not likely to net you enough cash for an iPod.

CATE   Then how will I ever get an iPod?

ME   You can do chores and save money.

CATE   Can I just eat the blood of Jesus and get my money?

ME   That's not how it works.

CATE   Yes, it does. My friends have iPods that they bought with the money they got from getting congratulations for eating Jesus.

ME   I know you understand what I'm saying here. I know you do.

CATE   What if God told you to get me an iPod?

ME   Still no.

CATE   Who was in charge before George Washington?

ME   I have no idea.

CATE   Somebody had to be.

ME   I've never thought about it.

CATE   You should. It was probably God.

ME   Probably. Or Jesus. Maybe Jesus' sister?

CATE   I bet George Washington had an iPod.

ME   What makes you think that?

CATE   Because even if he didn't eat Jesus, the president just gets what he wants.

ME   You should run for president someday.

CATE   I think it would just be easier to eat Jesus and get my money. Why are we in the iPod store if you don't want to buy me an iPod?

ME   I have no idea. You want to go get some ice cream?

CATE   I'd rather have an iPod.

TERRIFYING TOGETHERNESS:
Traditions, Tender Moments and Life Lessons

"Nothing says holidays like a cheese log."

—Ellen DeGeneres

Zach: Will you scoop me some ice cream?

Me: Sure, if you pour me a glass of wine.

Zach: I didn't want to get up though. I'd have to get up to pour you a glass of wine.

Me: Yes, and then you can get yourself some ice cream too. See how that works? We would both get what we want. Yay!

SUCK IT, SANTA CLAUS

When Zach was nine years old, he decided to use some of the Christmas money he had saved to buy the book *Twilight*. I know what you're thinking. He's nine years old and I'm letting him read fucking *TWILIGHT*? Well, I had heard enough about the campy vamp series not to be too worried about the content, AND I was done being nagged about taking him to the bookstore for the hundredth time. So off we went! I realize that most nine-year-olds are much too young to be reading lusty vampire lore, but my spawn wasn't your average nine-year-old. Of course THAT is another story; in THIS story, he wanted to read about vampires and I let him buy the goddamn book. He'd read all of the Harry Potter books, knew where babies came from (though not how they got there) and he hadn't believed in Santa Claus for years. Some moms may think all of this sad and wonder where his childhood went. I am not one of those moms. I'm not sad now and I certainly wasn't too sad then. If he had still believed in that bullshit mythical creature nonsense, he would have been doubly disappointed in the days to come, because this was Easter week, and I was about to come close to outing the Easter Bunny.

The book he'd nagged me about for a week, the book he HAD to have, turned out to be "more lame and boring than the Hardy Boys mysteries that Dad thinks are so cool." He made this statement after reading ten pages. Ten lousy pages and he wanted me to run him back to the store to return the book. Um, NO! I encouraged him to continue. He told me he'd rather suck a turd than read one more page of *Twilight*. I claimed that it couldn't be that bad and he quickly pointed out that since I hadn't read it yet, how the hell did I know it wasn't that bad? Touché!

So I picked it up and started reading; as a proud book snob, I'd know after a couple of paragraphs whether the book was really worthy of a trip back to the return line at the bookstore. After a quick "look-see," as I called it, I immediately fell deeply in love with Edward the sparkly vampire and the rest of the Cullen clan. I was so immersed in the story that I forked over the cash he would have gotten as a refund. Money well spent. I'da paid him twice that to continue avoiding the twenty things I needed to do in order to prepare for the Easter holiday. I'm such a procrastinator that I have actually run out of gas multiple times, and besides, I was loving the shit out of *Twilight*!

There was nothing I wanted more on that particular Thursday than to continue to indulge in the lusty tale of the brooding, undead Edward and the shy, clumsy Bella. I was hooked. Like a crack whore needs to bang out rock, I had come to NEED *Twilight* after the first hit. And since I had successfully whipped together many a holiday at the last minute, I threw frozen pizza and grapes at the kids for dinner and snuggled up with the book, letting all thoughts of ham and bunnies and eggs and cleaning fade away into the twilight (see what I did there?).

By Saturday, I was halfway into the ***fourth*** book of the magical and completely implausible series about the vamps and wolves in Forks, knowing damn well that I was way behind on my duties as the Easter Bunny. I told myself that I still had plenty of time to make Easter all pomp and circumstancy! There was just no way I could put my whole heart into the Easter Bunny stuff until I knew whether Bella Swan was going to die having her little monster baby.

And poor Edward, right? That sensitive bastard was a loose cannon and I was deep enough in fantasy to be confused as to whether or not I might actually BE a character in the book; you know, like the quirky BFF he talked to when Bella was being a whiny, insecure bitch (like she was ALL the fucking time, especially in *New Moon*), and who he would realize he was in love with all along after the mutant baby killed Bella by chewing its way out of her vagina. It could happen. Mmmmm . . . of course he would have to understand that I was married with children and . . . OH MY GOD! You see the problem here? I just needed to get through the book and back to reality.

I still had at least three hundred pages to read! Crap! I've been able to pee, eat and even feign interest in my kids while I'm reading, but I knew that I could *not* fill and hide Easter eggs and read at the same time. Don't get me wrong. I've got MAD holiday skills. I'm good. A lifetime of procrastination has only sharpened these skills—I can multitask like a motherfucker—but I'm just not THAT good (yet). Those plastic eggs weren't going to fill and hide themselves. The only thing I wanted to do less than stop reading my book and fill and hide the eggs was to have a mutant vampire parasite ripping its way out of my body, but who else was going to do it? The *real* Easter Bunny? God, I wished!

Around here, I am the Easter Bunny, the Tooth Fairy, Santa fatty Claus and whatever other make-believe bullshit fantasy hybrid assigned to whatever event or holiday is taking place. It's me, myself and I who always end up scrambling around last minute, making the materialistic mystical dreams of my children come true. It chaps my ass that these implausible beings take all the damn credit for all the cool stuff I say no to all the rest of the days of the year. I personally find the perpetuation of these myths to be tough, but necessary. It's tough not just because of the lying involved, but because it's labor-intensive to be a good liar. I'm not a fan of putting too much effort into something that isn't going to last forever, but childhood memories *do* last forever, even if the belief in mythical creatures does not, so labor I will! It takes a shitload of time to decorate, bake, shop, hide, wrap and stuff, and it always costs fifty-six times more than we budget for. See? TOUGH! It's also a thankless job. My efforts go completely unrecognized and mostly unappreciated, yet if I miss one little detail, everyfuckingbody notices. Why do I do it? Like I said, childhood memories last and I'm committed to making good memories for the fruit of my loins.

And for me, the stress over the cash and labor disappears the moment I see the sheer joy my kids experience during each and every holiday celebration. I love to relive the magic of childhood through my children: hearing them squeal with delight, and watching them practically kill themselves tripping over each other to get the most eggs in the Easter egg hunt or to open their Christmas presents is dreamy mom stuff. They get all spastic and jumpy and flushed from all the excitement and the inevitable sugar buzz and then predictably they melt into irritable, exhausted goo as the buzz wears off and the fun slows down. That's when I end up with the ultimate reward: a warm body, usually in some sort of character pj's, snuggled up in my lap or snoring in my ear next to me in bed.

Soon after they wake, they are off to guard their loads of teeth-rotting sugary treats and hoard the plastic toys from China in bedrooms and toy boxes already packed with long-forgotten shit that they were equally excited about once upon a time. All the recognition I really need is witnessing those entertaining and tender moments . . . and when they are occupied with all the new junk, I can sneak away and curl up with *my* presents, which are always piles of new books!

I know that some people actually refuse to entertain or maintain these magnificent charades with their crotchfruit. For them it's not just the labor involved. There are people who think that suggesting the existence of an itty-bitty fairy that collects dead hunks of calcium from under children's pillows in return for cold, hard cash is lying.

DAMN RIGHT, IT'S LYING!

I don't know many parents who don't sprinkle almost every interaction with their children from birth to at least age ten with harmless, sugary-sweet fibs. These stories aren't harmful; they actually encourage the imagination, wonder and intelligence of the developing minds of children. I adore the idea of prolonged innocence and awesome imagination, especially since my son didn't experience this blissful time for more than about five minutes. I desperately wanted to support my daughter's suspended disbelief for as long as possible. I would *not* burst her bubble of joyful naiveté like I did with her brother. Let me rephrase that: I would *not* burst her bubble of joyful naiveté like her brother FORCED ME TO DO while he was still practically a toddler.

When my son was only five years old, we were coloring at his midget-sized wooden play table. As he sat across from me on a tiny, red wooden chair he said—as calmly as if he was just asking me to pass the green crayon—"Mom, is Santa Claus real? I want you to know that if you lie to me, you'll probably go to hell. The Bible says that."

WHAT THE FUCK?

He had even brought God into this! Clever boy. His blue

eyes were like lasers, blasting into my brain and annihilating all the bullshit that was trying to move from my mind to my mouth.

His baby blues did NOT break contact with mine. The kid didn't even blink. He was a serious little guy by nature, and big on rule following. Since it was just the two of us that particular night, no husband or other kid awake and demanding attention to distract me, I was stuck. I would have given a kidney for the dog to have a seizure at just that moment. My heart was pounding. I was being challenged by a kindergartner in a button-down shirt and khakis wearing a superhero cape and nerd glasses so that he could look like Peter Parker, yet his eyes revealed the soul of an old man. I couldn't imagine him losing the magic of Santa at such a young age, but I had never outright lied to him when he asked me a direct question. EVER!

He didn't blink. The dog didn't seize. I was going to rip his childhood apart with one word. One tiny word had the power to change his life forever. Could I lie? Could I stand the heat in hell? I'd probably know most of the people once I got down there, but it's just so fucking HOT.

Lying makes me sweat and I hate being hot. The sweat is my "tell" and the little terrorist interrogating me had a smug smirk beginning to peel across his face, as he maintained his blink-free and fidget-less position across from me in his red midget chair. He knew the truth, but wanted to hear me say it. I knew I couldn't lie to him. I'm a shitty liar, but shitty liars are great stallers. We stall until we can distract or redirect so we don't have to lie. I wiped the sweat from my brow and fired my own unblinking blue lasers right back at him. "What do *you* think?"

His smirk turned into a full-face grin full of baby teeth.

"Woman, are you kidding? I can't believe you thought that I ever believed in any of that stuff."

Did he just call me "Woman"? I could hardly keep a straight face.

After a mere nanosecond of sadness (I think it was the baby teeth that threw me), I felt like a tremendous burden had been lifted! I expected some pouting or comment about feeling disappointed, or mad about being lied to, but there was nothing. He did not shed a tear. The kid was actually HAPPY and satisfied that he had some top-secret information that his sister and friends did not possess. He kept that smile plastered in the middle of his face, a face still plump with baby fat and the remnants of dinner smeared across his chin. Not just a little smile, but a big, toothy grin lit up the room. I joined him in Smile-ville! He was now my little enlightened one! I had to scoop him up for a squeeze to celebrate, but once I let him go, we had some loose ends to tie up.

I threatened him within an inch of his life if he were to spill the beans to even one of the true believers. "If you tell ANYONE I swear to god that *you* will be the one getting a little taste of hell. Are we clear?" He assured me it was no problem and I believed him. He'd had Lutheran guilt jammed up his ass on a daily basis at day care since he could crawl. He was more worried about God than me and that was just GODDAMMED dandy as far as I was concerned. That very night, he began his habit of strutting around with his little chest puffed up, making all kinds of over-the-top references to Santa Claus. Fresh with the secret, he made a habit of doing this in front of his sister whenever possible, followed by an obvious wink in the direction of any adult in the room, making sure to impress them with his maturity and knowledge.

The kid was ecstatic, and so was I. In my mind, helping my kid meet this milestone of childhood without scarring him for life was on par with getting him potty trained. But his sister was a different animal altogether. Four years later, I was still playing all the parts for her. And when I found myself so engrossed in book four of the epic love story of Edward and Bella, I was *not* in the mood to be the FUCKING Easter Bunny.

I WANTED TO KEEP READING!

Yeah, I said it—I'm a selfish and immature woman, not fit for motherhood! I wanted my own magic magnificence to continue without interruption, so I brainstormed a genius solution. I called on the boy to get his bunny on. You can call me selfish, but nothing makes my kid happier than running with the big dogs. He had been a proud gatekeeper of his sister's innocence for years and he was more than happy to help me keep her in the dark for another holiday. How could I deny him this joy? Plus I was going to pay him for his trouble.

That freeloading firstborn of mine was glad to earn his keep by doing the hippity-hop, filling and hiding Easter eggs for his sister for hours with shits and giggles to spare. This year, his baby fat was gone and big chompers replaced the little toofers that had grinned at me years ago when he became an official myth perpetuator. In between shoving as much chocolate in his gob as he could get away with while still having enough for his own eggs (which he was also filling and hiding), he plopped down on the couch, where I was devouring vampire smut, and hung out reading his own book. It was glorious, but the irony was not lost on me that my nine-year-old son was bearing the grown-up responsibility of keeping my preschool daughter's innocence alive while I myself wallowed in fantasy.

We were all winners that weekend, the whole fam-damily! I plowed through the entire *Twilight Saga* in time to scramble together some ham and green bean casserole with those crunchy onion bits on top for Easter supper, my daughter enjoyed another ridiculously overblown holiday, my husband didn't do jack shit, and my worldly and wiseass son chalked up another year of secret-keeping success (with only one nasty episode of ass-blasting diarrhea from the chocolate overdose, but that wasn't until after I was done with the books and even if it wasn't, I could read and rinse out shitty undies at the same time. I'd done it before).

I'll tell you another thing: even though I'm going to ride the wave as long as I can with my daughter, I won't be sad when she finds out the truth. Quite frankly, I'm tired of Cocksucker Claus the binge eater and a creepy, mutant rabbit with no pants getting all the credit for my hard work and generosity. I can handle a few more years of suspended disbelief, though. Now that I have my own personal elf hopping around my crib, I won't need to be Fatty Claus either, which will inevitably be my favorite present that Christmas!

IF YOU HAD FUN, YOU WON

Every spring the big event at my kids' school is "Field Day"! What's Field Day? you ask. Are you kidding? It's only the most exciting and most anticipated event of the year! The very pinnacle of what would otherwise be an anticlimactic last week of school! It's the only time when you can dunk your favorite or least favorite teachers in the dunk tank or throw pies at their faces without getting in trouble! All the grade school kids dress in color-coordinated T-shirts, binge on drippy Popsicles, run relay races, play outdoor games, toss water balloons and beanbags, get their faces painted and win prizes playing Bozo motherfucking Buckets! It's a smorgasbord of fantasticness! They spend the day using their "outside voices," throwing things at each other and running around without getting yelled at. Field Day is a day full of general amok-ness and kids fucking LOVE it.

Parents love it, too! Field Day is a whirlwind of activities that really poop kids out and better yet, they never come home with homework on Field Day! Tired kids + NO HOME-WORK means that there are two fewer things to fight about when they arrive home from school! Everybody wins. But the most fun is being a parent volunteer! I'm as busy as a hooker on nickel night at Field Day and it makes me look like a caring and involved parent just by showing up and staying the entire day. Makes people forget I don't do jack shit the rest of the year.

Yes, it is a big, social, ass-kissing, "look at what a good parent I am" day for the grown-ups. Parent volunteers get to spend the entire day rubbing elbows with faculty and staff, mingling with other parents and then talking badly about them once they are out of earshot. It's also the perfect venue for that sadistic pleasure known as embarrassing the crap out of one's spawn. To maximize the embarrassment of an older child (who HATES that you are volunteering and wishes you wouldn't), I recommend blowing kisses in his direction throughout the day, and waving to him yelling, "Hi, (insert most sugary-sweet nickname)! Mommy loves you soooooooo much!" I also make sure to swing by and smother MY kid with frequent hugs and love taps on his little sugar buns when he is trying to look cool in front of his friends or a cute girl. These fourth and fifth graders just don't appreciate the effort it takes to put this monstrosity of activity together, and they are teetering on deeming it very uncool. A little retaliation toward these ungrateful little snots is just good parenting and reminds them who has the upper hand.

Now, when you aren't harassing your older child, you are often trying to peel your younger kid off of your leg. The little ones are always ECSTATIC that you are there for the afternoon, and proudly want to introduce you to all their friends. The joy and excitement of the day sucks the beastly, oppositional, squirmy argumentativeness right out of them. You have to take full advantage of the limited time your little buggers will consider you anywhere close to cool, so I highly recommend that you stretch out the volunteer business for as long as they'll have you. First of all, you're creating a positive memory, which will lessen the amount of time they spend telling their future therapist how much you suck. Second, the little ones who belong to your friends and neighbors have no filter, so you can ask them all sorts of nosy questions about rumors you have heard about their families. They will tell you ALL the details and then some, especially if you are in charge of the Popsicles. It's a magnificent way for a sneaky suburban busybody mom to get the 411 about the bitches in the 'hood. WORD!

Another underhanded, selfish benefit for me is face painting. I must confess that I enjoy showing off my artistic talent while attempting to confuse young minds with plausible lies about myself. After painting what was possibly the fiftieth unicorn on a chubby cheek, I start telling the second graders that I trained and rode unicorns professionally before having children. I just love warping a young mind on a sunny spring day. It's precious and only slightly cruel to lie to little kids, but I just cannot resist! They are so gullible and adorable and I like the idea of them imagining me wrangling and soaring through the air on a mythical creature that farts rainbows, shits marshmallows and pisses glitter—GLORIOUS!

Sun and fun! My kids come home tired and sun kissed and I have successfully messed with and openly mocked a large number of people for hours on end. Yet there is one little something that just kills a small part of it for me. It's groovy that we all have fun, but the awards given at the end of the day are glaring examples of how parents and educators today are setting the lowest damn standards possible when it comes to achievement and effort. THIS is what makes me feel stabby, yet gives me the support I need to excuse my own naughty, sneaky and inappropriate behavior when I'm volunteering on Field Day.

Each year, a slippery green ribbon is given to every kid that says, "If you had FUN, you WON!"

BULLSHIT!

BULLFUCKINGASSSHIT!

IF YOU AIN'T FIRST, YOU'RE LAST!

I never tire of complaining about the way the schools treat kids these days. Nobody wins? Bullshit. Somebody fucking wins. There is *always* a winner, but winners just don't get recognized or celebrated for their hard work and accomplishments anymore. Some asshole decided that it wouldn't be fair and that kids who didn't win would feel hurt!

NO SHIT! Losing sucks and it's a part of life kids need to learn how to handle.

The pussification of kids today is nothing short of disgraceful. THEY NEED TO LEARN THAT WINNING IS IMPORTANT. Of course it's not everything, but it certainly is something and it should be recognized and celebrated! Do not serve the metaphorical cake of fun-ness without the metaphorical frosting of winning-ness. The kids are always the first to wonder why the fuck the cakes are bare.

My kids want to win. They realize that losing is a great motivator for trying harder and that winning does mean something. They know good goddamn well not to come crying to me if they lose because they haven't put the time and effort into doing what it takes to win, but if they are busting their humps and don't make the cut, I'll always be a soft place to fall and a voice of encouragement.

This Field Day stupidity lessens the coolness of an otherwise incredible day for kids and parents alike! Believe you me, every last one of those kids from at least second grade up knows good GODDAMN well who the winners were. I'm just so glad I can spend the day embarrassing my kids and lying about mythical creatures without rebuke from teachers or other parents, because if their dignity is the only thing they can lose on Field Day, at least they are learning SOMETHING about dealing with loss. Am I right? Of course I am.

Every year I show my kids the crap "awards" that I retrieve from their lunch boxes, pockets, or backpacks. My son usually has his award jammed into his shorts pocket along with the lint, candy wrappers and crumpled-up notes from his posse of admirers. My daughter shoves hers into her lunch box with the leftover juice from her mandarin oranges. We talk about the day and always agree that it was pretty rad and they are lucky to attend a school that encourages fun and celebration after a long year of hard work. There has never been a year when they have been disappointed, because Field Day is THE BOMBFUCK-ING DIGGETY end-of-the-year extravaganza for grade school kids. Of course, each year I make sure to ask them what they want me to do with their "awards." Even though I think they're crap, I give them a chance to have their say.

At the risk of revealing my high tolerance for grade school potty mouths, I'll share the boy's usual answer: "You can throw it out. Everybody wins, my ASS!" Not to be outdone (because she is incredibly competitive, especially with her brother), my daughter says, "Dump mine, too, Mom! You know that shit can't even be recycled!"

"Right," I say, "but not before using them to wipe my butt!" And THAT, I think, is truly one of my favorite parts of Field Day, because those ribbons are satiny soft.

I don't care if bitching about having to vacuum the sofas and deep clean the refrigerator can be construed as being ungrateful and having "first world problems." I hate both of those fucking chores with the force of a million beer farts and I don't care who knows it.

FUCKING FAMILY GAME NIGHT

Mom, in the laundry room, shoveling ice cream in her yapper with a cheap wine chaser.

Does this sound like the solved mystery to one of the now numerous different themes of the board game Clue? A hide-and-seek version of the game where the goal is to find out where mom is hiding and what she is eating and drinking so that she can get ten minutes to herself to regroup so that she doesn't *lose her fucking mind?* I think it's a very good idea for a game. I'd buy it. I'd play it with the neighborhood moms instead of fucking Bunco, not that I play Bunco, a game that I hate. I think at this point you can get a Sponge Bob version of Clue, where Patrick offs Mr. Krabs with Sponge Bob's special Krabby Patty spatula at the Krusty Krab, so I think there's a real market for a game called "Mom Escape!" I really think someone should create that game. The idea reeks of fun and money!

Anyway, the mom-hiding scenario is actually one that can frequently be observed after a night of board games at my house. The mom I'm talking about who is sitting on top of the dryer hogging down mint chocolate chip and washing it down with wine from a box is *me*. Yes, ma'am, you can usually (fine, always) find me in my special place with delicious treats after a few hours of high-quality family fun on what I like to call "Fucking Family Game Night."

Fucking Family Game Night is one of the few things that cause me to binge eat. I lose myself in the soothing sounds and the delightful vibrations of the dryer on my rump. To be honest, I'm so mentally exhausted after not yelling at anyone amidst the high-stakes competition aimed at expanding the minds and social skills of my children during Family Game Night, I might not notice if the dryer is even on, but it doesn't matter. I'm alone, drinking booze and eating comfort food and checking Facebook on my iPhone. That's what matters.

Growing up, it was a family tradition to have regular game nights with my family, and I hold warm fuzzy memories of these special times in my heart. I want to carry on this tradition with my own family, hoping my kids will feel the same way. Unfortunately, I'm not as good at keeping my cool as my mom was. She never yelled and she never lost patience with us while we tattled, cheated, whined and schemed. She just kept a big smile plastered on her face while everyone else was being jack-asstastic to each other even before the first dice had been rolled or card had been dealt. I asked her if she ever hid out after game night and she said that she didn't have to because she drank the entire fucking time. Well played, Mom. Well played.

I wish I could do that, but my kids spill any beverage that is within a ten-foot radius, no matter where they are. They are quite gifted in that way, and I want to grow their other gifts as well by spending time with them and encouraging them while having fun. Game night is parenting at its most intense, because it's one of those rare times you get to teach your kids cool life lessons that will benefit them forever without grounding them because they learned the life lesson "the hard way" by getting in trouble doing something outside of the house. Don't get me wrong—there is often trouble on Family Game Night, but games are the one thing that all four of us can actually do together where nobody feels left out or bored—even if we do occasionally fight like a gaggle of groupies trying to get backstage time with the lead singer of a rock band.

And so, despite the high level of irritation, anxiety and frustration this activity causes me sometimes (okay, most times), I firmly believe in the power of family game night as an opportunity not only to teach lessons about rules, strategy and cooperation in the safety of the home environment, but also to build tolerance, patience and understanding among family members. As Katy Perry says, "We fight, we break up. We kiss, we make up." Right on, Katy! That describes my family to a "T." Of course it's hard to say how *much* social skill and tolerance building actually goes on during these cutthroat games, but I'm sticking to my guns on this one. Even though the whole time I'm clearly a firework on the inside (see what I did there?), knowing some shit's inevitably going to go down, I'm just the opposite on the outside. I stay calm! That is because I know that *after* Fucking Family Game Night, I shall escape into the laundry room for a warm hug from the friends who understand me: wine and ice cream! And sometimes Katy is with me during this chillaxing time, because her songs frequently come up on the shuffle of my iPod that provides the soundtrack to my journey back to sanity.

On Family Game Nights, my family knows to leave me be in my postgame "decompression chamber" until I am ready to resurface, or at least until they get themselves ready to be tucked into bed for the night. Even when it's my husband's turn to do tuck ins, there's no guarantee that I'm off the hook because "Daddy sucks at tucking in," according to my kids. Of course this is a bold-faced LIE, meant to make sure to let me know that although they allow me a certain period of alone time to pull my shit together, I need to remember that I'm on call 24/7 and shouldn't EVER try to forget it.

The last time we had Family Game Night, we played Clue and Mr. Green sliced that unlucky bastard Colonel Mustard in the dining room with the knife. I'm not sure why or how it started, but after the mystery is solved, it's a twisted tradition in our family to identify the victim and speculate on the reasons for his or her grisly murder. I had a few scenarios in mind this particular night, as it was December and I had holiday brain. I suggested that Mr. Green was sick of the colonel only coming around when he needed money, or maybe they were just hammered at Christmas dinner and shit got weird. "Don't drink and play with knives at family parties, kids," I told them when they asked why I thought Mr. Green would kill a decorated military man like Colonel Mustard. There's always room for encouraging creativity and teaching life lessons, just a few reasons Family Game Night is SO important to me.

And the thing about my kids is that they do ask those kinds of questions. ALL THE TIME! The boy waxes all philosophical about killing and what it would look like if someone actually got shot with one of those old-fashioned revolvers, and the girl suspects that there was probably some boyfriend stealing involved with each and every crime, each and every time. But they never seem to tire of speculating about it and so I play along, all the while wondering if other families go into such detail while they play Clue or they just fucking play like normal people.

You can see why I seek out the solace of my laundry room hideaway to simmer down, perhaps by sucking down an entire pint of lemon sorbet I mixed up with cheap wine (one of my

276 | NICOLE KNEPPER

favorite postgame combos), can't you? Maybe you can't because your family doesn't talk non-fucking-stop while playing games, in which case I'd consider you quite lucky and now that you know how it could be, I'll bet you do too! So, although I really *like* to hide out for a good long time and do the wine/ice cream laundry room binge, I can't always get away with it. Especially on the nights that it actually IS my turn to do tuck ins. On those nights, I try really hard to choose a game where constant counting or deep strategy is required, which means there will be considerably less blathering and fighting amongst the Knepper clan. The more they have to concentrate, the less bickering there is, which means that it's fifty percent less likely that I'm vibrating like a has-been child star hooked on meth at tuck in time. I believe they subconsciously know this and cut me some slack on those nights, but actually they're probably just thinking about how they can stall their bedtime for five more minutes, twenty-five more times.

Once in a while, we introduce a new game and the "I must win" and "I hate change" members of the family immediately get stressed out. On those nights I have to pretend I have a stomachache so I can hide out in the bathroom for a few minutes at least three times during every game in order to get my mind right. There is no wine or ice cream in the bathroom, but I keep a steady supply of celebrity smut around to distract me from reality. It's better to escape into the amusing coverage of the Lohan family's latest antics than to have a nervous breakdown. Just reading about her hot mess of a mom and dad make me feel like Family Game Night is nothing short of heroic! And although I don't know exactly what a nervous breakdown entails, I assume that if I had one during Family Game Night, it would completely ruin the quality family time that I'm always trying so hard so create. Speaking of creating, I don't know what kind of sadist marketing guru invented the concept of "Family Game Night," but I'm sure it's the same asshole who decided that Polly Pockets and Littlest Pet Shops needed to have fifty thousand fucking accessories or the greedy dickhead of a toy company CEO who decided the price point for Legos (which is way too fucking high in my opinion).

I'm one of many gullible parents who seek to feel like less of a failure by providing my children with activities that don't involve sitting in front of a screen of some sort. I want the high-quality interpersonal shit that makes memories, no matter how difficult it is for me. Fortunately, the parenting "experts" claim that it's the quality and not the quantity of this togetherness that matters. Agreed! I think there is such a thing as too much togetherness. I don't agree simply because the experts tell me what I should think; I agree because in my experience, too much of a good thing is never good. Cavities, chafing and hangovers are just a few consequences of too much of a good thing gone bad. And yet for some reason I keep torturing myself by repeatedly insisting that we have Fucking Family Game Night, even though I almost always require isolation, ice cream and a big honking glass of wine in order to recover from all that quality togetherness.

I mentioned that I dislike Bunco—and I do, both the game and the catty gaggle of neighborhood gossips who play it—but I'm not really a game person in general. Actually, I hate them. I hate them almost as much as I hate being stabbed in the face with a fork. I find board games about as exciting as folding laundry or picking up dog shit. They are all methodical, predictable and boring. Merely thinking about Chutes and Ladders stirs up an irrational level of misdirected anger at inanimate objects. I'd rather color or do some crafts (or "craps" as my kids call them), but *they* want to play games, so I take one for the team. (Moms do that.) They love games so much so that we play them often, even when it's not officially Family Game Night. And believe me, each of them unknowingly engages in multiple behaviors that grate on my nerves and make them more painfully annoying than being tailgated or having pink eye. Are you thinking something like, "It can't possibly be that terrible. She has to be exaggerating"? You're right. It isn't always THAT terrible, but it's somewhere on the spectrum from slightly painful to excruciating depending on the vast instability of the numerous external variables that come with family life. You'll know I'm not exaggerating when I elaborate but beware: after reading this you could end up in the aforementioned laundry room scenario just to recover from the stress of the story. Don't say I didn't warn you.★

★(If you are lactose intolerant, a recovering alcoholic or both, remember that it's not important what you eat or drink when you are in seclusion as long as your eats and drinks have the ability to soothe the stabby out of you.)

Remember how I said that I desperately want to be a good mom and quality family time is one of the things good moms are supposed to provide for their ankle biters? Providing this quality time says to my kids, "See how much Mommy loves you and wants to spend time with you?" Sometimes I even get out the camera so that in the future I can provide proof of my good mom-ness. Game night is the type of family activity with the potential to merge quality with consistent quantity. And it is super cheap. Movies are another potentially sweet quality time, memory-making experience, but taking my family to the movies costs no less than half a car payment these days, and sometimes the stress of all the spilling and poking and bathrooming and people kicking our seats is as un-fun as tolerating each other's game-playing habits. Notice I said that these activities have *potential*; they are not sure things, because even good moms don't always model good coping skills in response to the stress of these efforts. Yelling "Seriously, sit the fuck down" to a kid hopped up on sugar from eating six boxes of candy before the movie even starts while sweat pours out of your eyeballs from racing back and forth to the bathroom because the movie theater popcorn gave one of your kids diarrhea is NOT an example of good coping skills. At home I have hiding spots where I can go to "cope." Games at home vs. movie at a theater? For me it's an obvious choice for the quality time win.

But you are still asking why this "win" of Family Game Night stresses me the fuck out, and drives me to drinking alone and binge eating.

Some of the stress comes with my promise to love my husband through sickness and health. I'm sad to report that he's one sick motherfucker. I didn't fully understand that growing up in a big, competitive family made him sick, as in pathologically competitive sick! I kid you not, the man pouts like a bitch if he doesn't get the Monopoly properties he wants (or I won't trade him). If it weren't for the fact that we made babies together and needed something cheap and easy to do as a family, I'd do practically ANYTHING to avoid playing any kind of game with him. When we were dating we played a lot of cribbage. After we married, I had to let him know that his postgame sulking was super unsexy. And it isn't just that he takes games way too seriously. Add to this his tendency to leave out important details when teaching an opponent a new game and his compulsion to cheat, and you'll understand the first of many reasons why couples game night turned into dinner and a movie and only includes the occasional hand of cards afterwards IF other adults are involved.

One of our kids inherited the cheat gene. Not only does

she look exactly like her father; our daughter has inherited her daddy's competitive, sneaky and sore-loser ways when it comes to playing games. She may be the youngest member of our family, but she possesses the cheatiest cheating skills that I have ever seen.

Cate would be a legend because of her unbelievable "luck" if she weren't such an obvious cheater. Even when she was still in diapers (and she was in diapers until she was five), she somehow managed to pull the Queen Frostine card on the very next turn after having to haul her gingerbread game piece ALL THE WAY back to old Gloppy in the molasses pit when playing Candy Land. How did she always manage to pull that card? Because she shoved it in the back of her fucking diaper at the start of the game! Now she always seems to have a wild card handy when playing UNO. She stores her "luck" in her underpants now that she's done with diapers and I think that's just as gross, even if there isn't the occasional poop smear on the card. I'm sure someday I'll look back and think it's hilarious that she hides cards practically in her butt crack, but now I just think it's irritating and disgusting. Cate also hates to lose. She might just hate it more than her father, and that's why the two of them become the Diabolical Duo each time we play a team game. THEY MUST WIN!

My son is not part of this cabal of double crossers. Zach (A.K.A. Mr. Manipulator, Master of Memorization and Rule Enforcer Extraordinaire) is the game cop of the family. His eyes are like security cameras that track and capture every player, every turn and every *move* in detail. He keeps the paper copy of the game rules in a conspicuous place to remind all the players that he's not tolerating any deviation from the norm. He checks and rechecks the rules and makes sure to keep the banker or the dealer honest. He counts each space that each player moves on the game board—OUT LOUD—letting each player know that if they want to cheat, they have to outsmart HIM, which is no small feat—believe me, I've tried. Not to win, but to bring an end to a painfully long game of Scrabble Junior or Yahtzee, sometimes I turned to the dark side. I admit it. And because of this, he treats me as if I'm in cahoots with his father and sister. Zach is not a cheater, and never gets mopey when he doesn't win, but he's going to make good goddamn sure that his reign of regulation is just as maddening and distracting as the bullshit behavior I have to endure with the other two.

Speaking of two, the two dogs manage to be at their most irritating as soon as they see us settling down to play a game. If we're on the floor, they walk over the game board or bring a toy so that we can play fetch with them. Then the roll of the dice, whoosh of a spinner or shuffling of cards seems to activate some internal switch that turns on their bodily functions. I'd rather miss my turn or fail to spot the devious maneuvers of the diabolical duo than clean up the piss the mutts inevitably leave on the carpet when ignored. Up and down I go, making sure that the woofers' needs are met.

I'm pretty sure that the game sounds trigger not only animal needs, but also hunger and thirst in my children. "Mom, can you get me a lemonade?" or "Let's have popcorn AND games!" are the kind of requests that can occur anytime during the game, but most often when we are deep into the game and the stakes are high. I'm not sure if it's a conscious ploy to distract me or just the usual constant need they have to be fed and watered, which is normal. At least the pediatrician said it is. Of course my husband is like, "Honey, as long as you're up . . ." and then requests something weird like nachos, which makes me grin around clenched teeth as I say to all of them, "What, are your legs broken, people? Let's pause the game and each get up to get ourselves a snack, shall we?" When we return to the game, everyone argues over whose turn it is. EVERY SINGLE TIME!

That inevitable argument is a nice segue into telling you about the fighting, misunderstandings, false accusations and "he/she is touching me" complaints of the kids. I'll gloss over the persistent, sexually suggestive comments from my husband. If I didn't know better, I'd think these people were in cahoots with the animals and they all secretly plan and rehearse until they have perfected these maddening behavioral performances. I may be a tad emotionally unstable, but I'm not crazy. Or am I?

Sometimes I feel like I *am* going totes cuckoo when I'm trying to keep my cool during all of this high-quality family fun time. It always ends up looking more like a scene written for some family sitcom, trying to cram as much chaotic dysfunctional entertainment as possible into thirty minutes, but it would have to be on cable because of the swearing and not so thinly disguised references to blow jobs and murder. I'm beginning to wonder if I am out of my fucking mind, perpetuating the delusion that somehow it will get better and maybe everyone will at least keep their shirts on and not spill whatever they are eating or drinking all over the goddamn game board.

I guess I'm just going to have to continue to rely on my decompression ritual until A) the experts decide that non-quality time is just as beneficial to building strong and healthy families as high-quality time, B) I can figure out some other cheap and easy way to create family togetherness or C) somebody actually kills someone else.

If I have to hide out for a bit on the dryer with ice cream and wine after a high-pressure, emotionally charged Fucking Family Game Night, well, I've earned it. Besides, it provides consistency for my children (they ALWAYS know where I'll be after game night—on non-tuck-in nights, of course), and good parenting is all about consistency, yo. Besides, I know of no other way to motivate myself to keep doing the damn game night thing.

Between you and me, I hope they tire of Family Game Night soon, before I move on to some really disturbing behavior like slamming Wild Turkey straight from the bottle while sitting inside the dryer sucking on all the candy wrappers and shredded tissues that I never seem to remember to get out of their pants pockets before I fucking wash them.

GIRL TALK

CATE   Mom, why can't you be like a real girl and be pretty?

ME   I've always been a tomboy. I don't like makeup, trendy clothes or shoe shopping.

CATE   You are not a boy, Mom. You don't have a penis.

ME   No! Tomboy is an expression describing a girl who likes sports and isn't super girlie.

CATE   Maybe your penis is hiding in your vagina and you don't even know it.

ME   Believe me, if there was a penis in my vagina I'd know it, sister!

THE LICE LETTER

Dear Parents/Guardians,

We are sending this letter to all parents to help educate you about head lice so that you can take steps at home to help prevent your child from contracting head lice. This is also a formal way to beg those of you who aren't doing your due diligence at home to get rid of it for fucking good so that you stop sending your infested kid to school. Seriously, some of you really need to get your shit together.

Sure, we all know that head lice don't spread disease and are not a serious medical condition, but GODDAMN if it doesn't feel like the plague, right? Those stubborn little fuckers are tricky, opportunistic and crawl faster than an unsupervised baby towards an exposed live wire.

Lice can't jump, fly or swim and they can't survive on pets (so they say), but we all know that kids don't seem to have a fucking clue about physical boundaries and are always all up in each other's personal space, and that, my dear parents, is how kids are spreading the bugs around at school. If you tell a kid NOT to do something, that thing is the first fucking thing they do, right? RIGHT? At school we tell them not to share brushes, hats, hair bands or personal items, and what do you think they do five seconds after the talk? HEAD-BUTT EACH OTHER and try on each other's hats. I know you understand. I'm sure they act like oppositional little shits at home too.

I think we can all agree that we would all have better luck stapling running water to a slab of ice than to get kids to follow directions, but we can't give up on you, the parents. We need your help. I know you think it's easier for us to deal with your kids' lice problems on top of all the daily bullshit because we get paid, but you are wrong. It may not cost us in cash dollars, but your little fuck trophy is only one of thirty or more kids in a classroom. The cost of handling thirty kids just like your crotchfruit or worse, all day, every day, having to be fair, appropriate, patient and encouraging is HUGE. How can we do all that *and* make sure they don't get hair bugs from the kid standing next to them in line for chicken nuggets in the cafeteria or bumping backpacks jammed into their tiny cubbies?

Right, we fucking can't. So act like mature grown-up parents and eradicate these little fucking hair bugs on your own turf, okay? I know it's hard. It's brutal and difficult and damn near impossible sometimes, but you have got to do your due diligence until you eradicate those little bastard bugs from your home and family members.

I know it's the first month of school and you're all like, "DUDE—ARE YOU FUCKING KIDDING? I just got the whiny little bastards out of my house after dealing with their shit day in and day out during the hottest summer on record since 1995." I hear you. I really do. Forgive me if I beg you NOT to shoot the messenger.

At the risk of minimizing your upset and invalidating your feelings and making myself sound like a total pussy in the process, I have to say that your stress is nothing compared to what I deal with every damn day as the administrator of this school. Some of you are helpful and understanding, but there are a good lot of you who are out of your goddamn minds. I have to sit with my thumb up my ass, listening to you bitch about whatever the complaint of the day happens to be. Just a few weeks ago I had no less than fifty of you idiots crying because you don't like the teacher assigned to your child this year.

It's not even October and I've already stepped up my nightly six-pack of light beer to a dozen jiggers of hard liquor. You people are tough to please, but you don't see me getting all up in your face and barking back at you when I'm not happy, do you? NO! I'm a fucking professional. Also, I don't want to get fired. I have a shitload of school loans to pay off. So, I'm asking you to do me a solid. I work my ass off—we all do here at the schoolhouse—and if we weren't around, you'd have to deal with your children year-round. I'm just asking you to do some really important shit right fucking NOW, so that both of us can breathe a little easier and itch a lot less as the school year progresses.

First of all, IF your kids have lice: JESUS CHRIST, DON'T SEND THEM HERE! I don't care what you use to kill those nasty little bloodsuckers, just fucking kill them. ALL OF THEM. Don't rush through the process. Drink as many alcoholic beverages as you need to settle yourself down while you pick, wash, comb and murder every last nit and bug crawling on your spawn.

Next, you need to understand that killing off the creepy crawlers on your kid's melon does not mean that you are done. I will repeat this. YOU ARE NOT DONE. Not by a long shot. You have to literally boil the shit out of your linens and vacuum the beds, the furniture and whatever the fuck else your kid has been near. Basically you have to scour your house from floor to ceiling, and put whatever you can't boil or bleach in plastic bags for a few weeks in order to suffocate the tricky little motherfuckers. Those little bloodsuckers are stronger than those vampires on *True Blood*.

It's a lot of work and you aren't in the clear for a good three weeks after you fumigate your crib. THREE FUCKING WEEKS! You have got to keep your peepers open all year, in fact, because lice are as common in the grade schools as naked text photos are on the cell phones of high school kids. (Don't even get me started on the debauchery and dysfunction in the junior high!)

I don't give a rat's ass if your mom or your cousin Shirley's sister-in-law Barbara told you something different about treating and preventing lice that contradicts the information we are sending home. BARBARA IS IGNORANT! She might not realize it, but she is also a total asshole for spreading lies and misinformation. The Barbaras of this world are one of the main reasons people aren't doing what they should be doing to treat and prevent the spread of lice. She doesn't know shit about shit and needs to be silenced. If you can't punch her in the throat to shut her up, at least ignore the crazy bitch, okay? The Centers for Disease Control folks may be assholes—I don't know them personally—but at least they aren't ignorant. They know about diseases and bugs and whatever kind of nasty thing you need to learn about, and trust me, having kids will guarantee that you will need to learn about all kinds of horribleness.

Seriously, people, Google some images of lice! DO YOU WANT THESE WICKED CREATURES CRAWLING ON YOUR KID OR YOURSELF??!!??!

So I am asking you to please look at the Centers for Disease Control's official information and treatment guidelines handout being sent home with this letter and read it carefully. Don't skim, *read*. If your kid did that, you'd be all, "Hey, stop doing everything half-assed." Set a good example, for crying out loud. Take notes. You can't just flick these little fuckers away like dandruff or kill them by putting mayo on your kid's head for an hour while he/she watches a few episodes of *Family Guy*.

I know that getting this letter sucks as much as listening to you complain about how your child isn't a rude little jackass but actually a gifted and talented mind that isn't being challenged by his shitty teacher. Let's meet each other halfway, okay? Quit sending your lice-infested spawn back here to reinfect his/her class, and in exchange, accept the enclosed coupons for buy one get one free twelve-packs of Miller Lite, boxed wines (white or red) and various whiskey blends, bourbons and distilled spirits from our local liquor depot. In case you find yourself too intoxicated to make a run to the drugstore to buy more lice shampoo, I am also enclosing the phone numbers of women from the PTA who have generously donated their services as designated drivers in lieu of having to participate in the fucking fall fund-raiser.

Sincerely,
Gal Smiley, "the PrinciPAL is your PAL" at Everyschool Elementary

BLACK FRIDAY BONDING

"SHUT UP!" my sister-in-law, Krista, bellowed, slamming her palms on the dining room table, making playing cards and beer bottles catch an inch of air as she threw her head back and started howling with laughter.

"NO, YOU SHUT UP!" I yelled back, laughing and choking on my wine and spitting it all over the cards in front of me on the table.

"NO, YOU SHUT UP!" Tears began running down her face, her laugh no longer a howl, but more of a choking, gasping, body-heaving type of thing.

"NO, YOU SHUT. . . ." But I couldn't finish. We were both sobbing and shaking with laughter.

Our husbands were shaking too, shaking their heads from side to side in that way people do when they have no words to express their disgust. I have no idea how many more "shut up" exchanges there were, because we were DEEEEEEEERUNK! Not buzzed, but full-on piss drunk.

It was Thanksgiving, and we were playing cards after attempting to make waste of a hundred thousand pounds of food. It's a tradition in our family to play cards after dinner during the holidays. It's a well-established fact that I'm not a huge fan of games or sitting still in general, but add wine and subtract kids and I can usually be persuaded to play a few hands of cards. Plus I love Krista. She's a goof, the kind of person who tries to make you laugh during a funeral, and then when you do, joins in with the people giving you dirty looks for being such an insensitive jerk. Not that she's ever done that kind of thing, because that would be wrong and terribly inappropriate.

Krista tells everyone to shut up, all the time. It's not because she wants them to shut up; it's just her response to anything that surprises her, in this case my admission that I had never shopped the Black Friday midnight sales. The yelling, however, I can only attribute to her inebriated-ness.

"SHUT UP! LIAR! YOU HAVE TOO!" I think she was really enjoying the novelty of yelling. I know I was. It was hilarious and she had me rolling. "OH MY GOD! YOU ARE GOING WITH ME TONIGHT!" she bellowed. Those last few words? Not funny.

I *hate* shopping. Even when I'm wearing my pj's, grocery shopping sans kids late at night with a travel cup of mommy juice, listening to Air Supply's greatest hits on my iPod, I strongly dislike it.

"No," I told her with as much seriousness as I could muster, considering I was fully blotto. "Ain't gonna happen."

"SHUT UP! YES, IT IS. OH THIS IS SO HAPPENING! YOU ARE GOING!" she yelled more, laughed more. She was torturing me. "Aw, come on. I've been looking forward to this since I found out you guys were coming for Thanksgiving this year!" Now she was using guilt? The girl was good. She was weakening my resolve. And besides, if anyone could make shopping fun, it was Krista. Notice I used the word "if," because as far as I'm concerned, shopping can't and won't ever be fun. If I didn't act fast, she was going to suck me into her fun vortex. It was time to start yelling again. "SHUT UP! NO, I AM NOT!

WHY DO YOU WANT PEOPLE TO DIE?" I screamed back, cracking myself up with the thought of how I would handle the crowds and chaos of Midnight Madness shopping on Black Friday.

"I can't handle a crowd of bargain-hungry psychos! I would kill or at the very least seriously injure someone. Some pushy extreme-couponing type will shove me one too many times and I will lose my shit. Or with my luck, the person I kill would be someone with an epic sob story and I'd become a notorious villain. Homicidal drunken maniac from Chicago injures innocent Hoosier shopper, a mother desperate to get the last set of Harry Potter Legos at half price because her kid's legs were chewed off by a coyote. Who knows? Either way, there's no way I could handle any of that dumb-fuckery!"

I was serious. I have no tolerance for crowds. I've experienced homicidal ideation when stuck in long checkout lines at the supermarket. It would totally ruin the rest of the holiday season if I ended up in jail for murder.

"You are going!" She was done yelling, but her tone was fierce. "You should experience this at least once in your life, you HAVE TO, you MUST! And besides, I NEED you because I need to get a ton of stuff! It'll be fun. I will make it fun!" She had gotten us both a piece of orgasm-inducing ice cream cake that her mother-in-law made every year, thinking it would melt my resistance.

Wrong to the NO. She could NOT make me go. But she was right about one thing. Doing most anything with her increased the chances that fun would be had.

She wasn't giving up. I continued to resist. "I can't do it. I WON'T!" I whined, shoveling cake in my face hole. "Besides, I'm sauced. You are sauced. Neither of us can drive." Eric knew damn well how I felt about shopping, so I looked to him for some backup. "Tell her, Eric! Tell her she can't drive all smashed! She's too juiced—look at her! We can't go!" I winked at him and pleaded with my eyes.

That's when the rat bastard betrayed me. "I'll drive you guys. Dave will follow me and leave a car in the parking lot for when you are done. By then you'll be fine to drive and you'll need the car for all the loot you score. You should go, Nic! Come on! Don't be a turd. It will be fun and you can get a jump on our Christmas shopping!"

Oh my god, did he just throw me under the fucking bus? TRAITOR!

Obviously, blood is thicker than marriage, I thought to myself. And what was this "our" Christmas shopping? When had he hauled his ass out to the mall, battling crowds in toy stores to find the stuff our kids had asked Santa for in their letters? Um, never. That's fucking when. Grr . . . I was now angry enough with him that I wanted to get away.

Fine, I would go with her. Really I had to. Not because my husband screwed me over and I wanted to kick him in the ding-ding, or even because I thought Krista would be mad at me if I stayed home. There was another important reason my resistance buckled like drunken, spaghettilike legs. The image of Krista and me, schnockered, bashing carts into big-butted bitches in Toys"R"Us at midnight put a big grin on my face. Now *that* sounded fun. *That* I could enjoy. Krista wouldn't let me kill anyone, and anyway, she worked at a bank, which meant she had access to bail money if something did happen. What the hell? I would approach the evening with an open mind. There had to be a reason people did this Black Friday business year after year.

I was done arguing. "Fine, you win. I will go."

"YEAH, YOU WILL, BITCH!" she yelled. I still wasn't sure if I wanted to hug her or hit her, but I would go shopping with her. "Good thing it's only nine thirty," I said. "We have time to keep getting our drink on." I hopped up and headed toward the fridge to get some wine.

"Hell no," Krista said, "let's get a pot of coffee going. We have to leave soon, you know, to get in line. I didn't even realize how late it was and if we don't hurry, we'll be waaaaaay far back in line. We want to be as close to the front as possible so we can get the tickets they hand out for hot items."

Did she just say "tickets?" And whoa now—did she say something about lines? Now I was shaking my head back and forth. I'd agreed to go shopping, not wait in line for three hours. Eric pulled travel coffee mugs out of the cabinet for us and filled them halfway with Baileys. That traitor was at the top of my naughty list, so this was a very wise move on his part if he ever wanted to get back in my good graces. Krista started rushing around like a maniac, looking for the newspaper with all the sale ads and her shopping lists. She wanted to have all her stuff ready to go. I didn't have squat! I hadn't given Christmas shopping one shred of thought up until the moment she started yelling at me about it. I shrugged and poured some wine, thinking I'd just kick back a bit until ~~Judas~~ Eric was ready to drive us to ~~hell~~ the mall.

When Krista was ready to roll, I slugged down the rest of my wine, took a quick trip to the loo and then headed for the car. As ~~Benedict Arnold~~ Eric drove us toward the mall, all I could think about was peeing. "What if we have to tinkle? Will we lose our place in line?" I asked.

She looked at me like I had just asked her if I could borrow her boobs for the day. "There will be no tinkling. You gotta hold it, girl. The stores aren't even open so there's no place to go other than squatting behind a car in the parking lot. You should have gone before we left the house."

I *did* go before we left the damn house! Now I was really worried. My bladder hadn't grown since sixth grade. I'd just had at least a bottle of wine and I was drinking a cup of coffee and Baileys, which meant I was worried I would need to pee sometime in the next few hours. What I should have been worried about was the fact that I had not worn a hat or gloves, or thought to bring them along either.

We stumbled out of the car and Eric drove away. As we walked toward some of the longest fucking lines I had ever seen in my life outside of an amusement park, I quickly became acutely aware of my drunken oversight. HOLY MOTHER OF GOD WHO WERE THESE LUNATICS AND DEAR BABY JESUS WHY DIDN'T I WEAR A HAT AND GLOVES? "I cannot believe I agreed to this," I hissed at her through my clenched teeth. "OH SHUT UP!" she yelled in response and started laughing her head off, which loosened me up quickly.

"OH MY GOD I AM SO FUCKING COLD. I'M GOING TO CATCH A YEAST INFECTION AND DIE!" I hollered back.

Krista grabbed my hand and started pulling me towards a line. "Did you say you are going to get a yeast infection from the cold?" she laughed.

"YES, YES, I DID SAY THAT! I'M GOING TO CATCH MY DEATH OF YEAST FROM THIS COLD!" I hollered, because I wanted her to join in the yelling fun again. Once we had our place in line, Krista started in with the Black Friday shopping tips. She explained that she couldn't yell them, because she didn't want to share her tricks with the others in line.

Oooohhh, okay, secrets. I understood that. She was a veteran, a professional sale shopper. I needed to listen. We huddled together and she gave me instructions.

"Okay, listen up! Soon the people who work here are going to come out and hand out tickets or vouchers for things like iPods, Tickle Me Elmo, or whatever crap is limited and in demand. It doesn't matter if you want whatever the voucher is for. Just grab it. Do you understand? Grab it! It might come in handy later," she whispered before taking a long pull on her travel cup full of boozy warm goodness. "Now what did I just tell you?"

Serious again? I think not. I was shivering and feeling a yell coming on. "OH MY GOD I THINK IT'S HAPPENED, THE YEAST! AND CONJUNCTIVITIS! THIS IS YOUR FAULT!" I barked at her, giggling.

She whipped out her phone and started dialing. "Who the hell are you calling?" I complained. "It better be a doctor because I have conjunctivitis and blepharitis and allergic rhinitis and . . ." I kept going, throwing out as many conditions ending with "itis" as I could think of.

"AND VAGINITIS AND TENDONITIS!" she added, covering the receiver with her hand, giggling. "Now shut up! I'm calling Nicole. She'll bring us hats and gloves and stuff. She lives close. I'll tell her to bring you some Vagisil, Bengay and ACE bandages." Ah, clever girl! I couldn't believe that either of us hadn't even thought about it! I don't care how trashed we were, as lifelong Midwestern girls, we knew better.

"NICOLE," she started yelling into her cell phone, "I NEED YOUR HELP. . . ." And she went on to tell Nicole where we were and what we needed, finishing with, "HURRY—WE CAN ALREADY FEEL THE YEAST AND CON-JUNCTIVITIS CREEPING INTO OUR VAGINAS!" Yes, indeed, Krista put the fun in dysfunctional and would be getting us some warm stuff soon. After about ten minutes with no call back from Nicole, we tried again. There was more yelling. I claimed my gall bladder was rotting and Krista was pretty sure she was starting to feel the effects of flesh-eating bacteria or possibly an ovarian cyst bursting. "NICOLE, YOU HAVE TO HURRY THE HELL UP OR ELSE WE ARE GOING TO DIE!" That should do it.

I was going to add that I felt my spirit trying to leave my body, but I realized that it wasn't my spirit. It was my pee. I was laughing so hard that I had started to leak a little pee. This was bad, the worst! If I held my pee for too long, I could die of a bladder infection. I crossed my legs and told Krista the sad news. I was probably going to die before we even got into the store. Of course I yelled the news, so that all the people who were already disgusted with our drunken debauchery might realize that I was potentially at death's door and take me seriously, maybe help find me a place to pee. One of these crazy bitches had to have a Poise pad in her purse, right? "IF I DON'T PEE, THE BACTERIA IS GOING TO SEEP THROUGH MY INNARDS AND POISON MY BLOODSTREAM AND I'LL DIE!" That stopped the Toys"R"Us lady handing out vouchers dead in her tracks. She held up the voucher and asked me if I wanted one.

"Oh, yes, I want a voucher for an iPod Touch! Gimme! Yep. Yes, please and thank you very much! And do you have a Poise pad or an adult diaper?" I asked her. She ignored me and moved on. No sense of humor, that one. The people surrounding us in line were duds too. We continued yelling about our cold-related illnesses and drunk-dialing Nicole, who was not returning our calls. "Krista, I'd pay somebody the price of an iPod for a potty to pee in. I'm dying. DON'T LET ME DIE!" I screamed just as Nicole and her younger sister, Courtney, rolled up next to the curb, honking the horn. Nicole hopped out of the car and gave us hats, scarves and mittens. Big poufy, clean, warm stuff! We rushed to put everything on and thanked her with hugs and a promise to return the favor someday. I wish we had asked her to bring a Poise pad or a diaper. I'd have put either one of those puppies on right then and there no matter who was watching. I gave Nicole the iPod voucher. I wasn't going to use it. Her sister had parked the car and joined us in line. If looks could kill, all four of us would have been dead as Courtney squeezed in line with us after parking the car. The people behind us were mad as hell. Krista and I had spent the last hour drunkenly yelling about the cold and now we had let people cut in line. I felt sort of bad so I tried to lighten the mood and joke around a bit.

"Aw, stop your bellyaching!" I yipped at a young girl behind us who was mumbling about how it was unfair that we let our friends cut in line. "If you got a problem with it, we can just take care of it right now! I'm from Chicago, bitch, and in my city, we kill people just for breathing too close. Are you rolling your eyes at me? I'll kill you with one finger!" I was laughing and holding up my pinky finger, but since I was wearing big old mittens, it didn't really have the effect I had hoped.

My travel cup was empty, my bladder was full and I was starting to feel the beginnings of ~~uric acid poisoning~~ a hangover, as the line started moving. Are you kidding, I thought, just when we get our winter gear we get to go inside? At least I'd be able to pee. I would live to experience the crazy Black Friday shopping, but now I'd have to worry about someone dying if it didn't go well. Please don't injure or kill anyone, please-please-please, I silently begged myself. It was go time; we were being let into Toys"R"Us. Krista reminded me to grab a cart and fill it with anything that looked like a good deal whether I wanted it or not. I could use random crap to bargain for the stuff I wanted if there wasn't any left when I went to find it.

When we walked in the doors, I was stunned. The store was set up so that cart traffic could flow in only one direction. It was a madhouse. Aisles were lined with boxes, creating one-way streets barely wide enough for the carts to pass through. FUN? No. This was a clusterfuck. People were shoving each other, grabbing toys with both hands like survivors of the zombie apocalypse desperate to snatch as much food as possible. Honestly, I couldn't think of even one thing I wanted for either of my kids. I wandered around until I found the bathroom, and of course there was a line. I considered just letting it go, peeing right down my leg. It would be nice and warm and who the fuck would even notice in the mass chaos and crowd of people? Had I not sobered up, I'm sure I would have done it, but I waited patiently for my turn and made a promise to myself that I would never, ever do this Black Friday shopping shit again unless I was wearing an adult diaper and five layers of clothing. Wait. No, I wouldn't. Nope, not even then. Never again would I engage in this asinine tradition. I think it took me half an hour to drain my bladder. Sweet relief. I walked out of the bathroom and into the chaos. Idiots were everywhere, crashing their carts into one another and giving each other the stink eye. Murderous Christmas, everyone!

Krista, Nicole and Courtney were off doing their thing, so I grabbed a cart and headed down an aisle. Fuck yeah—halfprice Harry Potter Legos! I tossed those bad boys and a few other boy toys in my cart along with a Leapster, a Barbie Hairstylist set, and a bunch of Christmas-themed candy for stocking stuffers. Aside from those items, I saw nothing so fabulously sale priced that I felt it justified freezing my tits off and almost dying from urine poisoning on Thanksgiving. My initial excitement fizzled out quick, and just like I predicted, there were far too many big-booty bitches carelessly bumping into me with their carts, elbows and twenty-pound duffel bag purses. If I wasn't so exhausted and happy to be mostly done Christmas shopping for my kids, I might have "accidentally" hopped up and kicked one of them in the middle of the back like a ninja or rammed my cart into one of their rear ends with as much force as I could muster, considering there wasn't much room to pick up speed in the jam-packed aisles. I was feeling scrappy.

Sure, it was fun to yell my face off and act like a lunatic in a town where nobody knew me. And I had to admit I'd enjoyed this long overdue night of irresponsible and immature fun, but it was not fun enough to make up for *this* horror show. "See? Nothing but dumb-fuckery," I said aloud to no one in particular. No, I would not do this again. Hell to the no. I was grinding my teeth and my hands were in tight fists. I needed to get out of the store and get out fast before my homicidal rage got the best of me.

I started weaving through the store, frantically looking for Krista. I was about to start yelling out her name when I spotted the most glorious, ridiculous and magnificent example of dumb-fuckery in the history of dumb-fuckery: S'mores the talking, three-foot-tall fucking toy pony with a toy carrot and brush! The thing actually neighed! Neeeeeeiiiigh!

"SHUT UP!" I screamed to nobody in particular. "SHUT THE FUCK UP!"

S'mores the toy pony melted my cold heart into mush. How could I be angry when something so gloriously happy was within my reach? I would get my girl a robot pony and make her Christmas the best she'd ever had!

Now I was big booty banging my cart down the aisle toward this ludicrous and offensively expensive toy equine! "I

HAVE TO HAVE YOU, S'MORES!" I hollered, giggling as I pulled a box off the stack and tried to balance the enormous thing on my cart. I struggled to keep it from falling, holding on to it for dear life. S'mores was half price! HALF PRICE! I would make my daughter the happiest little cowgirl on Christmas morning with this velvety lifelike horsie for only a hundred buckaroos. S'mores the magical pony made the madness finally make sense. Maybe this is why Krista was stoked about Black Friday shopping savings? Finding something so fabulous for such a bargain and anticipating Cate's squeals of excitement on Christmas morning got me thinking. Maybe I would do this again next year? Being prepared would make it tolerable, maybe even fun!

Now I had to find Krista! My niece, Maddie, would go apeshit over S'mores the pony too, but there was no way I could scoop another one up and put it on my cart. I was barely able to keep the one I had from toppling over. I was ready to start yelling out Krista's name. Why not? I'd been yelling all night anyway and the store was a mob scene! I was sure it would be the only way I would find her. I peeked around the gigantic box, trying to see where the hell I was going, and saw her right away. Hallelujah! She saw me and waved. The dork was trying to balance a massive box on top of her cart while moving through a herd of people to get to me. She had found S'mores, too! At the exact same time, we burst out laughing and screamed as loud as we could:

"SHUT UP!"

HAPPY BLOW YOUR
FACE OFF DAY

Who decided that the Fourth of July was a time for blowing up shit? That person is a fucking idiot.

I've read that fireworks were used to boost the morale of the troops during the Revolutionary War. That I understand. The soldiers were dealing with dysentery and typhoid on a daily basis. Ill-equipped, starving and freezing cold, these guys deserved a sparkly distraction. I mean who doesn't love a cheering up between bouts of explosive diarrhea? It wasn't like Vietnam, where they had an endless supply of prostitutes around to boost their "morale." I know I need a morale boost every Fourth of July. Trying to celebrate America's birthday when my morale is in the crapper is imfuckingpossible. I am stressed to the max, no matter how much wine I've drunk or how much meat on a stick I've enjoyed, because I spend Independence Day in the great state of Indiana, where fireworks are legal, and my husband, son, brother-in-law and nephew are all about blowing up EVERYTHING IN FUCKING SIGHT with absolutely no regard for their personal safety.

I spend the weeks leading up to the Fourth quoting statistics on firework-related injuries and deaths. I try to weave disgusting and terrifying stories about fireworks accidents into casual

304 | NICOLE KNEPPER

conversation. "You guys playing Xbox? Cool. Did you hear about that guy who got ahold of a batch of faulty fireworks? No? Well, he blew half of his face off, killed his dad, and his mom had to drive him to the hospital while he held his eyeball in his hand, hanging by thin strings of mucus from the socket."

My sister-in-law, Krista, is not only wise but also disciplined. She's the idiot whisperer. I've never seen a person handle idiots with the calm and confidence of Krista. Knowing damn well there's not a thing she can do when the boys get their brains in bombing-shit mode, she laces her beer with a Xanax and settles her buns in a comfy chair a safe distance from the firework staging area to witness the idiocy. When the injuries start rolling in, she's ready with the first aid kit and resists the urge to say, "I told you so." She's magnificent!

Not me.

I do not suffer fools gladly. I stomp around with my arms flailing in the air, ranting and complaining to nobody in particular until the urge to yell has passed and then either A) go inside and read a book until the idiots finish blowing shit up or B) sit down next to Krista and jabber complaints until my lips are numb or I'm too drunk to care.

I want to make it clear that I am not anti-fireworks. I like the glittery madness. I especially enjoy lying on a blanket and looking up into the sky while patriotic music blares in the background. What I *don't* like is being anywhere near the staging area where the fireworks are being set off by various male relatives. Every year I say the same thing: "You do realize that you don't get a second chance to NOT blow your fucking face off, right?" And every year I get the same response: none. Not even a glimmer of understanding communicated nonverbally through eye contact or body posture. The boys stand in front of me like they were just lobotomized and are waiting for Nurse Ratched to escort them to their rooms in the nuthouse. Like I said, they are idiots. Totally and completely mental.

I'm well aware of my tendency to overreact, but when it comes to explosives, is there really such a thing as being too careful? I think not. Exhibit A: two years ago, the idiots almost blew off my sister-in-law's ass. I can't decide what flipped me out more that night, the rogue fireworks shooting through Krista's legs, or my eleven-year-old son sauntering around lighting firecrackers like a little pyro.

Needless to say, I was already in a snit. The kids would not stop running towards where the dads were shooting off the fireworks. Keeping them corralled was maddening. The girls were waving sparklers three inches from each other's eyeballs just to be funny, and as soon as I stopped that insanity and sat down with Krista, the boys started shooting off fireworks at the end of the driveway. I was about to haul ass into the street to rip the lighter out of my kid's hand when he decided to take a break from exploding shit. Zach started walking up the driveway towards me. Good, this would save me the trouble of getting up.

Oh yeah, my kid was just strolling up the driveway, flicking the flame of the lighter on and off, burning the end of a stick. He was grinning, quite pleased with himself, and I could not believe he hadn't considered that seeing him play with fire wouldn't set me off like a firework. I'm a freak about safety, and fire safety has always been a hot-button issue with me. (See what I did there?)

BOOM! I went off like an M-80, screaming at him. "What do you think you are doing with a lighter? Youknowyouarenotallowedtohavealighterandyouarenotallowedtoplaywithfireever!" I screeched and grabbed the lighter out of his hand. He looked at me, incredulous, like I was speaking a foreign language. "Where did you get this lighter?" That seemed to register, although I think it's because he saw a way to redirect my rage.

"Dad said I could! Dad gave it to me! Dad . . ." Well played, mini-pyro-Judas. So, I screamed for my husband, and of course he denied it. They both gave me the lobotomy look. The husband was too focused on blowing up hundreds of dollars of explosives with my brother-in-law, Dave, to care much about my opinion, and I think Zach was just waiting to see if he was off the hook, if his lack of loyalty to his partner in crime would pay off. I shoved the lighter in my pocket, snapped around and walked silently toward the house. I had to get away before I went Nikki Nagasaki. I went inside and threw myself on the sofa, grabbed my book and started reading.

FUCKING IDIOTS!

Blow your damn faces off. I DON'T CARE! But I did care. I couldn't stay inside. I had a bad feeling somebody's something was getting blown off that night. I went back outside and plopped down in the chair next to Krista. "I don't know how you stay calm. Someone is going to get killed. Did you see Zach with the lighter? Like it was just his thang-a-lang, being a firebug. And your brother looking at me with that blank, clueless-as-a-box-of-rocks expression makes me want to strangle him! IDIOTS!"

As the mother of a boy and wife of a man-child, I'm used to dangerous stunts and general mayhem. Boys are nuts in the best way and most of the time I laugh. I'm not a helicopter parent, but explosives are just one of the areas where my usually flexible style turns into adamantium. No fire. NO discussion! I started yelling at the kids to come back up to the driveway, to stay far away from where the men-children were setting off the missile silo's worth of explosives purchased for the weekend. I had no problem being the bitch, the fun hater. On my watch, people, life and limbs stay put.

And then it happened. The sound was unmistakable, the "whoooooosh" coming directly towards us. There was no time to move out of the way before it hit. BOOM! The mortar firework flew between Krista's legs and under her chair, causing it to burst into flames. We leaped up and ran away from the chairs as the men charged up the driveway. As her husband stomped out the flames, I looked over at Krista and found that she was laughing uproariously. I started laughing too, but I always laugh when I'm nervous and holy shit I was nervous. "OH MY GOD! I FUCKING TOLD YOU GUYS THAT SOMEBODY WAS GOING TO GET SOMETHING BLOWN OFF," I screamed through my deranged chuckles. I knew it. I just knew it. Idiots.

After the fire was out and things calmed down a bit, I actually let the kids wave a few more sparklers (which burn anywhere from 1800 to 3000 degrees Fahrenheit, and are responsible for over fifty percent of all firework-related injuries) just to make sure there was nothing left for anyone to light on fire—I wanted the shit *gone*! My husband and brother-in-law were walking around like dogs that got caught pissing on the carpet, avoiding eye contact with me, cleaning up the smoke bomb and bottle rocket remnants off the street and lawn.

Happy Blow Your Face Off Day, idiots!

I think it's healthy for kids to hear both sides of an issue, just not this issue. I'll engage in dialogue with the hub over just about any topic related to the kids. It's surprising how different we feel about certain parenting issues, and we are good at seeing each other's point of view. I can be flexible, I've admitted when I'm wrong, and I've even agreed to disagree, letting my husband do certain things with the kids that I would never do. But I cannot be flexible about activities that could result in my kids getting their faces blown off, even if it is a treasured tradition on America's birthday. Let them boost their morale with Mountain Dew since I let them have that garbage only on special occasions. There's enough caffeine and sugar in one can of that horror to keep them buzzing for days!

I do know that as my kids grow, they need to learn to be around and use fire safely. I will keep trying to be a positive role model despite my husband's strong pyromaniacal influence. Fire is a necessary evil. Sadly, I think both my kids will inevitably carry on the idiotically American tradition of blowing shit up. I find it ironic that our country celebrates our freedom from tyranny by doing dangerous things that make us seem like ignorant children desperately in need of a levelheaded authority figure.

Celebrating our freedom makes me feel anything but free when I'm busy worrying about permanent injury or death. Because nobody actually got injured or died as a result of the near miss of his Aunt Krista's ass, I knew my son would be chomping at the bit to blow shit to bits the following year, arguing that he was old enough and mature enough and whatever nonsense he could think of. I knew damn well I would have a fight on my hands the following summer. Men seem to be instinctively drawn to all things destructive and weaponish. I understand this and do not harbor the delusion that my nagging rants will ever stop my boys from wanting to blow shit up, but I hope it will make them stop and think about it and get some safety measures in place before doing so.

After everything was cleaned up that night and all the sparklers were spent, the kiddos went inside to watch a movie. I poured myself a jumbo Captain Morgan and Coke and told Krista that I would be engaging in the illegal activity of taking one of her prescribed pills. Then I curled up with a book. I didn't want to play cards with the "grown-ups," and I needed to get away from the kids. I didn't give a shit how late they stayed up, what they ate or how filthy they were. Each of them still had their limbs and faces. I had only three hundred sixty-four days until I had to deal with pyromaniacs again, so I was going to spend the remainder of this one day with a buzz and a book—undisturbed by idiots and immersed in fantasy.

The following summer there was a drought, causing dangerously dry conditions. Several counties in Indiana banned the personal use of fireworks. "Happy Independence Day, everybody!" I squealed while numerous news anchors repeated the warnings about the dangers of fireworks and reminded the citizens of Allen County about the ban. I was free! Free from the stress, free from being called a nag, a worrywart and an overprotective mother hell-bent on ruining everybody's holiday fun. I celebrated my freedom by jumping up and down and yelling, "YES YES YES YES! Thank you, God, Jesus, Buddha, Allah, Krishna and all you other deities I'm allowed to worship because goddammit, I'm a fucking American!"

CONVERSATIONS with CROTCHFRUIT

DRAMA MOMMA PLAYS DOCTOR DOOM

ZACH   Mom, would you help me bandage up this cut on my knee? I think it's infected.

ME   HOLY SHIT! IT'S TOTALLY INFECTED! How did this get so bad? You have to tell me when you have a cut like this!

ZACH   I forgot.

ME   YOU FORGOT? Dude, you could lose a leg from infections like this! How can you FORGET something like this? Z, come on now, you are almost twelve years old. Do I need to check your entire bod from head to toe every day to make sure you keep your limbs until you reach thirteen?

ZACH   (Sheepish grin and shrug followed by screams when antiseptic hits the pussy gash on his knee) OUCH OUCH OUCH! MOM THAT HURTS OH MY GOD STOP!

ME   I'll stop if you want to lose this leg due to flesh-eating bacteria. You want that?

ZACH   No, but it hurts so baaaaaaaaaaaaaaaaaaaaaad!

ME   Well, suck it up, sucker! Save the drama for yo momma.

ZACH   You are my momma.

ME   That's just what I tell you so that you don't freak about being abandoned by gypsies on our front porch. No child of mine would let a wound fester like this. This explains why your real mom didn't leave a note. No common sense. That or she couldn't even write. Hard to say although I've often wondered about—

ZACH   Okay, stop it! Please! I get the point and I'll show you right away next time I get hurt. And by the way, I've seen the video of the day I was born about a thousand times so who's the drama momma?

ME   That video is all special effects. You think I can't Photoshop a video or use a fancy computer program to make fantasy come alive? It's getting real old the way you are constantly underestimating me and my mad skills.

ZACH   I underestimate you because you
talk like this all the time, Mom.
It's so weird. And annoying.

ME   There you go, calling me "Mom" again
after I told you that I'm not really your
mom. Now that's annoying.

ZACH   Are you done? Can I go?

ME   Yeah, you are all good for now but I
can't promise you won't lose this leg
'cause it's not looking good. Not good
at all . . .

Dear Family,

Please don't stop watching television to get up and help me bring groceries in from the car, and do continue to bark out requests and demands while I'm doing this task all by myself. This kind of thing makes me feel needed and important. My life is nothing to me if I'm not serving you.

Love,
Mom

ACKNOWLEDGMENTS

If you don't like this book, blame these bastards:

Pat McCauley—a friend who taught me how to capture lightning in a bottle. Jimmy Greenfield—a friend who believes I have talent and am possibly a decent human being despite my best efforts to prove otherwise. Jenny Bent—my agent. Girl, you kept me focused and forced me to "move my cheese." Tracy Bernstein—my editor, a singer of strange lullabies, sister in nerd-hood and wrangler of mass chaos. Spring Hoteling—genius graphic designer. Dagmar Engelbrecht Ladle—the person I need, my soul sister. Lisa Dulli Deese—you inspired this madness and feel it too. Amy Madden McEvilly—my guardian angel. Cathy Jepson Nichols—the voice inside my head. Melanie David Impastato—brilliant and brave and loyal, my role model for being a grown-up. Stacy Ray Shaffer—who knows what really matters in life and matters more to me than she realizes. Allison Berglund Ferarro—the most beautiful woman in the world. Janet Miller Masters—how I miss you. Jackie Castillo—nobody on the planet has your strength of heart. NOBODY. Krista Knepper Cocks, Tiffany Fregeau Kane and Lisa Knepper Eskridge—laughter and love bind us just as much as blood would if we were sisters instead of sisters-in-law. Kathleen Neil Wichman—my cheerleader who holds me accountable. Sarah Spinney Burke and Miriam Spinney, who have always been more like sisters than friends.

Julie Haas Brophy—for being generous with your knowledge and the single most unselfish source of support and reciprocity and friendship I have encountered throughout this entire process.

DC Stanfa and Melissa Wood for seeing it all before I did and telling me what to do. Karen and Charlie Jones—good friends who inspire me and encourage me from afar. Bill Knepper—who watches over me. John Ladle—for generously sharing your wife with me. Wendy Pharo—who is truly the mother of all the moms who drink and swear. Mike McCauley—new old friend and king of tech support.

To the Moms Who Drink and Swear Group Administrators, group members, friends and various bloggers I read, respect and adore. Thank you for being brave with your words, loyal to each other and inspiring to me.

To the devoted readers of my blog, tweets and silly status updates—it has always been hard for me to absorb the idea that you care what I have to say and have continued to support the MWDAS message of laughter and learning. I have tried to give us a voice and hope I will continue to earn your trust by never, ever compromising the spirit of what we have created together. I raise my glass to you all.

Thank you to the *Tribune* peeps Bill Adee, Belinda Englman, Wendy Wollberg and Jimmy Greenfield.

To my friends and fellow bloggers within the ChicagoNow blogging community—I am proud to be associated with a group of talented, passionate and authentic people and I am so grateful for your support and friendship.

To everyone at New American Library, thank you for taking a chance and believing in me.

My family: the Iidas, Kanes, Cocks, Kneppers, Eskridges Chaissons, and Great-grandma Beckstein. My brother, Jack, thank you for making sure I never lose faith.

The grown-ups who helped me grow the hell up: my dad, Jack Sr., my grandma, Buddy, and my father-in-law, Frank—I miss you so much. My mom, Judy—she knows why. My mother-in-law, Karen Treesh Knepper, she knows why too.

My husband, Eric—stay tuned for scenes, hon. Thank you for a million things, but mostly for hanging in there and believing in us. I like you and I love you.

My kids, Zachary and Catherine—you are everything to me and I will love you forever. I'm proud to be your mom. The most important thing I have ever done is to bring you guys into the world. I know you two will conquer it in your own special ways just by being the fascinating and brilliant human beings you are.

NICOLE KNEPPER was born in Peoria and raised in Naperville, Illinois. She attended Concordia University, where she earned a master's degree in professional counseling psychology and a master's degree in gerontology. For many years she worked as a licensed clinical professional counselor specializing in treating adolescents with chronic mental health issues and their families. In addition to the Moms Who Drink and Swear page on Facebook, you can read her wildly popular blog of the same name on the *Chicago Tribune* blog network, ChicagoNow. The Knepper family lives in Plainfield, Illinois, where their favorite activities include goofing off at home, going to the museums in downtown Chicago, and making waitresses miserable with their constant requests for extra napkins, dill pickles, lemon slices and drink refills.